Geography
for A2

CAMBRIDGE
UNIVERSITY PRESS

PUBLISHED BY THE PRESS SYNDICATE OF THE UNIVERSITY OF CAMBRIDGE
The Pitt Building, Trumpington Street, Cambridge, United Kingdom

CAMBRIDGE UNIVERSITY PRESS

The Edinburgh Building, Cambridge CB2 2RU, UK
40 West 20th Street, New York, NY 10011-4211, USA
477 Williamstown Road, Port Melbourne, VIC 3207, Australia
Ruiz de Alarcón 13, 28014 Madrid, Spain
Dock House, The Waterfront, Cape Town 8001, South Africa

http://www.cambridge.org

First published 2002
Reprinted 2003

Printed in the United Kingdom at the University Press, Cambridge

Typeface Minion 11pt/15pt *System* QuarkXpress®

A catalogue record for this book is available from the British Library

ISBN 0 521 89349 6 paperback

Design, page layout and artwork illustrations by Hardlines, Charlbury, Oxford.

The cover photo shows a tornado over the town of Cantrall, Illinois
© Sipa Press/Rex Features.

The publisher has used its best endeavours to ensure that the URLs for external websites referred to in this book are correct and active at the time of going to press. However, the publisher has no responsibility for the websites and can make no guarantee that a site will remain live or that the content is or will remain appropriate.

Contents

Preface

To the student

This book has been written to help prepare you for the People and Environment options module of OCR's Advanced GCE in Geography, Specification A. Not only does this module (No. 2684) require you to study two specific options from a total of four, it is also the module through which your understanding of connections between different aspects of the subject will be assessed. This type of assessment is described as *synoptic assessment*, and it takes place at the end of your course when you have completed your A-level studies in Geography. The People and Environment module is examined through a paper lasting $1\frac{1}{2}$ hours, during which time you will be required to write two essays, one for each of your two chosen options. This paper counts for 20 per cent of the overall A-level examination.

As you can see from the Contents page, this book has been divided into four parts, each corresponding to one of the four available options. After a scene-setting introduction, including a spider diagram illustrating links with other aspects of the subject, each part is subdivided into chapters which focus on the key topics within the option. Each chapter begins with a presentation of the key themes covered within that chapter.

Terms described in the Glossary on pages 220–22 are highlighted in **colour**.

Thinking synoptically

To cope well with the synoptic examination paper, you will need to develop the habit of thinking synoptically – a skill that this book supports. You may be familiar already with the term 'synoptic' from studying weather maps which are conventionally known as synoptic charts. Alternative terms meaning much the same are 'general summary' and 'overview'. They all have one feature in common: they focus on the interactions between one phenomenon and another, or between different parts of the same phenomenon. For example, a weather chart showing a depression brings together in one coherent picture a wide range of otherwise independent factors such as atmospheric pressure, wind direction, wind speed, temperature and precipitation. In effect, the chart reveals the meteorologist's understanding of how interactions among these variables combine to create a particular pattern and sequence of weather. Without this synoptic understanding the synoptic weather chart could not be drawn. Hence, for successful synoptic understanding across the areas of geography that you have studied, you will need to think in terms of the interconnections between them.

In practice, it often helps to think about the application of geographical knowledge. For instance, if you were planning the location of a new housing development, you would need to take into account a wide range of physical, economic and social factors. Drawing up the plans for the development would involve you in thinking synoptically about the links between as many of these factors as possible.

Within the introduction to each part, you will find three essay titles similar in style to those you will encounter in the examination for Module 2684. These titles have been worded to encourage you to think and write in such a way that the examiner will recognise your ability to pull different parts of the subject together, and to show how interaction between those parts may be just as important as the parts themselves.

Contributors to this book

Editor

Clive Hart, Education Consultant

Authors

Jane Dove, St Paul's Girls' School, London

Michael Raw, Bradford Grammar School, and Principal Examiner for OCR A-level Geography

Alisdair Rogers, School of Geography, Oxford University

Kevin Stannard, Eton College, Windsor

Part One

Geographical Aspects of the European Union

Introduction

The European Union (EU) is an economic and political grouping of 15 states which together cover most of western and southern Europe, and Scandinavia (Figure 1.A). With an economic output comparable to that of the USA, and twice as large as Japan's, the EU is, today, one of the world's three economic superpowers. The EU has four principal features and functions:

- The EU is a customs union. Barriers to trade between member states have been progressively abolished, and since 1993 the EU has operated a single market. Meanwhile a common external tariff protects EU industries from imports from non-EU members, although ex-colonies and many LEDCs have special dispensations.

- The EU has common policies which cover agriculture, fishing, iron and steel, regional development, transport, nuclear energy and environmental protection.

- In the late 1990s economic integration was taken a step further with the introduction of a single currency (initially encompassing all EU states except the UK, Denmark and Sweden), and a

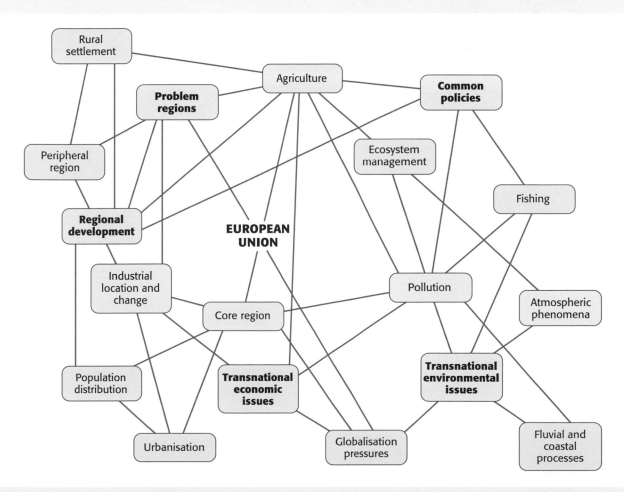

Thinking synoptically: the European Union

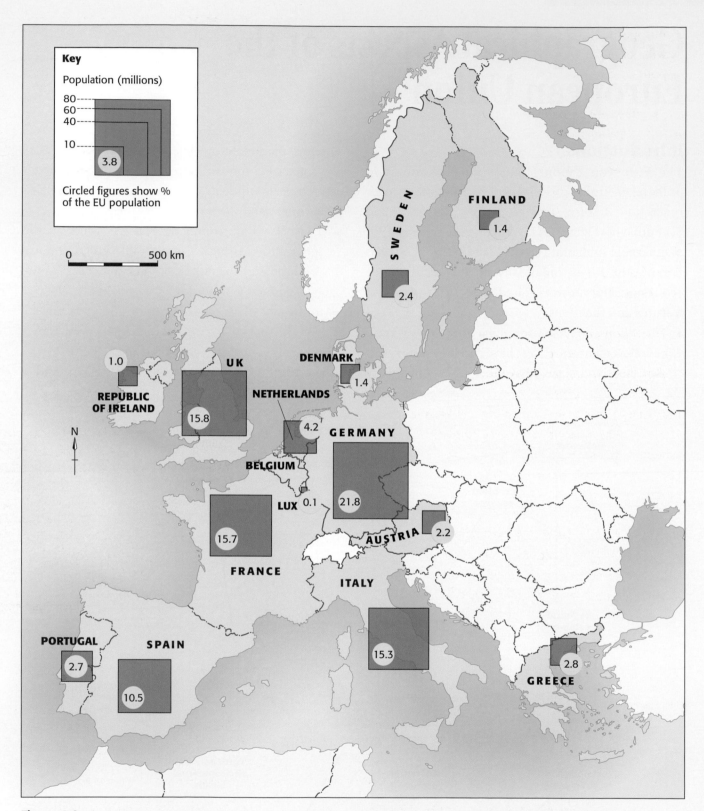

Key

Population (millions)

80
60
40

10

3.8

Circled figures show %
of the EU population

0   500 km

1.0

REPUBLIC
OF IRELAND

N

UK

15.8

DENMARK

1.4

SWEDEN

2.4

FINLAND

1.4

NETHERLANDS

4.2

GERMANY

21.8

BELGIUM

LUX 0.1

AUSTRIA

2.2

FRANCE

15.7

ITALY

15.3

PORTUGAL

2.7

SPAIN

10.5

GREECE

2.8

Figure 1.A

The EU member states and their population

European Central Bank. In the future EU countries will cooperate even more closely in areas of social policy, employment, foreign affairs, defence, international crime (e.g. terrorism, drug trafficking, illegal immigration, etc.)

- Five separate institutions are responsible for EU policy, government and legal affairs: the Commission, the Council of Ministers, the Parliament, the Court of Justice, and the European Council (Figure 1.B).

The development of the EU

The idea of a European Community took hold in the late 1940s. Europe, devastated by the Second World War, was in urgent need of reconstruction. Cooperation and closer economic ties among countries were considered to be the best way of reducing the likelihood of future armed conflict. The first step was the creation of a common market for the iron and steel industries (European Coal and Steel Community) in 1951. Then followed the Treaty of Rome (1957) which established the European Economic Community (EEC) of France, Germany, Belgium, Netherlands, Luxembourg and Italy.

The subsequent history of the EEC had two strands: first, the deepening of ties between member states through the adoption of common policies; second, the widening of the community from its initial 6 member states to 15 by 1995 (Figure 1.C).

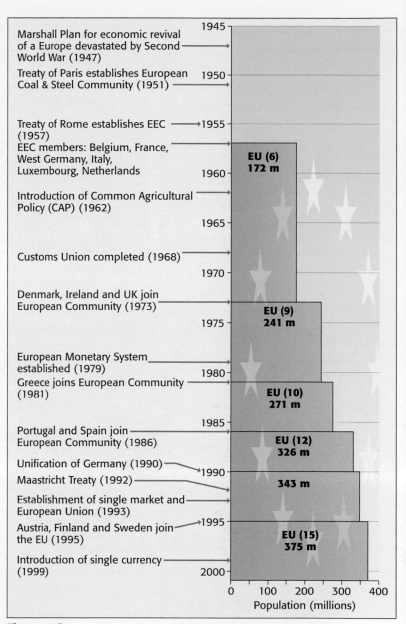

Figure 1.C

The development of the EU

Figure 1.B

The EU's main institutions

Institution	Function
Commission (Brussels)	Consists of 20 commissioners appointed by national governments for five years. Proposes legislation in the form of draft directives. Responsible for managing EU budget, and relations with other countries, including aid.
Council of Ministers (Brussels, Luxembourg)	Comprises cabinet ministers from all member states. Has legislative and decision-making powers. Responsible for common foreign and security policies, justice and home affairs. The Council ensures that national interests are represented. Considers proposals from the Commission.
European Parliament (Strasbourg)	626 MEPs. Considers proposals from the Commission. Responsible for legislation and controls EU budget. May veto legislation.
Court of Justice (Luxembourg)	Monitors the lawfulness of EU Acts and the compliance of member states with EU law.
The European Council	EU heads of state or government assisted by foreign affairs ministers and President of the Commission. Important role in the development of the EU and policy guidance. Adopts new directives which become law.

Geographical Aspects of the European Union

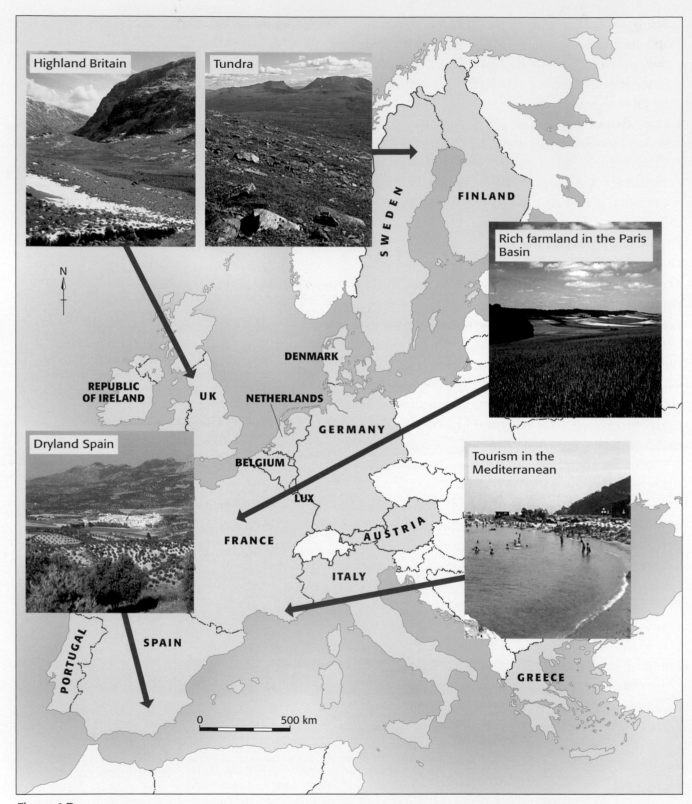

Figure 1.D

Natural environments in the EU

Size is an important economic advantage when competing in today's global economy. With a domestic market of 375 million people, and a combined gross national product (GNP) of $8 000 000 million, the EU's status as an economic superpower allows its member states (and especially smaller ones such as Ireland and Denmark) to compete on equal terms with the USA and Japan. This economic power also gives the EU more political influence on the world stage.

Natural regions

The EU extends across a wide range of latitude from southern Spain (latitude 36°N) to northern Finland, deep inside the Arctic Circle. The result is a series of distinctive latitudinal zones of climate, natural vegetation and soil. These zones are complicated by two key factors: relief, and the Atlantic Ocean. Mountain ranges such as the Alps, Pyrenees, Kjølens and the Scottish Highlands, and the pronounced oceanic influences in the west, combine to modify the basic pattern and create a wide range of different environments, some of which are shown on Figure 1.D.

Population distribution and density
Spatial patterns

Given the contrasts in the physical environment, it is hardly surprising that the spatial distribution of population in the EU is highly uneven (Figure 1.E). On the one hand average densities exceed 400 people/km^2 in regions such as the western Netherlands, south-east England, North Rhine Westphalia and Ile-de-France, but fall below 10 persons/km^2 in northern Sweden and northern Finland.

The distribution of population in the EU has a ring-like structure. There is a high-density core which covers southern and eastern England, the Low Countries, northern France, and southern and western Germany (Figure 1.F). Within this zone there are areas of extremely high density centred on major **urban agglomerations** such as London, Paris, Randstad, Brussels and Rhine-Ruhr. Surrounding the core is a zone of moderate density, known as the semi-periphery. This zone includes southern and western France, northern Italy, Austria, eastern Germany, Denmark, northern and western England and Wales. The outer or peripheral zone has the lowest density. It includes the Iberian Peninsula, the Mediterranean Basin, the western fringes (Ireland and Scotland) and the northern fringes (Sweden and Finland).

Urbanisation

The EU is one of the most highly urbanised regions in the world (Figure 1.G, page 8). On average nearly 8 out of 10 people in the EU live in towns and cities, and over one-quarter live in urban centres with a population in excess of 1 million. Ireland is the least urbanised country, but even there nearly 60 per cent of the population live in urban areas. In Belgium, the EU's most urbanised country, 97 per cent of the population are urban dwellers.

The momentum of past population patterns

The distribution of population in the EU is long-established. Today's population core – England, the Low Countries, northern France, north-west Germany and northern Italy – has changed little in the past 200 years. At the close of the 18th century the initial advantages of the core for people and economic activity included favourable environmental conditions for agriculture, local energy resources (especially coal) and access to the coast and trade. The survival of this distribution, withstanding changing political and economic circumstances, demonstrates both the inertia and momentum of past population patterns. Today, the core area of the EU has the greatest concentration of large towns and cities, a fact that largely explains its high average population density. The location of the EU institutions in Brussels, Luxembourg and Strasbourg, and the strength of the fast-growing financial service sector in the core, suggest that this pattern will continue in future.

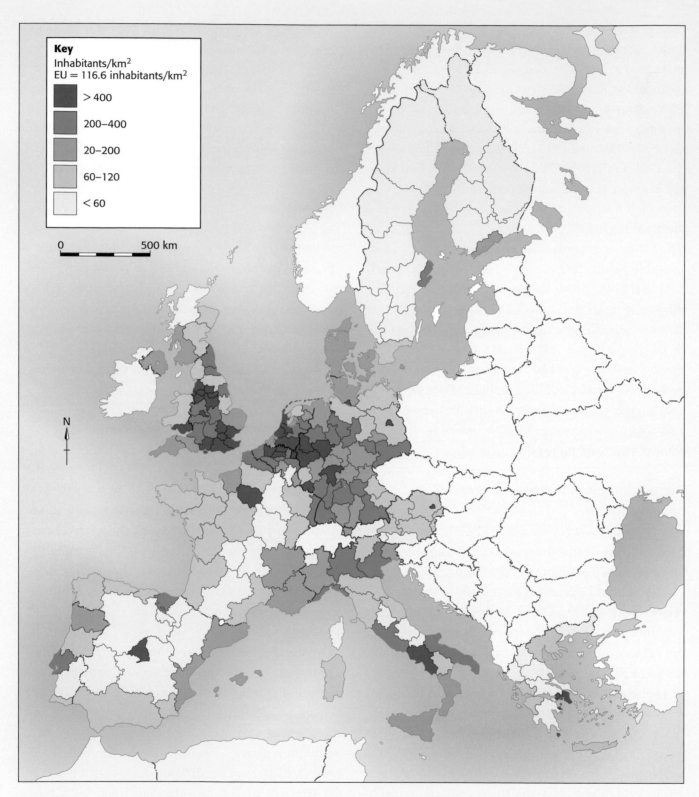

Key
Inhabitants/km²
EU = 116.6 inhabitants/km²

- > 400
- 200–400
- 20–200
- 60–120
- < 60

0   500 km

N

Figure 1.E
Population density in the EU, 1998

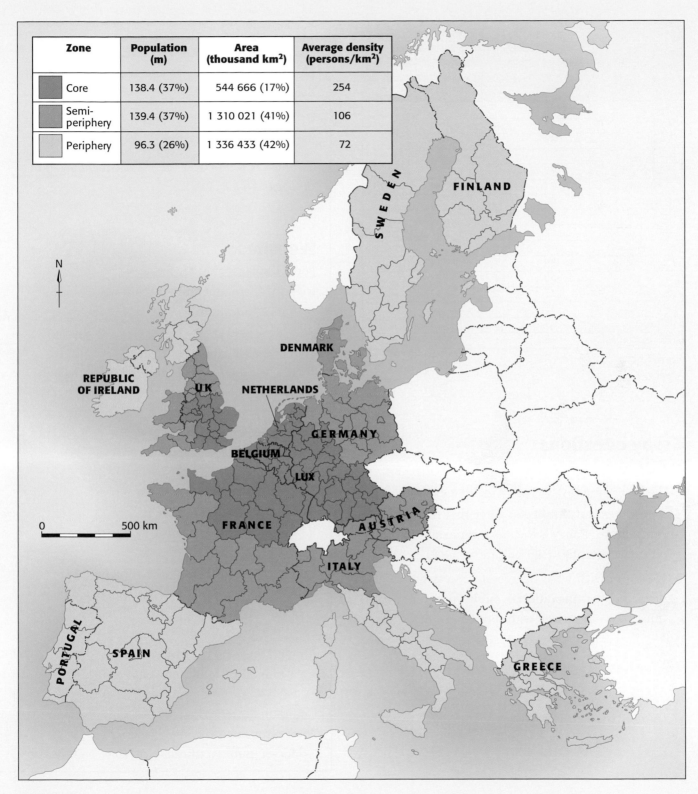

Zone	Population (m)	Area (thousand km²)	Average density (persons/km²)
Core	138.4 (37%)	544 666 (17%)	254
Semi-periphery	139.4 (37%)	1 310 021 (41%)	106
Periphery	96.3 (26%)	1 336 433 (42%)	72

Figure 1.F

The EU's zonal spatial structure

Country	% urban population	% population living in urban agglomerations > 1 million people
Austria	65	26
Belgium	97	11
Denmark	85	26
Finland	67	23
France	75	21
Germany	87	41
Greece	60	30
Ireland	59	0
Italy	67	19
Luxembourg	99	0
Netherlands	89	14
Portugal	63	57
Spain	77	17
Sweden	83	18
UK	89	23
EU average	78	27

Figure 1.G

The EU's urban population, 1999

Essay questions

1 Discuss the view that the prosperity of regions in the EU is largely determined by their accessibility.

2 To what extent would you agree that the Common Agricultural Policy is the most important influence on the geography of agriculture in the EU?

3 How and with what degree of success has the EU tackled its transnational environmental issues? Illustrate your answer with specific examples.

Suggestions for further reading

L. Collins 'Agenda 2000 and the enlargement of the EU: Part 1' *Geography Review* November 2000.

L. Collins 'Agenda 2000 and the enlargement of the EU: Part 2' *Geography Review* January 2001.

G. Nagle & K. Spencer (1996) *A Geography of the European Union* , OUP.

Websites

Population statistics for France:
www.ined.fr/population-en-chiffres/
    france/index.html

Population statistics for Sweden:
www.scb.se/eng/befovalfard/befolkning/befstor/
    befarlig/befarlig.asp

EU regional development funds and programmes:
www.inforegio.com/erdf/choice/ch_allp.htm

EU regional profiles:
www.are-regions-europe.org/
    VICARDS/index.html

EU regional policies and structural funds:
www.europa.eu.int/comm/dgs/regional_policy/
    index_en.htm

Immigration into the EU:
www.nidi.nl/pushpull/move/indexmove.html

Common Fisheries Policy:
www.europa.eu.int/comm/fisheries/
    doc-et_publ/factsheets/facts/facts_en.htm

Regional development in the EU

KEY THEMES

- The regional distribution of wealth in the EU is uneven, with a prosperous core and a relatively less prosperous periphery.
- The EU core is highly urbanised and dominated by service activities; the periphery is more rural, with greater dependence on traditional economic activities such as agriculture and fishing.
- The prosperity of the EU core reflects its high level of accessibility, favourable natural resource base, historical momentum and cumulative growth.
- While regional policies in the EU have had an important impact at different scales in the past 40 years, there are strong social and economic arguments for greater equality in the regional distribution of wealth within the EU.

Regional development policies

This chapter focuses on the regional disparities found within the EU. The causes of regional disparity are complex, but there is no doubt that geography, through relative location, accessibility and resource availability, has an important influence. Although all EU countries are comparatively well-off, there are significant regional variations in prosperity that raise issues of equality and economic and social justice, and which threaten the cohesion of the EU.

The EU has responded with a far-reaching development programme aimed at closing the gap between the community's rich and poor regions. Its regional policy aims to strengthen the cohesion of the community by closing the gap between the more developed and less developed regions. Large disparities in wealth between regions are undesirable on both economic and social grounds.

Economic and social arguments

Large regional disparities in levels of investment, employment and development mean an inefficient use of resources. Many core regions are overdeveloped, with congestion, labour shortages and soaring rents raising costs to businesses. At the same time, resources in the periphery are often underused. Migration from periphery to core merely amplifies the problems in core regions like south-east England, Ile-de-France and Randstad.

Social cohesion is more difficult to achieve when core regions in the EU have full employment, and peripheral ones (e.g. southern Spain, southern Italy) have unemployment rates in excess of 20 per cent. It is argued that people should have equal opportunities to employment whether they live in Surrey or the Saarland, Brussels or Brindisi.

Instruments of policy and assisted regions

The EU provides assistance to less developed regions through its four Structural Funds and its Cohesion Fund (Figure 1.1). These funds account for approximately one-third of all EU spending, as shown in Figure 1.2. Since 2000, the EU has defined two principal types of assisted area which receive regional development funding: Objective 1 areas and Objective 2 areas (Figure 1.3).

Figure 1.1

Funding for regional development, 2000–2006

Funds	Details
Structural Funds	
European Regional Development Fund (ERDF)	This is the most important fund. It takes up around one-half of the total budget for regional development. It gives financial assistance to EU regions that have a level of economic development which is lower than three-quarters of the EU average.
European Social Fund (ESF)	The ESF takes around one-third of the total budget. It gives assistance to improve human resources in the EU. The fund covers issues such as workforce adaptability, employability, equality and training.
European Agricultural Guidance and Guarantee Fund (EAGGF)	The EAGGF targets the agricultural sector. It promotes the modernisation of the agricultural industry and rural development.
Financial Instrument for Fisheries Guidance (FIFG)	The FIFG promotes the modernisation of the fisheries sector, e.g. fishing fleets, port equipment, the processing industry and aquaculture.
Cohesion Fund	
The Cohesion Fund is only available to EU member states that have a level of development which is lower than 90% of the EU average, i.e. Spain, Portugal, Greece and Ireland (being phased out). The Fund assists infrastructural projects such as the construction of waste management plants and improving road networks.	

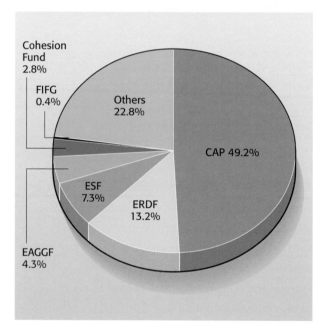

Figure 1.2

EU budget expenditure

In these regions projects to improve infrastructure, education, health and the environment receive up to 50 per cent of funding from the European Regional Development Fund (ERDF).

Objective 2: regions facing structural difficulties

Objective 2 covers four types of area: industrial, urban, rural, and areas dependent on fisheries. The criteria used to define those industrial and rural areas that are eligible for assistance are:

- **Industrial:**– unemployment above the EU average
    - higher percentage of jobs in the industrial sector than EU average
    - decline in industrial employment
- **Rural:** two of the following criteria:
    - population density less than 100 km^2
    - percentage agricultural employment twice the EU average
    - unemployment above the EU average
    - decline in population.

Objective 1: regions where development is lagging behind

Objective 1 assistance is available to the poorest regions, which are defined as those areas where per capita GDP is less than 75 per cent of the EU average. In 2001, 83 million people lived in regions with Objective 1 status (see Figure 1.4).

In 2001, 68 million people in total were covered by Objective 2 (see Figure 1.4). Objective 2 urban areas have a range of economic, social and environmental problems which include: high levels of poverty, unemployment, crime; low levels of education; dereliction and pollution (Figure 1.5). Areas which depend on fisheries receive Objective 2 assistance if they have experienced a significant reduction in employment in this sector.

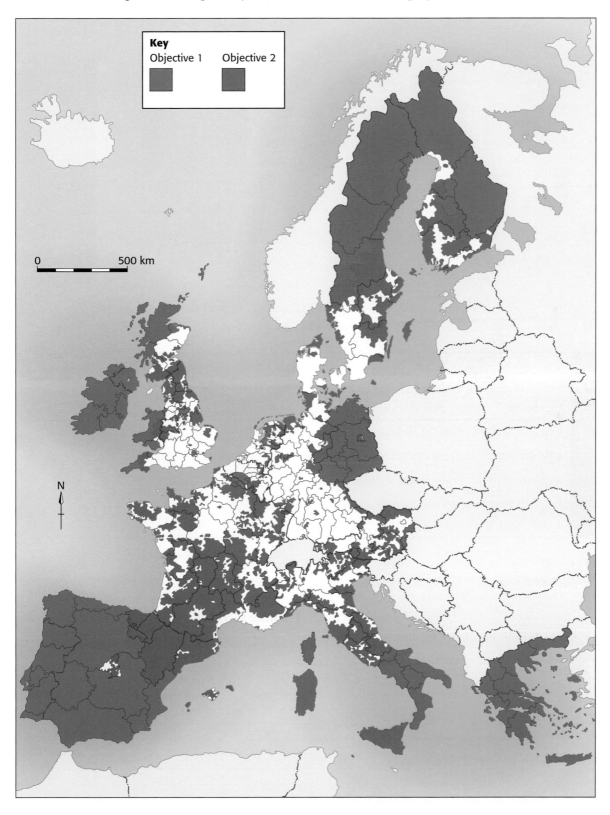

Figure 1.3
Assisted areas in the EU, 2000–2006

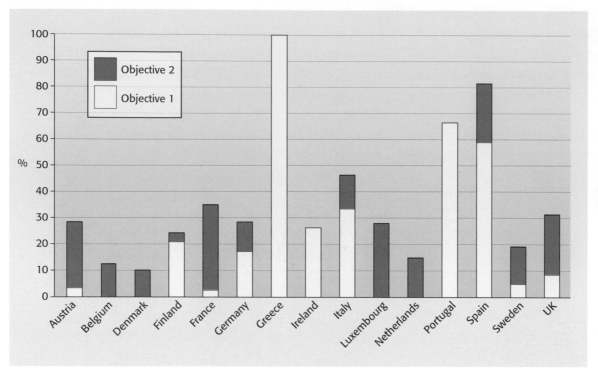

Figure 1.4

Percentage of total population in Objective 1 and Objective 2 regions

Figure 1.5

Signs of urban decay

Activity

1 Study Figure 1.6 and classify the regions into Objective 1, Objective 2 (industrial), Objective 2 (rural), and non-assisted areas.

2 Log-on to the European Regional Development Fund and Cohesion Fund website:

www.inforegio.cec.eu.int/wbover/overmap/uk/uk_en.htm

a Make a list of Objective 2 areas in your county (or adjacent counties).

b With reference to an OS map, decide the likely designation of each Objective 2 area, i.e. industrial, rural, urban, fishing.

Figure 1.6

Sample of assisted regions in the EU

Region	GDP per capita	Unemployment %	Popn change 1994–98 +/–	Population density km²	% employed in agriculture	% employed in industry
EU15 Average	100	9.3		117	4.7	29.6
Calabria (Italy)	61	28.7	–	137	7.5	24.5
Abruzzo (Italy)	82	10.1	+	117	2.9	11.2
Molise (Italy)	64	17.2	–	74	15.9	29.2
Liguria (Italy)	106	11.4	–	303	6.2	41.0
Galicia (Spain)	64	17.0	–	93	19.5	18.2
Limousin (France)	80	8.8	–	72	9.0	19.0
Thüringen (Germany)	70	17.2	–	152	3.6	34.5
East Riding (UK)	96	5.2	–	130	23.9	24.4
South Yorkshire (UK)	75	7.5	–	809	0.4	26.5

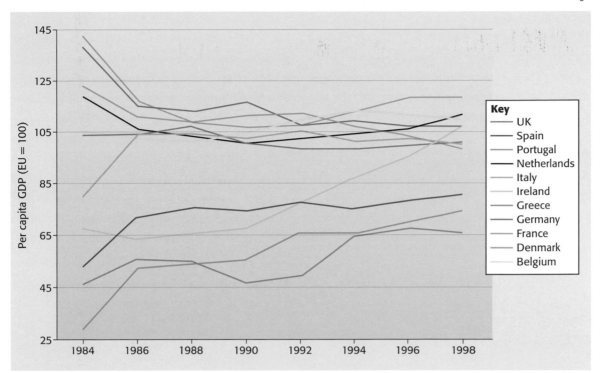

Figure 1.7
Changes in per capita GDP, EU12 (excluding Luxembourg), 1984–98

Key
— UK
— Spain
— Portugal
— Netherlands
— Italy
— Ireland
— Greece
— Germany
— France
— Denmark
— Belgium

The impact of EU policies on regional development

As already noted, the EU currently spends nearly 30 per cent of its budget on regional development. However, regional development has not always had such priority. Only after the expansion of the EU in the 1980s, with the accession of Greece, Spain and Portugal, did regional development assume greater importance.

It is not clear whether EU regional policies in the past 15 years or so have caused any narrowing of regional disparities across Europe. One problem is that a region's economic performance often depends on several factors, and it is not always possible to assess the impact of individual initiatives. For instance, rural regions in the EU, especially those in southern Europe, have benefited significantly from the Common Agricultural Policy (CAP); others have received support from a wider range of funding sources. Furthermore, governments of EU member states have their own regional policies and support mechanisms – assisted areas, grants, tax concessions and so on – all of which may be combined with direct EU support.

National scale

At the national scale, it is clear from Figure 1.7 that the poorer EU countries made significant progress between 1984 and 1998. This trend is best exemplified by Ireland (Figure 1.8). In 1984 Ireland's per capita GDP was 33 per cent below the EU average; by 1998 it was 8 per cent above. Portugal, starting from a lower base, also made impressive progress, as to a lesser extent did Spain and Greece. Thus while the difference

Figure 1.8
Ireland's economic boom: Dublin's financial district

between the richest and poorest EU states was 114 per cent in 1984 (EU12 excluding Luxembourg), in 1998 it had been reduced to 63 per cent. This economic convergence, closing the gap between rich and poor countries, is a signal achievement of the EU.

Regional scale

At the regional scale the convergence of rich and poor is less obvious. Many of the EU's poorest regions – in Spain, Portugal, Greece and eastern Germany – grew strongly in the 1990s, and closed the gap with their richer counterparts. However, in other parts of the EU, notably in southern Italy, southern France and northern UK, poorer regions did less well and their relative position worsened (Figure 1.9). None the less, the overall picture is positive: there appears to have been some narrowing of regional disparities in the EU in recent years, as Figure 1.10 suggests. The sample of 58 regions shows that almost two-thirds of the poorer regions (defined as having a per capita GDP of 90 per cent or less of the EU average)

Figure 1.9

Per capita GDP in some of the EU's poorer regions, 1986–88 and 1996–98

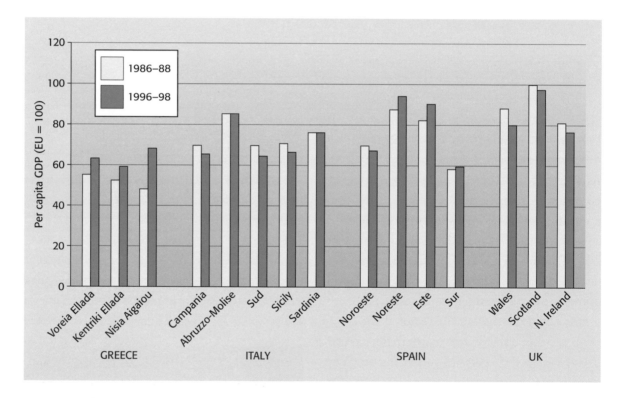

Figure 1.10

Changes in per capita GDP in 58 regions in EU12: 1988–98

	No. of regions experiencing increase, no change or decrease in per capita GDP		
	Increase	**No change**	**Decrease**
Regions with per capita GDP ⩽ 90 (EU average = 100)	13	2	8
Regions with per capita GDP > 90 (EU average = 100)	14	0	21

Activity

1 Summarise the changes in per capita GDP in EU12 countries between 1984 and 1998 shown in Figure 1.7.

2 'Although the gap between rich and poor regions in the EU has narrowed, the poorest regions today are the same as those 15 years ago.' Discuss the accuracy of this statement.

either increased or maintained their GDP per capita between 1988 and 1998. The comparable figure for the more prosperous regions (i.e. a per capita income of more than 90 per cent of the EU average) was just over one-third.

Regional disparities in the EU

There are major disparities in regional economic well-being within the EU. These disparities are measurable using regional **GDP per capita** (Figure 1.11) and levels of regional unemployment (Figure 1.12).

GDP per capita

GDP per capita is an indicator of output from a country or region, and is a frequently used measure of development. However, at a regional scale, per capita GDP values must be used with caution. In the EU, cities such as Luxembourg, Bremen, Hamburg, Vienna, etc. have inflated GDP values because of net commuter flows. Production in these regions is much higher than is possible with the resident population. Equally, GDP per capita is understated in those regions where large numbers of commuters live. An example of this occurs is Flevoland, adjacent to Randstad, in the Netherlands.

Richest regions GDP per capita (EU average = 100)		Poorest regions GDP per capita (EU average = 100)	
Inner London (UK)	243	Ipeiros (Greece)	42
Hamburg (Germany)	186	Extremadura (Spain)	50
Luxembourg	176	Dytiki Ellada (Greece)	53
Brussels (Belgium)	169	Peloponnisos (Greece)	53
Vienna (Austria)	163	Analtolki Makedonia Thakri (Greece)	55
Munich (Germany)	161	Ionia Nisia (Greece)	56
Frankfurt-am-Main (Germany)	154	Thessalia (Greece)	57
Ile-de-France (France)	152	Andalucia (Spain)	58

Figure 1.11

The EU's richest and poorest regions, 1999

Lowest regional unemployment (%)		Highest regional unemployment (%)	
Åland (Finland)	2.1	Calabria (Italy)	28.7
Berks, Bucks, Oxon (UK)	2.2	Andalucia (Spain)	26.8
Utrecht (Netherlands)	2.3	Extremadura (Spain)	25.5
Centro (Portugal)	2.4	Ceuta and Melilla (Spain)	25.5
Luxembourg	2.4	Sicily (Italy)	24.8
Oberösterreich (Austria)	2.7	Campania (Italy)	23.7
Noord Brabant (Netherlands)	2.8	Dessau (Germany)	20.9
Surrey; East & West Sussex (UK)	3.0	Halle (Germany)	20.5

Figure 1.12

The EU's lowest and highest levels of regional unemployment, 1999

	Activity
1	Investigate and describe the geographical distribution and the nature of the regions with: **a** high and low per capita GDP values (Figure 1.11), and **b** high and low levels of unemployment (Figure 1.12).
2	Describe and comment on the range of regional disparity shown in Figures 1.11 and 1.12. Are there any apparent connections with your findings from (**1**)?

The distribution of rich and poor regions

Figure 1.13 shows that at the continental scale the geography of wealth in the EU has a simple pattern – a rich core and a relatively poor periphery. The poorest regions have a per capita GDP that is 75 per cent or less of the EU average. In 1998, 40 of the EU's 205 regions were in this category with a combined population of 71 million. The poorest region – Ipeiros in Greece – had a per capita GDP of just 42 per cent of the EU average (see Figure 1.11). At the other extreme, the wealthiest region, Inner London, had a per capita GDP almost two and a half times that of the EU average.

The main concentration of the EU's poorest regions (excluding overseas territories and islands) is in southern Europe, in Greece, Spain, Portugal and southern Italy (see Figure 1.14). However, poor regions are not confined to southern Europe. Germany's eastern *Länder*, which formed part of communist bloc until unification in 1989, have a per capita GDP that

Figure 1.13
GDP per capita in the EU's structural zones

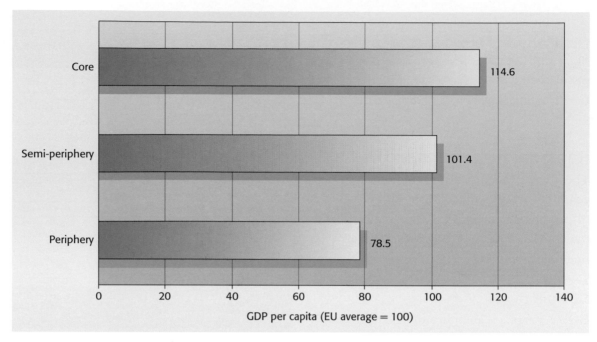

Core 114.6
Semi-periphery 101.4
Periphery 78.5

GDP per capita (EU average = 100)

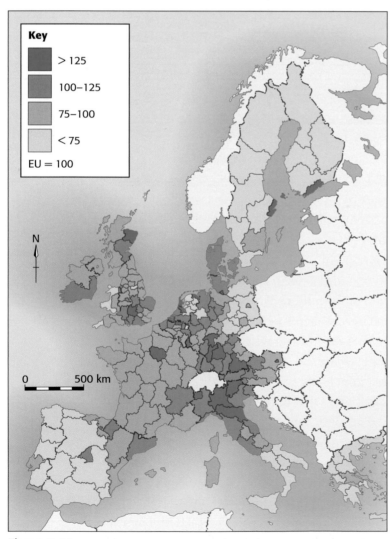

Figure 1.14

Variation in GDP per capita in the EU, 1998

Key
> 125
100–125
75–100
< 75
EU = 100

N

0   500 km

is 25 per cent below the EU average. In 2001 the UK had some of the poorest regions in the EU: Cornwall, South Yorkshire, Merseyside, and West Wales & The Valleys.

The wealthiest regions are focused on major urban agglomerations. Most are located in the EU core (e.g. London, Paris, Frankfurt, Brussels). Even so, there are wealthy urban regions in the periphery and semi-periphery, notably in northern Italy, and around Vienna, Hamburg, Stockholm and Copenhagen.

Regional unemployment

Regional unemployment is an important indicator of economic health and well-being (Figure 1.15). Levels of unemployment in the EU's poorest regions are more than 10 times higher than in the wealthiest regions. Regions of high unemployment often have a low per capita GDP. High levels of unemployment are a persistent feature of many regions. Unemployment is most acute in the periphery, and in particular in Iberia, the Mediterranean Basin, eastern Germany and northern Scandinavia. High unemployment is also found in two types of region within the semi-periphery: ex-coalfield and de-industrialised areas such as north-east England, Nord Pas-de-

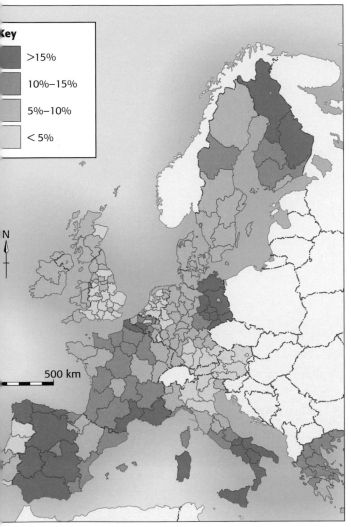

Figure 1.15

Unemployment in the regions of the EU, 1999

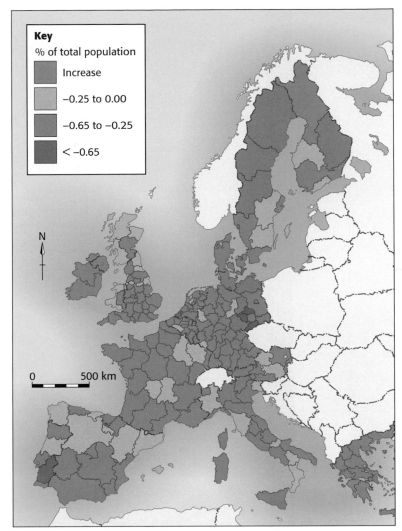

Figure 1.16

Population change in the regions of the EU, 1994–98

Calais (north-east France) and Wallonia (South Belgium); and the rural upland areas such as the Massif Central and the North Pennines.

Population change

In general the poorest regions in the EU have for many years suffered **depopulation**, as illustrated in Figure 1.16. The prosperous city regions in Germany and northern Italy are an exception to this trend. In these regions population decline is due to the decentralisation of population into surrounding commuter hinterlands. Hamburg's population, for example, declined by 0.05 per cent between 1994 and 1998. A similar trend occurred in Bremen, Düsseldorf and Berlin in Germany, and in Milan and Venice in Italy.

Elsewhere, depopulation is the result of long-distance migration from rural and de-industrialised regions in the periphery and semi-periphery towards the EU core. In some regions **natural decrease** has contributed to population decline. Natural decrease is widespread in Iberia, eastern Germany, Italy, Greece and northern Britain. Current forecasts suggest that natural decrease will affect 90 per cent of all EU regions by the year 2025. Out-migration, which is age-selective, also contributes to natural population decrease.

Activity

1. **a** Using the classification of core, semi-peripheral and peripheral regions shown in Figure 1.F (page 7), and referring to Figure 1.15, complete a copy of the table Figure 1.17.

   b From the data you have entered on Figure 1.17, test the hypothesis that 'unemployment is higher in the periphery than in the core'.

   c Compare Figures 1.14 and 1.15 and describe the relationship between regional per capita GDP and regional unemployment.

2. With reference to the EU, describe and explain the demographic factors that influence population change, taking into account depopulation, net migration change and natural decrease.

3. Study Figure 1.18 which shows rates of unemployment in 47 regions of the EU where the population declined in 1999.

   a Describe the relationship between unemployment and the rate of population decline.

   b State and explain two ways in which unemployment could result in depopulation.

4. Study Figure 1.19 and describe the socio-economic profile of regions with a population decline.

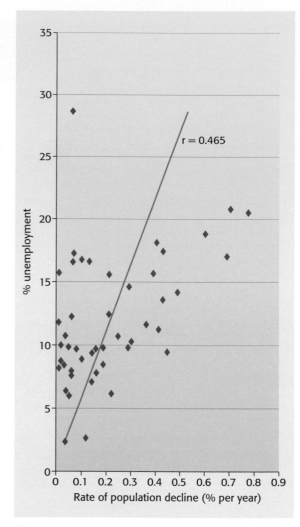

Figure 1.18

Unemployment and population decline in the EU, 1999

	Number of regions with unemployment rates of:			
	< 5%	5%–10%	10%–15%	> 15%
Core				
Semi-periphery				
Periphery				

Figure 1.17

Unemployment in the EU

Explaining regional disparities

The EU's regional disparities can be summarised at the continental scale as 'a prosperous core and a less prosperous periphery and semi-periphery'. While there are exceptions to this pattern, this simple model provides a framework for understanding regional disparities in the EU.

Five factors influence regional disparities in the EU: historical development, localised resources, cumulative growth, employment structure, and accessibility.

Historical development

During the past 200 years, the concentration of population, cities and wealth in the EU core has changed little. By 1830 the core cities of London (1.5 million), Paris (0.8 million) and Amsterdam (0.2 million) were already the leading centres of foreign trade, manufacture and banking. Great cities grew where agricul-

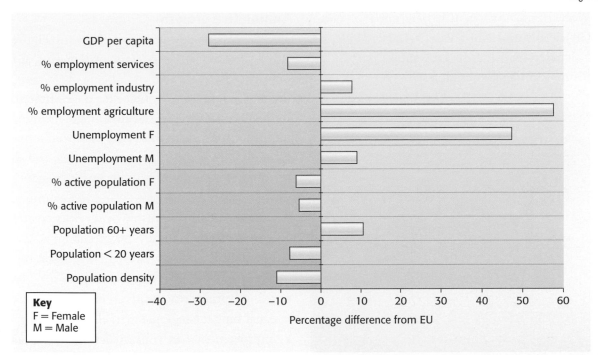

tural productivity was high and where trade routes met. These advantages favoured the growth of urban centres in Ile-de-France (Paris), central Germany and the Low Countries. Moreover, from the 16th century trade shifted from the Mediterranean to the Atlantic seaboard of Europe, favouring the growth of port cities in the core region such as London, Amsterdam and Antwerp.

Localised resources

Agriculture

In the EU, agricultural productivity tends to decrease with distance from the core. Climate and relief favour agriculture in regions such as the Paris Basin, the Low Countries, southern England and central Germany. The length of the growing season diminishes with increasing latitude, placing limits on agriculture. These limits are compounded by mountainous relief in Scotland, northern England and central Sweden, and by high rainfall and acidic soils. In the Mediterranean Basin the annual summer drought imposes constraints on agriculture. Traditional Mediterranean agriculture based on olives, wheat, vines and sheep sustains only low levels of productivity (Figure 1.20).

Figure 1.20

Traditional Mediterranean farming: simple methods and low productivity

Industry

In the 19th century industrialisation polarised on the coalfields of the core and on the semi-periphery. The coalfields attracted industries such as steel, textiles, chemicals and heavy engineering. The employment opportunities they created led to massive in-migration and the growth of huge urban agglomerations such as Rhine-Ruhr (i.e. Dortmund, Essen, Gelsenkirchen), the West Midlands (i.e. Birmingham,

Wolverhampton), South Belgium (i.e. Liège, Charleroi) and Nord Pas-de-Calais (Lille, i.e. Valenciennes). Figure 1.21 shows part of the Rhine-Ruhr agglomeration.

Figure 1.21

Heavy industry at Essen, Germany, in the late 19th century

Cumulative growth

The process of **cumulative causation** (Figure 1.22) provides an important explanation for regional disparities. Growth begins in regions that have an initial advantage for development. In the EU core these **initial advantages** included natural resources, such as coal and productive farmland, trade routes, access to the sea, and so on. Once development is underway it triggers a series of virtuous growth cycles. For example, new investment in industry or services creates employment which in turn may result in:

- population growth (through in-migration) increasing the size of the labour pool
- rising prosperity and spending power, expanding the regional market
- improvements in infrastructure, such as public transport, utilities and other services
- the growth of **external economies**.

The combined outcome of these developments is further investment. Thus the process is a cumulative one, with growth reinforcing further growth.

Spatial impact

Cumulative causation has important spatial effects. In its early stages it leads to the emergence of a prosperous core and a rather less

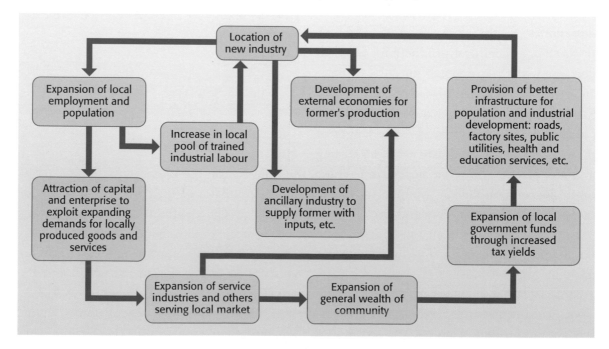

Figure 1.22

The model of cumulative causation

prosperous periphery. Potential growth in the periphery is diverted to the core, with its better infrastructure, skilled workforce and larger market. Eventually these so-called **backwash effects**, which boost development in the core, are replaced by the gradual spread or 'trickle-down' of wealth from the core to the periphery. This phase occurs when the core becomes overdeveloped. Burdened by traffic congestion, high labour costs and high rents, the core loses its attraction for inward investment.

The evidence for **spread effects** in the EU and growth in the periphery is unclear. On the one hand Ireland's economy, fuelled by massive foreign inward investment by high-tech industry and software companies, has grown spectacularly in the past 20 years. Once the poorest country in the EU, today Ireland's per capita GDP stands 8 per cent above the EU average. At the same time the recent success of Sweden and Denmark in securing major inward investment, and the attraction of Portugal's low labour costs to foreign manufacturers, lend further support to the reality of spread effects.

On the other hand the Mediterranean Basin still remains relatively underdeveloped in economic terms. With the exception of those regions that have localised resource advantages for tourism and agriculture, such as Andalucia, there have been few signs of wealth spreading outwards from the core to this part of Europe.

Employment structure

Agriculture and manufacturing

The uneven distribution of wealth within the EU is also influenced by regional employment structures. Excessive dependence on agriculture is associated with below-average prosperity, high unemployment and population decline (Figure 1.23).

Agriculture accounts for nearly 10 per cent of employment in the periphery, compared with 3.5 per cent in the semi-periphery and just 2 per cent in the core. Given that agriculture is a declining industry (Figure 1.24), its

	% unemployment	% employment in agriculture
Ile-de-France (France)	10.3	0.2
South-east England (UK)	3.2	1.3
Hessen (Germany)	6.7	1.7
Bavaria (Germany)	5.0	4.1
Sicily (Italy)	24.8	9.1
Sur (Spain)	25.1	11.7
Sud (Italy)	24.8	12.0
Centro (Spain)	17.6	12.0
Kentriki Ellada (Greece)	11.0	32.5

Figure 1.23

Percentage unemployment and employment in agriculture in selected EU regions, 1999

	Employment (millions)		
	1975	1999	% change
Services	48.1	78.2	+ 63
Manufacturing industry	40.9	33.7	−17
Agriculture	7.6	3.8	−49

Figure 1.24

Sectoral employment trends in the EU, 1975–99

link with unemployment and population decline is not surprising. It is a similar story in many manufacturing regions. Figure 1.24 also shows that employment in manufacturing declined by 17 per cent between 1975 and 1999. Long-established industrial regions such as the Saarland and South Belgium experienced severe unemployment through **de-industrialisation** with the sort of consequences illustrated in Figure 1.25.

Figure 1.25

De-industrialisation and dereliction in northern England

Services

Services dominate EU economies both in terms of wealth created and employment (Figure 1.26). Services create more than half the total output or 'value added' in the EU, and it follows that regions based on service economies are significantly more prosperous than those that rely heavily on agriculture and manufacturing. These service-oriented regions are most strongly concentrated in the core. While employment in agriculture and manufacturing has declined in the past 25 years, the growth of service industries has been spectacular. For example, 95 per cent of all inward investment in Denmark in 2000 was in the service sector, particularly in financial and business services. Services also play an important part in manufacturing industries, from market research and product design, to quality control, advertising and accounting.

Accessibility

Figure 1.27 shows overall accessibility to population within a 250 km radius of any location in Europe. The core area of the EU stands out as the area of highest **population potential**. Parts of the Low Countries and adjacent areas of Germany have access to more than 61 million people. The area approximated by the core in Figure 1.27 has almost immediate access to at least 50 million people. Population potential decreases with distance from the core. Within the EU, population potential is reduced to around 20 million in southern Europe, western Ireland and northern Scotland, and to less than 11 million over large areas of Sweden and Finland.

In a sense, Figure 1.27 summarises the geographical variations in the market potential of the EU. The main market for industry and services is in the core region which has the largest pool of skilled labour, the most developed infrastructure and external economies. Political intervention aside, it is safe to assume that the core is the most attractive area for investment. Access to markets, as illustrated by population potential, is therefore a further influence on the uneven distribution of prosperous and less prosperous regions in the EU.

Figure 1.26

Financial services buildings in the City of London

Figure 1.27

Europe: population potential within a 250 km radius of any location (millions)

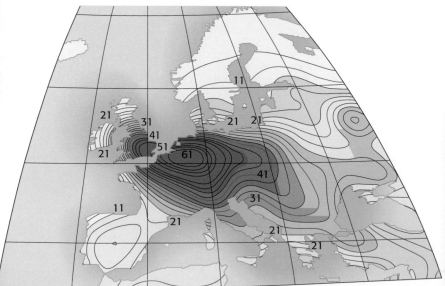

Activity

1 Weigh up the evidence which suggests that the EU has a prosperous core and a less prosperous periphery. Does it suggest that a core–periphery structure is a reality across the EU?

2 'Rich core and poor periphery.' Explain why this view of the economic geography of the EU is an oversimplification.

3 Describe the importance you would attach to physical geography in explaining regional disparities in wealth across the EU.

2 Problem regions in the EU

KEY THEMES

- Problem regions in the EU are often geographically isolated and located in harsh physical environments, for example Andalucia in Spain and Norrbotten in Sweden.
- Some regions have severe economic problems caused by de-industrialisation, structural change and globalisation, such as South Yorkshire.
- EU policies have had variable success in tackling regional economic problems within the community.

The nature of problem regions

In this chapter the characteristics of problem regions in the EU are examined through three case studies. Two of the regions studied – Andalucia in southern Spain, and Norrbotten in northern Sweden – are remote from the core of economic activity in western Europe. Their peripheral location has, in the past, deterred inward investment and encouraged out-migration. But their problems do not end there. Harsh climatic conditions make farming all but impossible in Norrbotten, and in Andalucia they contribute to low agricultural output. Assistance from the EU's Structural Funds aims to make these regions more accessible, to diversify economic activity, and to allow them to develop their comparative advantages.

The third region – South Yorkshire – also lags behind most other regions in the EU, but for different reasons. Its problems are structural. An early centre of industrialisation in Europe, for most of the 20th century South Yorkshire's economy remained overdependent on a narrow range of heavy industries. De-industrialisation in the 1980s brought heavy job losses in staple industries such as coal and steel. The region has still to recover. It needs economic assistance from the EU to re-build and diversify its economy.

 ## Case Study: Andalucia – a peripheral region on the move

Factfile

- Andalucia (Figure 2.1) is a predominantly rural region situated on the periphery of the EU.
- One-quarter of the value of Spain's agricultural output comes from Andalucia.
- Andalucia is the largest of Spain's regions: it is comparable in area to Portugal, and has a population of 7.3 million.
- Andalucia is Spain's poorest region, with a per capita GDP barely 60 per cent of the EU average.

- Andalucia has Objective 1 status and receives generous funding from the ERDF.
- In the 1990s Andalucia experienced a boom: its economy expanded faster than the rest of Spain and because of net migration gain its population grew by 6 per cent.
- 'Poles of development' around Seville, Cordoba, Granada and the Costa del Sol (Malaga, Almeria) attracted significant investment in the 1990s.

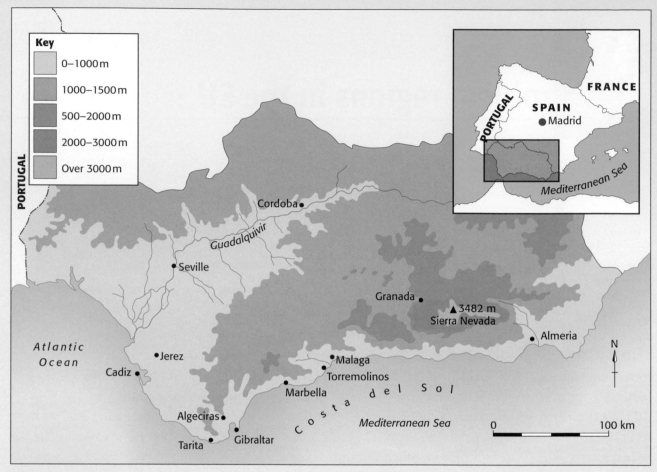

Key
	0–1000 m
	1000–1500 m
	500–2000 m
	2000–3000 m
	Over 3000 m

PORTUGAL

FRANCE

SPAIN
● Madrid

PORTUGAL

Mediterranean Sea

Cordoba ●

Guadalquivir

Seville ●

Granada ●
▲ 3482 m
Sierra Nevada

Almeria ●

Atlantic
Ocean

Jerez ●

Cadiz ●

● Malaga
Torremolinos

Marbella

Costa del Sol

Algeciras ●

Mediterranean Sea

0   100 km

Tarita ●   ● Gibraltar

N

Figure 2.1

Andalucia, southern Spain

Obstacles to development

Until the 1980s a number of factors contributed to the relative backwardness of Andalucia:

- Isolation: its transport links were poor – it took 12 hours by train from Malaga to Madrid, a distance of some 450 km.
- Antiquated farming: well adapted to the scorching heat of summer (mean July temperatures between 25 and 27°C) and drought along the Mediterranean coastlands, but inefficient and low in productivity.
- Little industry, apart from the mass tourism of the Costa del Sol.
- Lack of skills: by the mid-1980s only one-third of Andalucians had completed secondary education.
- A low level of enterprise and an unwillingness of banks to invest in new businesses.

Economic development
Agriculture

Andalucia's economy remains overdependent on agriculture (Figure 2.2). Nearly 12 per cent of employment is in the agricultural sector, compared with 7 per cent in Spain as a whole. Efforts are being made to raise the productivity of agriculture and to increase the added value of food products. Spain is the world's biggest producer of olive oil (heavily subsidised by the EU), and 80 per cent of this output comes from Andalucia, particularly from the Guadalquivir depression. Traditionally, most raw olive oil has been exported. Today, the processing, bottling and branding of olive oil, and of similar products such as mayonnaise and fruit juice, take place in the region, giving added value and providing much-needed jobs in the manufacturing sector.

Figure 2.2
Traditional olive groves in Andalucia, southern Spain

In lowland regions drip irrigation and mechanisation has transformed the drylands into areas of intensive cropping. Around Almeria, irrigation has led to a boom in vegetable production giving rise to scenes like that in Figure 2.3. In this region alone, 45 000 hectares are under plastic, producing courgettes, tomatoes, green peppers and other vegetables for export all year round. Exports are worth £1 billion a year. Intensive vegetable-growing employs 30 000 immigrant workers and also supports food-processing businesses. The industry takes advantage of the sunny climate (300 days of sunshine a year) and local groundwater. However, there are concerns about the industry's sustainability. Irrigation has led to falling water tables, and chemical fertilisers have polluted groundwater resources. Unique, semi-desert ecosystems have been destroyed and parts of the Cabo de Gata Natural Park are threatened.

Industry

Although Andalucia has one-fifth of Spain's population, it accounts for only 10 per cent of the country's industrial output. Attempts to diversify the region's economy have led to the successful introduction of high-tech industry. Technology parks were established at Seville and Malaga in 1993. Seville's Cartuja '93 park has attracted dozens of companies involved in biotechnology, computer science and aviation. At the start of 2001 the Malaga technology park employed 3000 people (half of them graduates) in just under 200 companies, most of them involved in IT (Figure 2.4). The attractions of Malaga include the 300 days of sunshine a year, relatively low wages, and EU funding. It is hoped that the high-tech cluster at Malaga will act as an 'incubator' for new businesses and attract inward investment from **transnational corporations (TNCs)**. The recent boom in industry in the region has helped reverse the traditional out-migration of young people to more prosperous regions in Spain.

Andalucia is also a leader in the generation of solar energy. There are thousands of square metres of solar panels in the region taking advantage of the reliable and plentiful sunshine.

Tourism

Much of Spain's development of mass tourism in the 1960s and 1970s took place on the Costa del Sol in Andalucia, particularly in resorts such as Torremolinos (Figure 2.5) and Marbella. The tourism boom was fuelled by the region's accessibility by air, its relatively low costs, distinctive culture,

Figure 2.3
Intensive vegetable production under plastic, near El Ejido, Almeria

Figure 2.4
High-tech industry in Malaga, Andalucia

warm and sunny climate and extensive coastline. Although tourism remains a leading activity, it is a mature industry with limited potential for further growth. Today the accent is on raising quality and moving the industry up-market (i.e. attracting fewer but higher-spending tourists). Meanwhile, attempts are being made to encourage a more sustainable tourism, to promote tourism during the winter and to develop the industry away from the coast.

Figure 2.5
La Carihuela beach, Torremolinos, southern Spain

Andalucia's development programme 2000–2006

As one of the EU's poorest regions, Andalucia qualifies for Objective 1 funding from the ERDF. More than half the cost of the region's development programme for the period 2000 to 2006 (Figure 2.6) will come from the EU, with a contribution from the ERDF of around £1.8 billion. The remainder will come from the Spanish government.

The priorities of the 2000–2006 programme are to reduce further Andalucia's isolation, invest in industry and tourism, modernise agriculture and raise skill levels through training. There is a strong emphasis on investment in transport and communications, especially motorways, rail electrification, ports (Algeciras, Tarifa), airports (Malaga, Seville, Jerez) and telecoms. Energy and water supply infrastructure are also targeted for investment.

Conclusion

Despite recent progress, Andalucia lags behind most other EU regions. So far development has been patchy and uneven. The problem is how to alleviate deep-rooted poverty and unemployment in much of the countryside. The successful introduction of high-tech industry and irrigation agriculture in pockets such as Seville, Malaga and Almeria is part of the answer. These **growth poles** generate employment and prosperity which could eventually spread throughout the region. Meanwhile a focus on improved infrastructure and human resources through training should make the region more attractive for future investment. Andalucia has many natural assets, not least its climate and coastline. These assets, which are not dissimilar to those of the booming sunbelt states of the USA, are grounds for cautious optimism for the future.

Activity

1 With the aid of an annotated outline map of Europe, explain how Andalucia's situation on Europe's periphery may have caused its development to lag behind that of other regions in the EU.

2 Examine the possibilities for future growth in Andalucia and for closing the wealth gap between it and other EU regions. Present your findings by means of a table with columns headed 'Possibilities' and 'Constraints'.

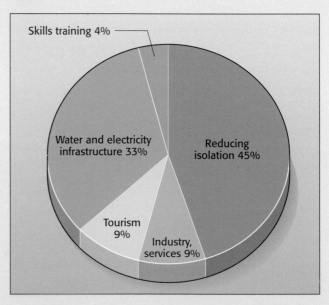

Figure 2.6
Andalucia: development programme spending, 2000–2006

Factfile

- Norrbotten is Sweden's most northerly *län* or county (Figure 2.7).

- It is a vast, sparsely populated region equal to the combined areas of Ireland and Belgium.

- Its population density – less than 2 persons/km² – is the lowest in the EU.

- Two-thirds of Norrbotten lies within the Arctic Circle.

- Norrbotten's total population is just over 250 000.

- Norrbotten's most populous municipality – Luleå – has 70 000 inhabitants; two-thirds of the region's population live in the coastal towns.

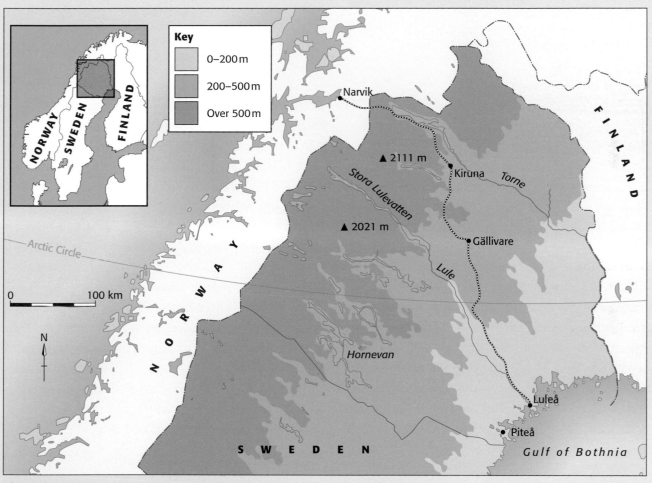

Key

	0–200 m
	200–500 m
	Over 500 m

Figure 2.7

Norrbotten, Sweden

Geographical problems

The geography of Norrbotten has had a direct influence on its development. The main obstacles to development are the region's remoteness, harsh physical environment, and low population density (Figure 2.8).

Remoteness

Even within Sweden, Norrbotten is remote: it is almost 1000 km by road from Sweden's capital, Stockholm, to Luleå. Within the wider context of Europe, Norrbotten, situated 2000 km from the core area of the EU, is by any measure on the extreme periphery.

Figure 2.8
Harsh physical conditions in northern Sweden

Physical environment

Norrbotten's northerly latitude means long hours of darkness in winter and temperatures that often plunge below –20°C. High mountains to the west shut out milder air from the Atlantic Ocean, and contribute to the region's cold winters. Temperatures are low enough for pack ice to form along the Gulf of Bothnia in winter. Coniferous forests dominate the areas of lower relief (below 500 metres) on the Baltic Shield. Elsewhere much of the land is boggy and mosquito-ridden in summer. In the far north, and in the mountainous west, tundra – dominated by low-growing shrubs, lichens, mosses and herbs – replaces the forest.

Norrbotten was the last part of Europe to be deglaciated. Glaciation has contributed to the harshness of the environment. Ice scoured the land, exposing large areas of bedrock and depositing sand, gravel and moraine on the surface. With the exception of the coastal fringe, the effects of glaciation, climate and relief make most of Norrbotten uncultivable.

Population density

Isolation and the harsh physical environment are largely responsible for Norrbotten's low population density. However, the region's small population is itself an obstacle to development. Densely populated regions such as Rhine-Ruhr and Ile-de-France attract investment because they offer investors a large workforce with a varied skills base, provide a large local market, and support vital external economies through inter-firm linkages and the urban infrastructure, e.g. transport, housing, utilities.

Economic and demographic problems

Norrbotten's geographical problems (which are shared with neighbouring Västerbotten and northern Finland) have been instrumental in causing the region to lag behind the rest of Sweden and much of the EU. In 1999, per capita GDP was 4 per cent below Sweden's average, and unemployment at 12 per cent was high even by EU standards. The region's economic problems have contributed to a steady decline in population since the early 1980s. This depopulation, caused both by natural decrease and net migration loss (Figure 2.9), has been most severe in the smaller centres of population away from the coast, as shown in Figure 2.10. Migration from Norrbotten is selective, with disproportionate numbers of women and young adults moving away.

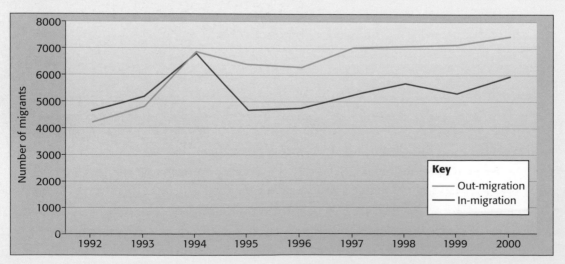

Figure 2.9

In-migration and out-migration: Norrbotten 1992–2000

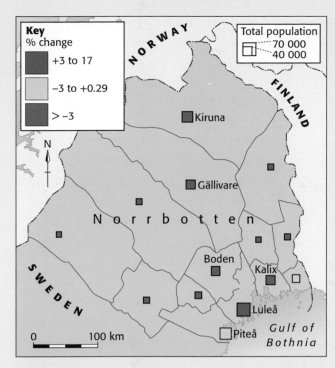

Figure 2.10

Norrbotten: population change 1991–2000

Activity

1	Study Figure 2.11 and calculate the crude birth rate and crude death rate for Norrbotten (remember to multiply births and deaths by four to arrive at an estimate for the year).
2	Assuming the rates of migration in Figure 2.11 remain unchanged, calculate the overall net migration change in Norrbotten likely to be experienced over the next 10 years.
3	Based on the rates of natural population change and net migration change, calculate the percentage change in Norrbotten's total population by 2011.
4	What proportion of this population change is likely to result from **a** natural decrease **b** net migration?

Total population	Births	Deaths	In-migration	Out-migration
255 834	635	683	1017	1367

Figure 2.11

Population change in Norrbotten: 1 January – 31 March 2001

Economy – dependence on primary industries and the public sector

The importance of primary activities

Primary industries such as hydro-electric power (HEP), agriculture, forestry and mining have traditionally been the mainstay of Norrbotten's economy (Figure 2.12). However, these industries have limited employment potential; together they account for no more than 6 per cent of all employment in the region.

Figure 2.12

Iron ore mining at Kiruna, northern Sweden

One-quarter of Sweden's HEP is generated in Norrbotten. Powerful rivers such as the Lule, and large glacial lakes, provide ideal conditions for the generation of hydro-electricity. Agriculture is restricted to the coastal fringe. Farms are small (20 to 30 hectares) and specialise in milk production.

Europe's largest deposits of iron ore are at Kiruna and Gällivare in Norrbotten. Twenty-two million tonnes of iron ore a year are exported by rail through the ports of Luleå on the Gulf of Bothnia, and Narvik in Norway. Other important mineral ores include gold, silver and lead. Norrbotten has huge potential for further development of its mineral reserves and is likely to attract significant inward investment from foreign mining companies in future.

Manufacturing and services

For many years Norrbotten has received economic support from Sweden's regional policies. In consequence, two out of every five jobs in the region are in the public sector, especially in services. For example, local government and government-owned industries are the region's leading employers, providing 11 000 jobs. Steelmaking, based on local iron ore, employs 1500 people at Svenskt Stål in Luleå. Development policies have promoted investment in footloose high-tech industries (biotechnology, medical technology, aerospace) and information technology. These industries employ around 4000 people. The Luleå technology university, established in 1994, is designed to strengthen the cluster of high-tech businesses in the region (Figure 2.13). Even so, the start-up rate for new businesses in the private sector is low, and small manufacturing enterprises (SMEs) find development difficult.

Figure 2.13
Luleå University of Technology, northern Sweden

Norrbotten and EU development policies

By the standards of the EU, Norrbotten is not a poor region. Its per capita GDP, for example, exceeds all the regions in the UK apart from the South East, and it is well above the 75 per cent threshold normally required for Objective 1 status. However, the region's isolation, harsh environment and low population density create unique problems which cannot be solved without government intervention. Hence Norrbotten (and neighbouring Västerbotten) are included in the EU's Objective 1 programme for 2000 to 2006.

Objective 1 programme for Norrbotten: 2000–2006

The programme (with a budget of £600 million) aims to create new jobs in order to reduce unemployment and enable people to live and work in Norrbotten (and Västerbotten), Figure 2.14. Financial assistance from the EU's Structural Funds covers 40 per cent of the programme's cost. The remainder comes from the Swedish government and the private sector. The priorities are: commercial and industrial development; improving infrastructure; skills and employment development; rural development (including fishing and aquaculture); nature and culture; and the Sami programme. The Sami are the indigenous people of northern Scandinavia who have a unique culture based on reindeer herding. For many years, measures designed to preserve and develop Sami culture and traditional activities have featured prominently in EU and Swedish development policies for the far north.

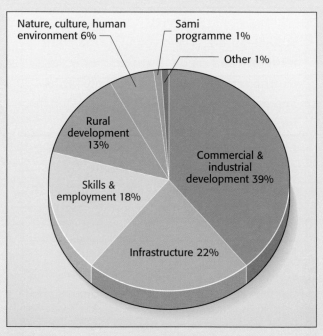

Figure 2.14
The Objective 1 programme for northern Sweden, 2000–2006

Activity
Write a critical appraisal of the view that: 'Geography is responsible for Norrbotten's status as a region lagging behind the rest of the EU'.

- South Yorkshire in northern England is a highly urbanised, industrial region (Figure 2.15).
- Most of its 1.3 million inhabitants are concentrated in the county's regional centre, Sheffield, and in Rotherham, Doncaster and Barnsley.

- In 1998 South Yorkshire had the lowest level of disposable income in England.
- Between 1971 and 1997 South Yorkshire lost 60 per cent of all its industrial jobs.
- The region suffered a population decline of 0.02 per cent between 1994 and 1998.

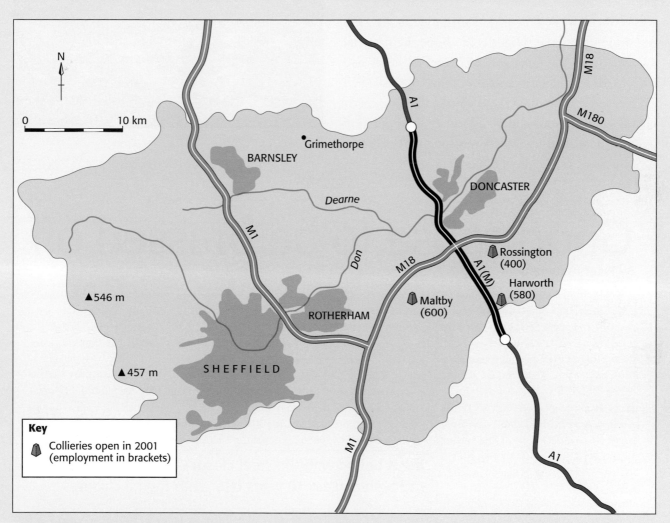

Figure 2.15

The South Yorkshire region

Industrial development

The industrialisation and urbanisation of this region took place in the 19th century. The South Yorkshire coalfield and local deposits of iron ore ensured rapid industrialisation. Industrial development was highly specialised, and focused on a small number of heavy industries, especially coalmining and iron and steel.

De-industrialisation

The vulnerable nature of highly specialised regional economies became apparent in the 1970s and 1980s when South Yorkshire's staple industries collapsed. Between 1978 and 1998 industry shed 177 000 jobs; 42 000 went in the steel industry alone. Employment in coalmining fell from 30 000 in 1988 to just 1500 ten years later.

The steep decline of coalmining created severe deprivation in mining communities such as Grimethorpe near Barnsley, and widespread social exclusion (Figure 2.16). Although South Yorkshire gained 96 000 jobs in the service sector, the workforce was reduced by 92 000 or one-fifth overall. By 1998 unemployment was 50 per cent above the national average and the amount of derelict land had increased to five times more than the national average. Not surprisingly, South Yorkshire has experienced a net migration loss and steady depopulation over the past 20 years. The newspaper article, Figure 2.17, sums up the plight of the region.

Figure 2.16

A socially deprived area in South Yorkshire

Good cause to be brassed off

By Peter Hetherington

Not so long ago, it was in England's industrial heartland. Work was hard but relatively plentiful and earnings above the national average.

Now most of the coal mines and steel mills have closed, the once-thriving villages that house the workers lie partly abandoned, and South Yorkshire has become one of England's poorest areas. Not even its fame as the setting for the most successful British film of all time, *The Full Monty*, can do much to help.

This week, after months of lobbying in Brussels by the four councils in the area, the European Union is expected to officially classify the county as one of its most deprived areas, alongside parts of eastern Germany, Sicily, Crete, Galicia in Spain, and Merseyside.

South Yorkshire should qualify as a so-called Objective 1 area, eligible for substantial aid to create jobs, improve training and redevelop derelict sites. To qualify, GDP must be no more than 75 per cent of the EU average. South Yorkshire scores 70.7 per cent, according to figures just released, placing it below Merseyside, England's only other Objective 1 area.

'On these figures, there is no doubt it is among the poorest areas currently in the EU,' said a European Commission

'It got belted with the steel closures in the early eighties and belted again 10 years later with the pit closures.'

spokesman. 'The economic comparisons with east Germany are striking.'

Kostas Georgiou, the researcher employed by the South Yorkshire's four councils to prepare its submission for Objective 1 status, said the area had deteriorated enormously in 20 years. 'The worst problem was the pace of

change – it happened so quickly and it is difficult to adjust. Twenty years ago it was a relatively thriving area. Big companies and the pits literally closed overnight.'

Richard Caborn, Minister for the Regions and MP for Sheffield Central, said his county had suffered a 'double whammy'. 'It got belted with the steel closures in the early eighties and belted

again 10 years later with the pit closures.'

The case for help from the EU is very strong. He said local councils had been stunned by new research showing the scale of South Yorkshire's economic problems. 'It is much worse than we thought.'

Figure 2.17

Extract from *The Guardian*, 16 March 1998

South Yorkshire and EU development policies

The decline in South Yorkshire's economic fortunes has been particularly rapid in the past 20 years or so. In 1979 the region's per capita GDP stood at 95 per cent of the EU average. It then fell every year between 1979 and 1996 until the average for the period 1995–98 reached 73 per cent, putting South Yorkshire on a par with Mediterranean regions such as Basilicata and Corsica. In 1999 the EU recognised that South Yorkshire was one of the EU's poorest regions, and granted it Objective 1 status.

The Objective 1 programme

South Yorkshire is included in the EU's Objective 1 programme for the period 2000 to 2006. The EU's Structural Funds will provide subsidies to the region amounting to between 40 and 50 per cent of the development programme. Overall the EU will pump around £740 million into South Yorkshire between 2000 and 2006. With government and private money matching the EU's commitment, the total invested in the region should amount to £1.5 billion. The Objective 1 programme revolves around five priority areas:

- encouraging new growth and high-tech sectors
- modernising businesses and promoting innovation
- developing a highly skilled, ICT-literate workforce and tackling the problems of access to employment and social exclusion
- developing a number of strategic enterprise zones and business districts in urban areas and encouraging small manufacturing enterprises (SMEs)
- improving the region's road infrastructure and access to capital and funding for SMEs.

Conflict between EU and government policies

A recent report suggested that South Yorkshire's Objective 1 programme would do little more than stop the region's relative decline. Adding just 2 per cent to per capita GDP, the programme would keep the region's GDP at 74 per cent of the EU average.

Development is complicated by government policy. The government wants new factories to occupy **brownfield sites** – derelict land left by de-industrialisation. The problem is that many brownfield sites in South Yorkshire (Figure 2.18) are poorly

Figure 2.18

Derelict land in South Yorkshire

connected to the motorway network. Moreover, government policy discourages industrial development next to motorways.

In Barnsley, the local development agency wants to build new factories on **greenfield sites** next to junction 37 on the M1. Good transport links are crucial to a business success. Despite generous subsidies, an industrial estate in the Dearne Valley (see Figure 2.15) remained empty until a link-road to the motorway was built.

Conclusion

South Yorkshire, unlike Andalucia and Norrbotten, is not on the geographical periphery of the EU. Its economic problems stem from neither remoteness nor a harsh physical environment. Rather, they can be attributed to an unfavourable employment structure, dominated until recently by declining steel and mining sectors.

Thanks to local energy and mineral resources, regions such as South Yorkshire enjoyed a **comparative advantage** over other EU regions until the mid-20th century. However, specialisation and over-dependence on heavy industries led to prolonged decline. This decline accelerated in the 1970s and 1980s. Today the region is still adjusting to the massive de-industrialisation which occurred at that time. The EU's regional policies, together with those of the British government, are intended to revive a region that lags behind the rest of the UK, and most of the EU. Recovery – as demonstrated by Merseyside which has been an Objective 1 region since 1994 – will be a slow and painful process.

Activity

1 Compile a table to summarise the main features of the three problem regions – Andalucia, Norrbotten, South Yorkshire – described in this chapter. Use the following column headings:

Per capita GDP, Unemployment, Population change, Physical environmental problems, Accessibility, EU-assisted area status, Development programme, Achievements.

2 Prepare a presentation for delivery in class addressing the following question: 'To what extent do the problems of less prosperous regions in the EU have common causes?'

3 Common policies in the EU and their geographical impact

KEY THEMES

- The EU states have common policies for agriculture and fishing.
- In the past, the Common Agricultural Policy (CAP) has led to massive food surpluses and environmental degradation in the EU.
- Recent reforms of the CAP have promoted a more environmentally sustainable agriculture and have sought to bring food production in line with demand.
- The Common Fisheries Policy (CFP) aims to create a sustainable fishing industry in the EU and to provide economic support to fishing communities.
- The CFP has failed to stop overfishing in EU waters and to halt the economic decline of many fishing communities.

Common policies in the EU

At the heart of the EU are a number of common policies covering agriculture, fishing, regional development and trade. These policies have had a profound effect on shaping the geography of the EU in the past 40 years.

Agriculture and fishing are the economic activities most closely regulated by EU policies. Both the Common Agricultural Policy (CAP) and the Common Fisheries Policy (CFP) have been targets for severe criticism. The CAP has resulted in overproduction and food surpluses, at considerable cost to the environment. Meanwhile the CFP has failed to resolve the problem of overfishing and to achieve sustainability in the EU fishing industry. In recent years, reform of both the CAP and CFP has taken place. It remains to be seen whether these reforms can establish an effective balance between production and conservation, and create sustainable agriculture and fishing industries within the EU.

The importance of agriculture in the EU

As far as economic output and employment are concerned, agriculture in the EU is a relatively minor economic activity. It contributes less than 2 per cent to GDP and employs just 4.7 per cent of the EU's working population. Agriculture is relatively most important in southern Europe. However, only in Greece does agriculture's share of total national output exceed 5 per cent, while in 1996 only Greece, Portugal and Ireland had more than 10 per cent of total employment in agriculture.

Agriculture has more significance as a land user. Just over 40 per cent of the land area of the EU is used for arable, pasture and permanent crops (Figure 3.1).

The Common Agricultural Policy

The CAP absorbs nearly half of the EU budget. Although this proportion fell steadily during the 1990s (see Figure 3.2), it is still remarkable

Figure 3.1

Land use in the EU

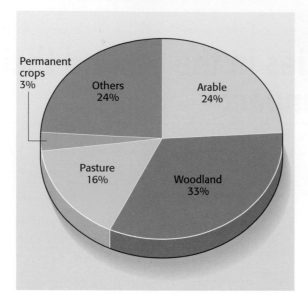

Figure 3.2

The CAP as a percentage of the EU budget, 1993–99

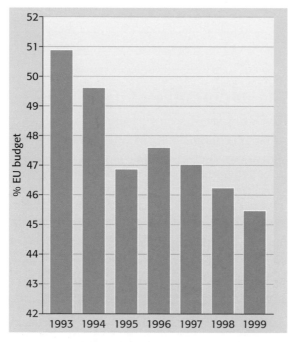

Funding the CAP

Money for the CAP is paid by the European Agriculture Guidance and Guarantee Fund (EAGGF). There are two sections to this fund: guidance and guarantee. The guarantee section accounts for 90 per cent of CAP expenditure. All market support expenditure – such as intervention buying and direct payments, as well as some environmental and forestry payments – is paid for by the guarantee section. The guidance section has traditionally paid for structural grants for farm improvements, including irrigation and land consolidation.

Reform of the CAP

In the past 40 years the CAP has been reformed on several occasions, most recently in 1992 and 2000. These reforms were variously a response to changes in the membership of the EU, mismatches between product supply and demand, and concern about the impact of agriculture on the environment. The CAP is complex. It has four main strands: price management, direct producer aids, supply controls, and structural and environmental payments. This structure is summarised in Figure 3.3.

Changes in agriculture in the EU
Declining agricultural workforce

In 1997 there were 14.5 million full-time workers in agriculture in the EU. Two-thirds were concentrated in southern Europe (Figure 3.4), in Italy, Spain, Portugal and Greece. Much of the farming in southern Europe is labour intensive and, compared with central and northern Europe, farms are small and inefficient. One-half of all farms in the EU are in Italy, Greece and Portugal. In these countries farm sizes average between 5 and 9 hectares. The UK has the biggest holdings, averaging 70 hectares, with 17 per cent exceeding 100 hectares.

There have been massive reductions in the EU's agricultural workforce in the past 20 years or so. Employment in agriculture fell by 36 per cent in the EU15 countries between 1980 and

that an industry which plays a relatively minor role in the economy of the Union so dominates its spending.

The CAP aims

Introduced in 1962, the CAP aims to:

- increase agricultural productivity and ensure a fair standard of living for agricultural communities
- stabilise markets
- ensure food security
- produce food at reasonable prices for consumers.

Price management	
Guaranteed price and intervention	A guaranteed market price is set each year. If the market price falls below the guaranteed level (e.g. £62/tonne for wheat and barley in August 2001), the EU buys the produce at the guaranteed price. This process is known as intervention buying; the produce is stored and sold at a later date.
Import levies	Imported produce from non-EU countries is subject to a levy, which increases its costs. These levies protect EU farmers against cheaper imports.
Export subsidies	These subsidies help farmers export products at competitive prices.

Direct producer aids	
Direct aids and market support	Direct payments to farmers per tonne of crop produced.
Deficiency payments	Payments based on the difference between the market price and the intended level of payment to farmers.
Livestock premium	Producers of sheep, suckler cows and beef cattle receive payments at a fixed rate per animal.
Area payments	Arable farmers' incomes are supplemented by payments per hectare of arable land (e.g. £308/ha for oilseed in August 2001).

Supply controls	
Quotas	Since 1984 dairy farmers have been charged a levy if they produce more than a fixed quota of milk. In other sectors – sheep, beef cattle, sugar beet, tobacco – limits have been placed on the amount of subsidy farmers can receive.
Set-aside	In the arable sector, farms only receive direct area payments if farmers remove part of their arable land from production (at least 10 per cent). Set-aside payments in 2001 were £255/ha.

Structural and environmental payments	
Structural assistance	Funds are available to improve farm structures and profitability, including grants for farm improvement, diversification into non-farm activities, assistance in difficult hill areas, and marketing and processing. In southern Europe funds are available to encourage the amalgamation of small farms.
Environmental aid	There are schemes to encourage environmentally-friendly farming. Grants are available for conservation, reducing pollution, and to promote traditional farming in environmentally sensitive areas.
Woodlands	Farmers who convert agricultural land to woodland receive payments to compensate for loss of income.

Figure 3.3

The CAP 2000–2001: how it works

1997. In fact, 1 million farmers gave up their holdings between 1990 and 1995 alone. The causes of this decline were:

- the general fall in farm incomes owing to lower prices for agricultural products
- an ageing population of farmers, with a disproportionate number reaching retirement age
- advantages of large farms (scale economies, CAP subsidies) which absorbed smaller ones.

Although the movement of labour out of agriculture is evident everywhere in the EU (Figure 3.5), the biggest shake-out will occur in southern Europe during the next 20 years. Here the full

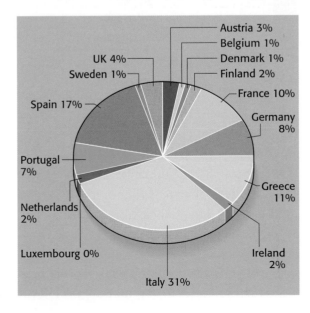

Figure 3.4

The EU agricultural workforce

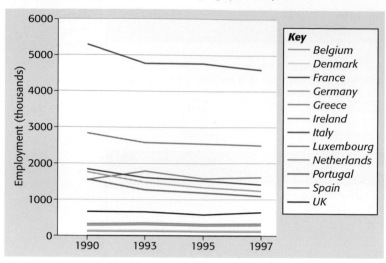

Figure 3.5

Employment change in agriculture (EU12), 1990–97

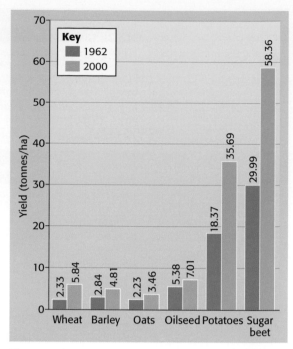

Figure 3.6

Changes in average crop yields (EU15), 1962 and 2000

impact of modernisation through mechanisation and farm amalgamation will take effect. Moreover, almost two-thirds of all farmers in southern Europe are over 55 years of age. With imminent retirement, thousands of smallholdings are likely to disappear, and a massive fall in the farm population, accompanied by migration from the countryside, looks inevitable.

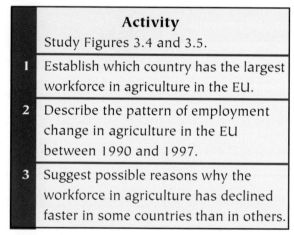

Activity
Study Figures 3.4 and 3.5.
1 Establish which country has the largest workforce in agriculture in the EU.
2 Describe the pattern of employment change in agriculture in the EU between 1990 and 1997.
3 Suggest possible reasons why the workforce in agriculture has declined faster in some countries than in others.

Rising production

Yields for all major crops have risen sharply since the establishment of the CAP in 1962. For example, wheat yields which averaged 2.33 tonnes/ha in 1962 had soared to 5.13 tonnes by 1990. Although yields then began to level out, wheat yields reached 5.84 tonnes/ha by the year 2000 (Figure 3.6). Other crops and livestock products such as beef, pork and milk all show similar increases.

The CAP is primarily responsible for these spectacular increases in output. Until the reform of the CAP in the early 1990s, the system of guaranteed prices and intervention buying gave farmers a market for their products regardless of the level of demand. The intensive use of agro-chemicals (fertilisers and pesticides) was also partly responsible for the increase in yields; Figure 3.7 shows how wheat yields and nitrate use rose in step with one another. The use of

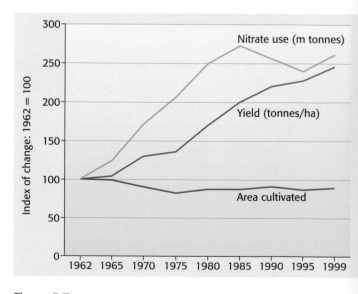

Figure 3.7

Wheat yields, wheat area and the use of nitrate fertilisers (EU15), 1962–99 more advanced machinery and the increase in the number of larger, more efficient farms further contributed to improvements in output.

Activity
With reference to Figure 3.7:
1 Describe the changes that occurred in wheat yields between 1962 and 1999.
2 State evidence suggesting that increases in the total production of wheat in the period 1962–99 was the result of the intensification of production rather than its **extensification**.

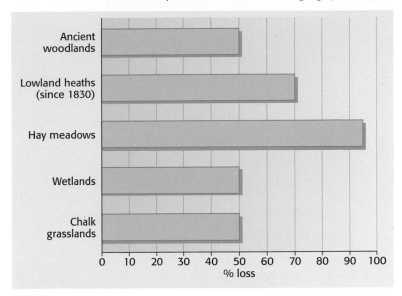

Figure 3.8

Loss of habitats in the UK, 1945–98

Surpluses

The CAP system of guaranteed prices and intervention buying fuelled increases in production and led to huge surpluses of grain, beef, dairy products and wine. The cost of storing and disposing of these food 'mountains' provoked widespread criticism of the CAP. The European Commission responded by introducing supply controls (Figure 3.3) and reforming the CAP in 1992.

Environmental impact

Increases in output in the 1970s and 1980s were achieved at considerable cost to the environment. Important wildlife habitats were lost through the intensification of farming and their conversion to farmland – see Figure 3.8 for the loss of habitats in the UK. Wetlands were drained, chalk grasslands ploughed, ancient woodlands and hedgerows cleared, and traditional hay meadows (Figure 3.9) were replaced by sown grasses.

These changes had disastrous effects on populations of plants and animals. They were compounded by the use of agro-chemicals. Herbicides removed plant species that competed with crops but provided valuable food sources for insects, birds and mammals. Nitrogenous fertilisers washed from the soil contaminated streams and groundwater

Figure 3.9

A traditional flower-rich pasture in Wensleydale

supplies. Water courses were also polluted by animal waste produced by intensive pig and poultry operations. A report by the Royal Society for the Protection of Birds produced in the late 1990s showed that European countries with the most intensive farming suffered the most rapid decline in bird populations. The decline was most severe in those EU countries where agricultural intensification had been driven by the CAP. Arable regions such as East Anglia and Brittany, with traditional landscapes of small fields and hedgerows, were fundamentally altered. The removal of hedgerows meant a loss not only of habitat but also of ancient cultural landscapes.

Agriculture is an important sector in the economy of Brittany, and Brittany is one of France's leading farming regions (Figure 3.10). Although the region has only 6 per cent of France's agricultural area, it accounts for nearly 14 per cent of the country's output (by value) of agricultural products. Intensive livestock farming dominates the region's agriculture. Brittany has over half of France's pig herd, produces nearly a quarter of the country's milk and is also the EU's leading producer of poultry meat. A typical pattern of land use resulting from this mix of enterprises is shown in Figure 3.11.

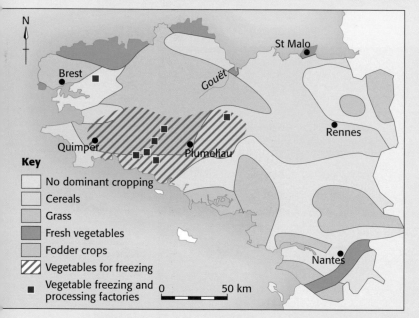

Figure 3.10

Brittany: agricultural land use

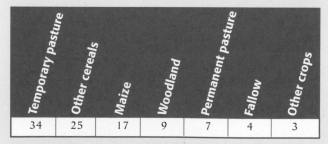

Temporary pasture	Other cereals	Maize	Woodland	Permanent pasture	Fallow	Other crops
34	25	17	9	7	4	3

Figure 3.11

Percentage land use in the Gouët drainage basin, north-west Brittany

Brittany has been strongly affected by changes in EU agriculture in the past 40 years. Milk quotas in 1984 led to a move away from milk production and an emphasis on intensive pig and poultry farming.

Pasture land was converted to arable to grow cereals (maize, wheat and barley) for fodder. The CAP also encouraged intensive arable farming, with farmers raising yields by the use of agro-chemicals and hedgerow removal.

The environmental impact of intensive farming

Intensive farming in Brittany has caused severe environmental pollution and changed the traditional rural landscapes of the region.

Pollution of water by intensive arable farming

The Gouët basin near Saint-Brieuc in Brittany illustrates how intensive arable farming has polluted water resources. Leaching of chemical fertilisers from arable land has concentrated nitrates and phosphates in the Gouët River, making the water unsafe for drinking. Pesticide levels are similarly high and phosphate enrichment has caused algal growth and **eutrophication**.

The severity of pollution from chemical fertilisers and pesticides depends on crop types and locations.

- Fallow and winter wheat are unable to fix nitrogen in soils fertilised during the autumn, even if the balance of nitrogen fertilisers is correct.
- The volume of pesticides and phosphates entering streams and rivers via run-off depends on slope angles, the distance these substances travel before reaching a stream channel, and on the amount of crop cover in winter.

Today around half of Brittany is designated as a **nitrate vulnerable zone**. Under this designation the CAP compensates farmers for reducing their inputs of nitrates and other chemical fertilisers.

Pollution of water by intensive livestock enterprises

The massive growth in intensive pig and poultry farming has greatly increased the amount of animal waste. Currently the volume of slurry generated is too great for the soil to absorb safely. Too many animals and too little land mean that inputs of organic nitrate exceed the safe level (170 kg/ha) over large areas of Brittany. It is known that high nitrate levels in drinking water present a public health threat, particularly to vulnerable groups such as pregnant women and babies. Despite EU directives in the 1970s and 1980s aimed at controlling nitrate use, France has been slow to respond.

Landscape change

Intensive arable farming driven by the CAP has transformed the rural landscape of large parts of Brittany in the past 30 years (Figure 3.12). The traditional rural landscape in Brittany, known as **bocage**, comprised small irregular fields bounded by hedgerows (Figure 3.13). This type of landscape was ill-adapted to modern arable farming. Small fields are inefficient for farm machinery. Hedgerows, which occupied 10 per cent of the agricultural area, shaded field margins and reduced yields.

Since the 1960s hedgerows have been removed and widely scattered plots belonging to different farms have been consolidated. Meanwhile as older farmers have retired, farms have been enlarged. All these changes, assisted either directly or indirectly by the CAP, have transformed Brittany's rural landscape.

Landscape change has also affected ecosystems. The disappearance of hedgerows has destroyed valuable habitats for wildlife and has modified the hydrology. Hedgerow removal has reduced interception and transpiration and increased run-off, with implications for soil conservation and stream flow. At the same time, rapid run-off has increased the risk of drought during periods of low rainfall.

Figure 3.13

Bocage landscape in Brittany

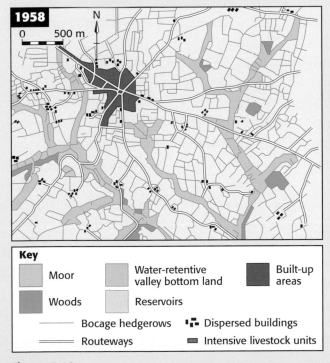
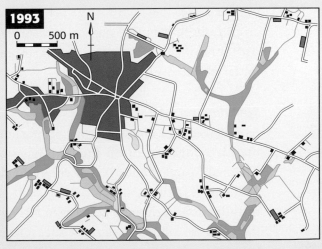

Figure 3.12

Change in landscape features to the south and east of Plumeliau, Brittany, 1958 and 1993

Activity

1 Study Figure 3.12 and describe, with possible explanations, the changes in land use and the agricultural landscape around Plumeliau.

2 Explain how an integrated approach that views farming as part of an ecosystem might solve some of the environmental problems caused by farming in Brittany.

3 To what extent might the CAP be blamed for the environmental problems caused by farming in Brittany?

Changes to the CAP in the 1990s

Since its inception in 1962 the CAP has had to adapt to meet a number of challenges.

Surpluses

Problems of surplus production have been addressed primarily by quotas and the set-aside scheme. Milk quotas, introduced in 1984, have successfully limited milk production. The set-aside scheme pays farmers to take arable land out of production (see Figure 3.3 and Chapter 9), and by reducing the arable area output has been lowered, bringing the supply of cereals and other arable crops into line with demand. Since 1992 policies have placed more emphasis on fixed area payments (e.g. per hectare of crop) rather than price support measures (e.g. per tonne of crop), thus reducing the incentive for farmers to overproduce.

Spending on CAP

As illustrated in Figure 3.2, the proportion of the EU budget spent on the CAP has slowly declined from around 70 per cent in the mid-1980s to less than 50 per cent in 2001. The introduction of direct payments to farmers at the expense of price support measures has helped to reduce the cost of the CAP. This trend will continue: reforms of the CAP in the year 2000 recommended further price cuts for most crops and livestock products.

Environment

During the 1990s the environment assumed much higher priority within the CAP.

- Set-aside land has encouraged wildlife, and recent modifications of the scheme are likely to increase further the benefits to the countryside (see Chapter 9, Figure 9.21).
- The promotion of organic farming has helped to de-intensify agriculture and reduce the harmful effects of chemical fertilisers and pesticides.
- Compensatory allowances, originally confined to less favoured farming areas (i.e. the uplands) have been extended to areas where specific environmental conditions impose restrictions on farming, such as in national parks.
- Subsidies are available for the conversion of arable land to woodland and for farming in both nitrate sensitive zones and environmentally sensitive areas (Figure 3.3).
- Premiums for cattle and sheep are increased where farmers maintain low **stocking densities**.
- Direct aid payments are conditional on compliance with environmental provisions.

Rural development

The CAP aims to maintain the viability of rural communities, provide work opportunities in rural areas, and modernise agriculture. Under the Guidance Fund, money is available to farmers:

- in less favoured areas (LFAs) where development is lagging behind (Figure 3.14)
- for agricultural improvements such as irrigation and land consolidation (e.g. in Andalucia)
- for diversification into 'off-land' enterprises such as tourism.

Figure 3.14
Hill farming in a less favoured area

The CAP in retrospect

Although much criticised, the CAP has undoubtedly fulfilled its key aims. Its success in raising food production has made the EU self-sufficient in most livestock products and temperate food crops, which has greatly increased the Community's food security. The CAP has also given farmers unprecedented stability of prices and income, providing a secure economic framework in which they can operate. But these benefits, though considerable, must be set against significant drawbacks:

- The CAP has been very costly. Taxpayers have been hit twice: first through huge subsidies given to farmers; and second through artificially high prices for food. One estimate suggests that the CAP costs an average family £700 a year in higher food prices.
- Until recently the CAP accounted for more than half of all EU spending. Critics argue that farming, which employs less than 5 per cent of the EU workforce and contributes no more than 2 per cent to GDP, enjoys a privileged position shared by no other industry.
- Subsidies have enabled small, inefficient farmers to remain in business.

- Large and efficient farms, able to compete effectively in world markets, have often received the biggest subsidies.
- Import levies protect EU farmers from lower-cost producers in non-EU countries, and export subsidies give EU farmers an advantage in world markets. Advocates of free trade (including the World Trade Organisation) argue that this situation is unfair. The policy discriminates against non-EU farmers and increases prices to consumers in the EU.
- The CAP, particularly up to the end of the 1980s, had a degrading effect on the environment. Price support encouraged intensification which destroyed wildlife habitats, changed the appearance of rural landscapes, and polluted water resources with agro-chemicals.

These criticisms have prompted reform of the CAP. As a result food surpluses disappeared in the 1990s, agriculture was de-intensified, and environmentally-friendly policies achieved greater prominence. More reform is likely. In the front line are both further reductions in the cost of the CAP to the taxpayer, and modifications to the protectionist policies which have hitherto shielded EU farmers from world competition.

Activity
Review this part of the book dealing with agriculture in the EU (pages 35–43) and write an assessment of the advantages and disadvantages of the CAP over the past 40 years.

Fishing in the EU maritime areas
Background

Fish are a natural resource and fishing is a primary economic activity. Although fishing in the EU contributes less than 1 per cent of GDP and employs fewer than 250 000 people directly, it supports other shore-based activities such as fish processing, boat building and fish marketing.

In some EU coastal regions, especially in Scotland, Portugal, Denmark and the Mediterranean, whole communities depend on the fishing sector. The general decline of the fishing industry in the past 20 years has created long-term economic problems in these communities. These problems, which include poverty, unemployment and lack of job opportunities, are comparable to those found in coalfield communities and remote rural areas.

Sustainable exploitation of fish resources

Resources that have common ownership, such as the seas, oceans and the atmosphere, are the most difficult to regulate. While countries have exclusive rights to develop offshore deposits of oil and gas in a 320 km zone, they have no such control over fish resources. Fish are a mobile resource, often migrating long distances. They cannot be managed in the same way as fixed offshore resources, and unlike oil and gas are not owned by any one country. Two factors make fish particularly vulnerable to over-exploitation: their common ownership, and a perception that as a **renewable resource** they are inexhaustible.

The regulation and **sustainable** exploitation of fish stocks are only possible where all parties agree. For example, if country A decides to conserve stocks by reducing its fishing effort by 20 per cent, but others continue to fish as normal, their catches will increase at the expense of country A. In other words, the actions of country A will not stop overfishing and will cause its fishermen to lose out. The inevitable outcome of this situation is that country A and all other countries will continue to fish unsustainably until the fishery is exhausted. To some extent this is what has happened in EU maritime areas since the early 1980s.

The Common Fisheries Policy (CFP)

The CFP, introduced in 1983, is the main instrument for managing the fishing industry in the EU. Its principal aim is to make fishing sustainable. There are three strands to the CFP: quotas or total allowable catches (TACs); reductions in the fishing effort; and economic support for fishing communities (Figure 3.15).

Activity	
1	Consult the Glossary (pages 220–222) and note down the definitions of the terms 'renewable resource' and 'sustainability'.
2	Explain the difference between a renewable resource and an inexhaustible resource.
3	Explain how the physical geography of Europe has influenced the development of the EU's fishing industry.
4	Amplify the statement: 'Every fisherman is vulnerable to the actions of others'.

Figure 3.15

The Common Fisheries Policy

The Common Fisheries Policy	
Quotas	Annual quotas set – total allowable catches (TACs) for countries, fish stocks and fishing zones. For example, for 2001, UK North Sea quotas were cut by 45% for cod, 21% for haddock, and 32% for whiting compared with the previous year.
Reducing the fishing effort	The fishing effort is the size and power of fishing fleets multiplied by the number of days spent fishing. Fishing effort is controlled by reducing the size of fishing fleets and by limiting the number of days spent at sea.
Economic assistance to fishing communities	Since 1993 EU money available for restructuring the economies of areas heavily dependent on fishing have been channelled through one fund – the Financial Instrument for Fisheries Guidance (FIFG). In 1996 the so-called PESCA initiative also gave these areas access to money from the other Structural Funds. In 2000, fishing communities that faced structural difficulties were included in either Objective 1 or Objective 2 programmes. Economic assistance from the FIFG and the Structural Funds is mainly targeted at diversification, job creation, re-training and education.

EU fishing in crisis in the 1980s and 1990s

During the 1980s and 1990s there was mounting evidence of the unsustainability of fishing in EU waters.

- Catches of whitefish such as cod, haddock and hake declined by 43 per cent between 1985 and 1999 (see Figure 3.16). During this period all the main fisheries – flatfish, pelagic fish such as mackerel and herring, and shellfish – suffered decline. By 2000, cod stocks in the North Sea were just one-tenth of their 1970 level.

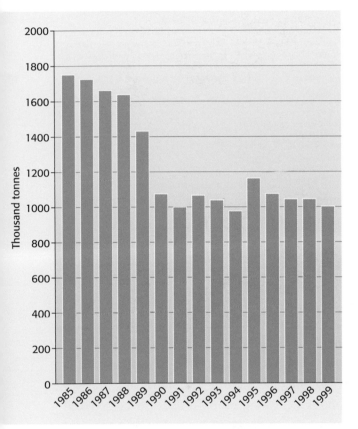

Figure 3.16

Catches of cod, haddock and hake (EU12), 1985–99

- By the end of the 1990s, so few cod were available that fisherman in the North Sea could not even achieve their quotas.
- An increasing proportion of smaller, immature fish was caught. This trend threatened spawning and the replacement of fish stocks.
- As larger species such as cod became scarce,

smaller fish (e.g. mackerel, sardines, anchovies) became more numerous and fishing moved down the food chain. The catch of shrimps and prawns is now nearly as important as that of large fish. Eventually even the smaller species will be depleted and already some countries are looking at the possibilities of harvesting plankton which supports the entire marine food chain.

- Herring stocks crashed in 1976 and only recovered after a total ban on fishing.
- In June 2000, all nine commercial fishing stocks in the North Sea were declared to be 'outside safe biological limits'.

Some experts believe that it may already be too late for some fish stocks to recover; that even an outright ban on fishing certain species would have little effect. Evidence of overfishing of cod on the Grand Banks of Newfoundland – once the world's most prolific cod fishery – indicates that if fish populations are depleted beyond a certain level they may never recover. In 1992 the cod fishery on the Grand Banks was closed; eight years later the cod had still not come back.

Reasons for declining fish catches

Declining catches mainly result from overfishing, although marine pollution and destruction of habitat by trawling also play a part, as described in Figure 3.17.

Overfishing is caused by excessive fishing effort. There is currently a mismatch between the size of fishing fleets (97 000 fishing vessels in the EU in 1999) and available resources. Too many fishing vessels, which are too efficient at catching fish, spend too long at sea. Indeed many fleets have been modernised (often with financial assistance from the EU) in the past 20 years, making them even more effective in catching fish. Modern trawlers (Figure 3.18) can pinpoint fish shoals by sophisticated radar and satellite technology. The largest are giant, floating freezer factories, capable of landing 50 tonnes of fish per hour.

Atlantic fish stocks in peril, survey reveals

Paul Brown
Environment correspondent

Two-thirds of the fish stocks in the north-east Atlantic and all of the commercial species in the North Sea are over-exploited and in danger of disappearing, according to a report released yesterday in Copenhagen.

In the first comprehensive look at the state of the seas along the European coastline, the depletion of fish stocks was the main concern but pollution from the oil industry and other human sources was also serious.

There have been regional reports of some coastal areas, Irish and North Seas before the Ospar Commission, a 15-nation treaty organisation that deals with pollution in European waters and the health of the seas, but never one covering the whole region.

The report reviews evidence from the Arctic to the Straits of Gibraltar and from Greenland to the Kattegat, concluding that in some areas pollution had been reduced but overall, the seas faced many threats.

Apart from overfishing, trawls were causing serious damage to the sea bed, destroying many species including rare corals which were being smashed. Anti-fouling paints used on the bottom of ships were continuing to cause serious problems, with shellfish changing sex and colonies being destroyed. For the first time, there were serious concerns about the effect of global warming on the seas – on fish spawning, the disappearance of wetlands and potential for flooding low-lying areas.

Among the other findings was the threat to wild salmon stocks of escapes from fish farms resulting in interbreeding and parasites; serious damage to sea bed and marine life by large-scale dredging for sand and gravel; litter from ships strangling and drowning birds, turtles and dolphins, and the discharge of oily waste and bilges from ships which has led to 100 exotic species being released and breeding in European waters.

Although heavy metals like cadmium, mercury and lead had reduced, PCB pollution was still a serious problem. Stored in body fat, PCBs could make some birds and mammals sterile. North Sea flatfish were developing tumours because of contamination. Oil and gas installations were causing pollution and marine life was reduced within two miles of platforms.

The report was launched in Copenhagen by the Danish environment minister, Svend Auken, the host of the five-day meeting of Ospar nations. He said it was a hopeful sign that the combined efforts of 15 countries had managed to reduce pollution in many areas but despite this there were many serious areas of concern.

According to the report, 40 of the 60 main commercial fish stocks were 'outside safe biological limits.' This meant too many adults were being killed to leave viable breeding stock. All nine species listed from the North Sea, including cod and haddock, came into this category despite EU efforts to limit catches.

Of special concern were the deepwater fish, not previously caught, but now trawled to replace overfished species. The scabbard, roundnose grenadier and argentine found along the continental shelf edge are now regularly found in British supermarkets.

Euan Dunn, RSPB marine police officer, said: 'Knowledge of these deepwater species is in its infancy. With their slow growth and low breeding rate they are highly vulnerable to over-exploitation.' Dr Dunn said the report was 'a wake-up call to the EU'.

The World Wide Fund for Nature said in a statement that global warming was potentially the most serious threat to species in the north-east Atlantic. It said the report showed the seas were severely degraded and a greater sense of urgency was required.

Figure 3.17

From *The Guardian*, 1 July 2000

Figure 3.18

A modern trawler in EU waters

Activity

Read the article in Figure 3.17 and compile a table that describes and explains the threats to fish stocks in the north-east Atlantic.

Managing the EU fishing industry

Without an effective common fishing policy to regulate catches and ensure sustainability, fisheries in the EU maritime area will eventually collapse. With them will go thousands of jobs in fishing and related onshore industries.

The CFP attempts to ease pressure on fish stocks by (a) setting annual quotas for catches and (b) reducing the overall fishing effort. Quotas are agreed for annual catches of individual species in particular fishing zones. For example, the UK North Sea cod quota was cut from 34 360 tonnes in 2000 to 18 930 tonnes in 2001.

Quotas by themselves, however, are not enough. Fishing effort must also be reduced either by scrapping vessels and reducing the size of the fishing fleet or by limiting the number of days at sea, or both. While the CFP sets targets for reducing the fishing effort of EU member states, it is up to individual governments to choose how to meet them, either through scrapping or tying-up its vessels. To date, just over half the total reduction in fishing effort has been achieved by scrapping vessels; between 1992 and 1996 there was a 7 per cent cut in the size of the EU fleet. Tie-up programmes now account for a 45 per cent cut in fishing effort.

North-east Scotland is the leading fish-catching region in the UK, as illustrated in Figure 3.19. In 1999 there were nearly 2800 fishermen in the region. They supported around 4700 local jobs in the fish-processing sector – around one-fifth of the total in the UK. In Fraserburgh, 8 of the town's 15 largest employers are fish processors.

The region's four main fishing ports are Peterhead (Figure 3.20), Fraserburgh, Buckie and Aberdeen. Cod, haddock and other whitefish landings dominate the total catch worth around £140 million a year. Peterhead is the largest whitefish port in the EU, landing 98 000 tonnes in 1999. Shellfish (lobsters and prawns) account for 22 per cent of the total catch by value, and the remainder comprises mackerel and herring.

The decline in fishing 1993–99

Figure 3.21 reveals the sharp downturn in employment in the fishing industry experienced during the 1990s in north-east Scotland. Nearly a thousand fishermen lost their jobs between 1993 and 1999 – a much steeper decline than in the rest of the UK. Worst-hit was Buckie, with a 63 per cent fall in fishing jobs.

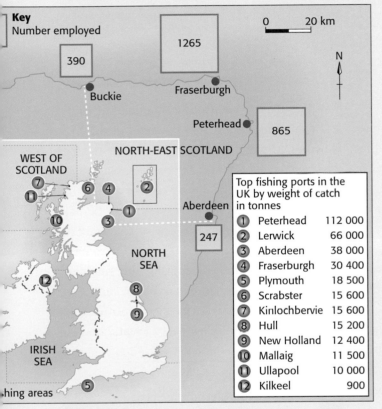

Key
Number employed

Top fishing ports in the UK by weight of catch in tonnes	
① Peterhead	112 000
② Lerwick	66 000
③ Aberdeen	38 000
④ Fraserburgh	30 400
⑤ Plymouth	18 500
⑥ Scrabster	15 600
⑦ Kinlochbervie	15 600
⑧ Hull	15 200
⑨ New Holland	12 400
⑩ Mallaig	11 500
⑪ Ullapool	10 000
⑫ Kilkeel	900

Figure 3.19
The UK's leading fishing ports, and employment in the fish-catching sector of north-east Scotland

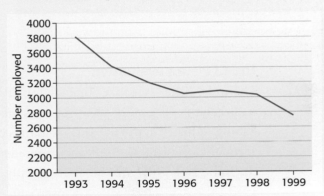

Figure 3.21
Employment in the fish-catching sector, north-east Scotland, 1993–99

The decline in fish landings caused job losses in the region's fish-processing factories. Here, fish processing suffered badly compared with other parts of the UK; elsewhere this sector showed a significant increase in employment of 14 per cent. The decline of fish processing in north-east Scotland was part of a general shift of the industry from the traditional fishing regions towards the main markets in southern Britain – see Figure 3.22.

The impact of the CFP

Reductions in quotas and fishing effort have had a severe impact in regions such as north-east Scotland that depend heavily on fishing and related industries. Massive cuts in cod, haddock and whiting quotas in 2001 created further unemployment, not only in fishing but also in boat repair businesses, fish processing and local fish markets. In January 2001 the cod recovery plan for depleted North Sea stocks meant a complete closure of a number of fishing grounds in the North Sea between February and April. Meanwhile a decommissioning scheme aimed

Figure 3.20
The harbour and docks at Peterhead, Scotland

at reducing fleet capacity by 20 per cent added to the gloomy prospects of the fishing industry in north-east Scotland.

Economic assistance from the EU

Owing to their narrow dependence on fishing, Peterhead, Buckie and Fraserburgh are included in the EU's Objective 2 programme. Inclusion means that they receive economic assistance from the FIFG, and also from the EU's Structural Funds. Through the principle of matching funding (financial assistance from the EU matched by similar funding from the British government), money is channelled into north-east Scotland specifically to restructure fishing, diversify economic activity, create new jobs, introduce new technologies and re-train the workforce.

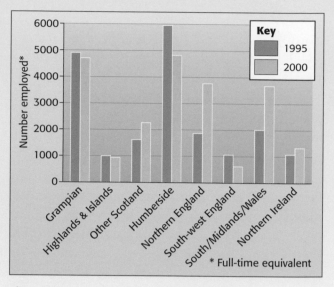

Figure 3.22

Employment in fish processing, 1995 and 2000

The CFP – an evaluation

There is little evidence that the CFP has succeeded in its goal of creating a sustainable fishing industry in the EU. Indeed many critics argue that the CFP is, itself, the main cause of the industry's problems. Since its inception in 1983, the CFP has allowed overfishing to continue to the point where some fisheries are on the verge of collapse. Quotas, fleet reductions and restrictions on the number of days spent fishing have done little to reverse this trend.

There is no doubt that the CFP is controversial and has met strong opposition from both fishermen and member states. Negotiations on quotas between the European Commission and governments frequently result in compromises that tend to ignore the advice of scientists and lead to further overfishing. Meanwhile monitoring quotas and preventing illegal catches is difficult.

Individual governments must also accept some blame, including the failure to cooperate with the CFP. For instance, between 1996 and 1999 the UK fishing fleet was cut by only 1 per cent, instead of the 11 per cent promised by the government. Meanwhile, the CFP paid British shipowners £70 million a year to build new boats. The EU argues that subsidies to shipyards support not only the 18 000 fishermen's jobs in

the UK, but also 50 000 jobs in shipbuilding yards and fish-processing plants throughout the EU. However, these subsidies increase the fishing effort and make sustainability even less likely.

Fishermen recognise the need for a sustainable fishing industry but feel that the CFP has failed to deliver. As fish are a resource in common ownership, they argue that progress towards sustainability can only be made if fishing policies are devolved to the national scale. Such policies have demonstrably succeeded in Iceland in the past 25 years.

Activity

1 Using a suitable tabular layout, compose a series of bullet points comparing and contrasting the CAP and CFP under the headings:
• Main features • Key differences in approach • Successes • Failings • Future prospects.

2 Conclude your table with a concise, reasoned paragraph agreeing with, or rejecting, the suggestion that the differences between the two policies are just a function of the differences between the resources they seek to manage.

4 Transnational environmental and economic issues and the EU

KEY THEMES

- Transnational issues in the EU are both environmental and economic.
- Effective action to solve transnational environmental problems in the EU (e.g. pollution) requires the close cooperation of member states.
- Transnational economic issues concerning trade involve the EU's external relationships with the global community.
- The EU's protectionist policies towards agriculture are at odds with the liberalisation policies of the World Trade Organisation (WTO).
- Foreign direct investment (FDI) and foreign transnational corporations (TNCs) have both advantages and disadvantages for the EU.

Transnational environmental issues

Some environmental problems affect people in several countries and are known as transnational problems. Within the EU, transnational environmental problems give rise to issues such as the pollution of the sea, international rivers and the atmosphere, and the depletion of fish stocks (see Chapter 3, page 45). In the past 10–15 years, the EU has made significant progress in tackling many of these problems.

The relatively small number of EU states, and their roughly equal economic status, has made agreement relatively easy. More difficult to solve are transnational problems at the world scale. Issues such as global warming and ozone depletion involve the entire world community, making agreements particularly hard to achieve.

The first section of this chapter focuses on three pressing transnational environmental issues within the EU: pollution of the North Sea, pollution of the River Rhine, and acid rain.

Case Study: Managing the North Sea ecosystem

Factfile

- The North Sea (including the English Channel) occupies a shallow enclosed basin on the continental shelf of north-west Europe (Figure 4.1).
- The North Sea increases in depth from an average of 30 metres in the south, to more than 200 metres in the north.

- The North Sea catchment area has a population of more than 185 million, and includes some of Europe's largest cities and industrial regions, e.g. London, Paris, Randstad, Brussels and Rhine-Ruhr.
- Industrial and domestic wastes from the catchment, together with intensive fishing, have put severe pressure on the North Sea ecosystem.

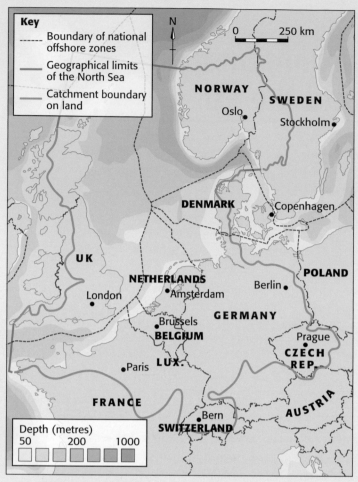

Figure 4.1

The North Sea and its catchment area

Pollution of the North Sea

Until the 1980s there were no attempts to regulate the discharge of pollutants into the North Sea. The North Sea was routinely used as a sink for the disposal of industrial and domestic wastes by the surrounding states. However, by the early 1980s it was clear that the North Sea ecosystem was being degraded. Rivers such as the Rhine, Thames and the Elbe discharged huge quantities of chemical and organic pollutants. Toxic wastes were being incinerated and dumped at sea. The development of offshore oil and gas fields in the 1960s added to the pollution load.

The impact of pollution on the North Sea ecosystem included:

- eutrophication caused by inputs of nutrients such as phosphorus and nitrogen; nutrient enrichment also caused harmful algal blooms, and a lack of oxygen near the sea bed killed many benthic fish (i.e. bottom feeders)

- accumulation of hazardous substances such as heavy metals and polychlorinated biphenyls (PCBs) in predatory fish, birds and mammals at the end of food chains (Figure 4.2)

- dumping of sewage sludge which destroyed all life on the sea bed in some inshore areas.

Added pressure comes from the fishing industries of EU states and Norway, as described in Chapter 3. Trawling has destroyed sea bed habitats and over-fishing has brought several North Sea fish stocks to the verge of collapse.

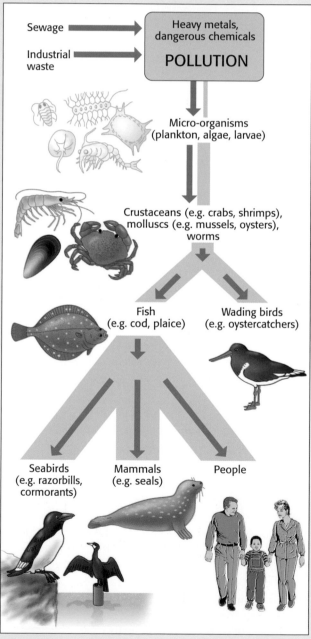

Figure 4.2

Accumulation of poisons in North Sea food chains

Managing for sustainable development
Pollution control

Pollution of the North Sea arose partly because it is an international resource and not the responsibility of any one nation. The development of a concerted international policy to combat pollution began in 1984 with the first North Sea Conference. All the North Sea states were represented, together with the European Commission and various non-governmental organisations (NGOs). Controls were placed on inputs of chemical fertilisers from farm run-off, the dumping and burning of toxic waste at sea, and oil spillages (Figure 4.3).

Figure 4.3

Oil rig in the North Sea

Ecosystem management

Pollution control to protect the physical environment remained the focus of successive North Sea Conferences up until 1995 (see Figure 4.4). The 1995 conference was a watershed. Future policies would adopt a holistic approach: the focus would be on the North Sea ecosystem, including plankton, fish, birds and mammals as well as the physical environment. Protecting the physical environment is essential to securing the health and **biodiversity** of the living members of the ecosystem, as well as helping to ensure the sustainability of North Sea fish stocks. However, sustainability also requires the integration of environmental policies with the Common Fisheries Policy (see Chapter 3). So far environmental controls have proved easier to implement than those on fishing.

Conclusion

Concerted action by European states to protect the North Sea environment has been largely successful. The North Sea example shows that sustainable management of international resources rests on cooperation between interested states and other stakeholders. However, the North Sea is more than just a physical environment: it is a complex ecosystem which includes both physical and biological components and numerous interactions among them. Protecting the physical environment of the North Sea makes little sense unless the biological environment is also managed. As noted in Chapter 3, the EU fisheries policy has, so far, singularly failed to protect fish stocks and biodiversity.

Figure 4.4

Achievements of North Sea Conferences

Issue	Achievements
Nutrient inputs	In 1987 agreement was reached to reduce inputs of phosphorus-based and nitrogen-based pollutants by 50 per cent. The phosphorus target was reached. Nitrogen inputs – the result of run-off from arable land – proved more difficult to control.
Hazardous substances	In 1990 limits were set to reduce the input of 36 hazardous substances (including heavy metals and chlorinated hydrocarbons such as PCBs) by 50 per cent. These substances accumulate in estuaries, sea bed sediments and organisms. Significant progress has been made, especially in reducing inputs of pesticides. Some pesticides have been phased-out, and production of PCBs ended in 1999. The aim is to stop all input of hazardous substances within one generation.
Tributylin (TBT)	TBT, derived from anti-fouling paints used on ships' hulls and responsible for sex changes in some shellfish, is to be phased-out by 2003.
Offshore oil and gas	A 1990 agreement eliminated all routine oil pollution from oil installations. The dumping of disused oil installations in the sea was banned in 1995.
Dumping and incineration	These activities, which figured prominently in the first North Sea Conference, have been banned and have now ceased.

	Activity
1	Study the map of the North Sea (Figure 4.1). On a simple outline of the North Sea basin, add brief notes to show where and how the physical geography of the North Sea might exacerbate pollution.
2	Construct a table to show the possible conflicts of interest between the principal uses of the North Sea, i.e. fishing, oil and gas extraction, recreation, conservation of wildlife, discharge of industrial and domestic waste.
3	Add explanations to your table stating why some of these uses are in conflict.

Case Study: The Rhine – managing an international river

Like seas and oceans, many large rivers are international resources. In fact, rivers, such as the Rhine, that extend across two or more countries drain 47 per cent of the world's total land surface. These international rivers are shared resources and often give rise to conflicts about water quality and water quantity.

Fact file

- Western Europe's longest river: it is 1320 km from its source in the Alps to its mouth in the Netherlands (Figure 4.5).
- The Rhine's discharge at the German–Dutch border averages 2200 cubic metres/second (cumecs); its maximum and minimum recorded discharges are 13 000 cumecs and 600 cumecs respectively.
- The Rhine is an international river: its drainage basin includes parts of Germany, France, Switzerland, Netherlands, Luxembourg and Austria (Figure 4.6).
- The Rhine drainage basin covers nearly 200 000 km^2 – an area similar in size to England and Scotland.
- 60 million people live in the Rhine catchment, which is one of the most urbanised and industrialised in the world.
- The Rhine is fed by glaciers and snowfields in the Alps which, together with glacial lakes, give an unusually stable flow, with relatively few extremes.

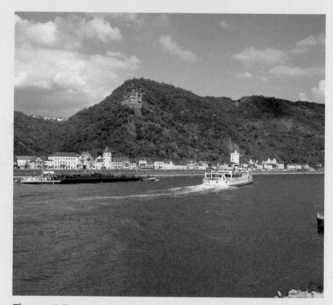

Figure 4.5
A typical stretch of the River Rhine in central Germany

A multifunctional river

Figure 4.7 shows that the Rhine and its tributaries fulfil several different functions. Nearly 20 million people in the Netherlands and Germany depend on the Rhine as a source of drinking water. Major industrial concentrations on the Rhine and its tributaries abstract water for cooling and processing. Electricity is generated by hydro-electric power (HEP) stations in France and Switzerland, and in the Netherlands farmland is irrigated with Rhine water to prevent saltwater intrusion from the sea. Recreation is important on the Upper Rhine, from

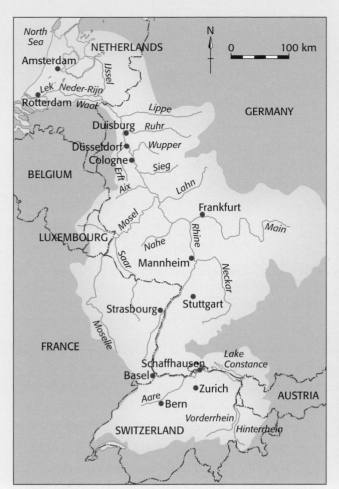

Figure 4.6

The Rhine drainage basin

	Switzerland	France	Germany	Netherlands
Drinking water			✖	✖
Process water	✖	✖	✖	✖
Irrigation				✖
HEP	✖	✖		✖
Amenity	✖		✖	✖
Fishing				✖
Navigation	✖	✖	✖	✖
Sewer	✖	✖	✖	✖

Figure 4.7

Functions of the Rhine catchment, by country

Lake Constance to Schaffhausen in Switzerland, and important wetlands for wildlife near the river mouth are supported by Rhine water. The Rhine is also the busiest inland waterway in the world: Rotterdam near the river's mouth (Figure 4.8) and Duisburg in

Figure 4.8

The port complex at Rotterdam, the Netherlands

the Ruhr are respectively the world's largest sea and inland ports. Finally, and less attractively, the Rhine is used as a sewer for the discharge of industrial and domestic wastes.

Because the Rhine serves so many functions, conflicts have inevitably arisen between different users. Most of these conflicts centre on water quality. Pollution of the river upstream with industrial and domestic wastes conflicts with the need to abstract water for drinking and irrigation downstream. Water polluted by industrial effluent damages wetland habitats, and dams built across the Rhine and its tributaries for HEP prevent the migration of salmon and sea trout. Meanwhile, land use changes in the catchment can also give rise to international issues: for instance, urban encroachment onto flood plains, and deforestation, both speed up rates of run-off and increase the flood risk downstream. Severe floods in the Netherlands in 1995 were, in part, a result of this process.

Death of the Rhine: 1950–86

Water quality in the Rhine deteriorated significantly between 1950 and 1986. International efforts to regulate discharges of pollutants made little impact during this period. The main polluters were chemical industries in Germany and Switzerland, and potash mines in Alsace and Lorraine. Untreated sewage, and the run-off of nitrate and phosphate fertilisers and pesticides from arable land, and organic waste from livestock farming, added to the pollution load. By the end of the 1970s, and for much of its length, the Rhine was biologically dead. Oxygen levels in some reaches had sunk too low to support fish life. Heavy metals such as mercury, cadmium and lead, and dangerous chemicals such as PCBs and benzene, contaminated the river and its sediments.

The turning point came in 1986, when a fire at the Sandoz chemical plant near Basel in Switzerland caused a lethal cocktail of pesticides, mercury and other toxic chemicals to spill into the Rhine. The results were catastrophic. Virtually all fish and insect life was destroyed for 100 km downstream, and the abstraction of water for livestock and human consumption in Germany and the Netherlands was suspended. Experts predicted that it could take 30 years for the river to recover.

Cooperation and planning by Rhineside states

Attempts by Rhineside states to work together and manage the River Rhine as an international resource date back to the 1950s with the establishment of the International Commission for the Protection of the Rhine (ICPR). Before this time individual states acted unilaterally, with little concern for their neighbours downstream. Although the European Commission joined the ICPR in 1970, progress remained slow. Meanwhile the condition of the Rhine continued to deteriorate.

The Sandoz fire brought about a change of attitude. Environmental awareness suddenly increased, and there was a new determination to confront the pollution problem. The immediate outcome was the Rhine Action Programme (RAP) of 1987. In the RAP the Rhineside states agreed for the first time to adopt an integrated approach to the management of the river. This approach meant more than simply improving water quality. The RAP covered all aspects of the Rhine ecosystem, including physical, chemical and biological processes and the river's wildlife.

Tough targets were set for reducing pollution. Discharges of hazardous substances were to be slashed by half by 2000; water quality was to improve sufficiently to allow salmon to return to the Rhine, also by 2000. In addition, safety precautions were to be tightened to prevent the dumping of toxic waste. In the long term, the Rhineside states aimed to restore the natural ecosystem (including its original flora and fauna) to large parts of the Rhine catchment.

The re-birth of the Rhine

Since the establishment of the RAP, spectacular progress has been made in cleaning-up the Rhine and its tributaries. Between 1986 and 1992, annual measurements taken near the Dutch border showed that mercury levels fell from 6 tonnes to 3.2 tonnes, cadmium from 9 tonnes to 5.9 tonnes and PCBs from 390 kg to 90 kg. By 1996 lead and dioxin levels had been cut by 70 per cent, and chrome and nickel by half. Modern treatment plants have made river water safe to drink again. Indeed water quality improved so rapidly that in 1996 – four years ahead of schedule – the first salmon returned to the Rhine after an absence of 50 years. Meanwhile, international chemical companies such as Hoechst, Ciba-Geigy, Bayer and BASF, eager to promote an environmentally responsible image among consumers, have donated millions of dollars to reduce pollution.

None the less, some problems remain. The Rhine still contains high levels of nitrogen and phosphorus. Today these substances are the main source of pollution in the river and the Rhine accounts for one-third of the input of these nutrients into the North Sea. Pollution from fertilisers used in intensive farming is especially difficult to control. In the Rhine delta in the Netherlands, toxin-filled mud, dredged from the port of Rotterdam and dumped in the 1970s, is still a problem.

Acid rain pollution

Acid rain is a pollutant that does not respect political boundaries. Sulphur dioxide and nitrogen oxides – the two main pollutants that form acid rain – are easily dispersed by the wind. Heavily industrialised regions in northern Germany and northern Britain, for example, 'export' acid rain to neighbouring states situated downwind, such as Sweden and Norway. As a consequence these countries suffer the consequences of acid rain pollution which include damage to lakes, forests, soils, wildlife, human health and buildings. Acid rain was only recognised as a global problem in 1979 when the Convention on Long Range Transboundary Air Pollution was signed. Since then several worldwide initiatives have followed – see Figure 4.9.

Date	Details of initiative
1985	Protocol agreed by 21 states to reduce their emissions of sulphur by 30% between 1980 and 1993.
1988	Protocol signed by 25 countries to limit emissions of nitrogen oxides to 1987 levels by 1994. Some countries (including Sweden) committed to 30% by 1998.
1994	Second sulphur protocol including 26 countries and the EU to reduce emissions by 2000 to 50% of 1980 levels. The protocol was based on a new principle of critical load, i.e. the amount of acid deposition that different ecosystems can tolerate.
1999	Protocol, based on a critical loads approach, which set targets for 2010 for the emissions of sulphur dioxide, nitrogen oxides and other pollutants. For the first time an integrated approach, covering acidification, eutrophication and ground-level ozone in ecosystems, was used.

Figure 4.9

International cooperation on the acid rain problem

Formation of acid rain

Acid rain is precipitation that has been polluted by sulphur dioxide (SO_2) and oxides of nitrogen (NO_x). In the atmosphere, these oxides react with water vapour to form sulphuric acid and nitric acid. Eventually the chemicals reach the ground in rain or snow, or as dry depositions. Although both SO_2 and NO_x occur naturally in the atmosphere, concentrations have greatly increased as a result of urbanisation and industrialisation.

Sources of acid rain

The main source of acid rain is the burning of fossil fuels. Coal-fired power stations and heavy processing industries, particularly those concerned with iron and steel and non-ferrous metals, release sulphur dioxide which is carried by the wind. More than half of nitrogen oxides come from vehicle exhausts. Ammonia, another nitrogen compound which contributes to acid rain, is largely derived from livestock farming.

Case Study: Acid rain in Sweden

The effects of acid rain

Scandinavia, especially Sweden and Norway, has been badly affected by acid rain pollution. About 10 000 of Sweden's 85 000 lakes are so acidified that sensitive organisms cannot survive in them. Worst affected is south-west Sweden. Here in the most acidified lakes, all aquatic life, including fish, snails, crustaceans and phytoplankton, has died out.

Large areas of forest in south-west Sweden are also acidified (Figure 4.10). Where soil acidity falls below pH 4.4, potentially toxic metals such as aluminium are released. Meanwhile acidification disrupts soil chemistry and the nutrient cycle, and depletes soils of essential bases such as calcium and magnesium. All these processes weaken the vegetation and cause forests to die.

Buildings and historic monuments, especially those constructed from limestone and sandstone, suffer accelerated chemical weathering due to acid rain (Figure 4.11). Even granite is affected.

Prehistoric rock carvings in granite at Tanum, a World Heritage Site on the west coast of Sweden, have been weathered by acid rain. In urban areas concentrations of oxides of sulphur and nitrogen contribute to respiratory disease. Soil acidification has also been responsible for the release of mercury and aluminium from soils and the contamination of drinking-water supplies.

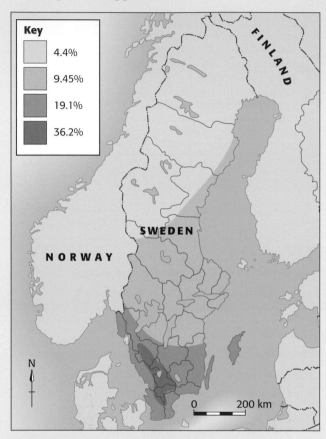

Figure 4.10

The proportion of Swedish soils with a pH of less than 4.4

Figure 4.11

Chemical weathering on Furness Abbey, Cumbria

Geographical origin of acid rain pollutants

Almost 90 per cent of the sulphur deposition in Sweden originates from other countries, principally from Germany, the UK and Poland (Figure 4.12). External sources also account for over half of Sweden's nitrogen oxide deposition: again much has its origin in Germany and the UK.

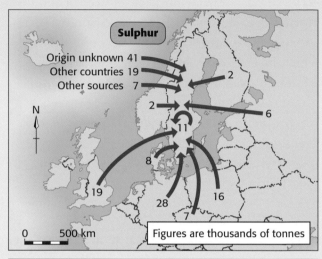

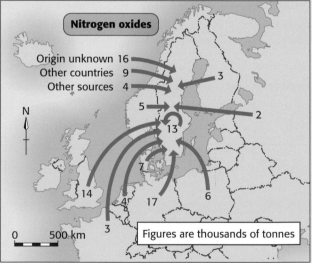

Figure 4.12

Sources of sulphur and nitrogen deposits in Sweden, 1997

Tackling the acid rain problem

Sweden

Sweden cannot resolve the acid rain issue on its own. Even so, it has taken the lead in reducing emissions of sulphur dioxide and nitrogen oxides. For example, Swedish emissions of sulphur dioxide fell from 900 000 tonnes in 1970 to 69 000 tonnes in 1997, a cut of 92 per cent in 27 years. This reduction was achieved by minimising sulphur in oils, increasing the use of nuclear energy, introducing the cleaning of flue gases in power stations burning fossil fuels, and imposing a tax on sulphur emissions. A similar tax on the emission of nitrogen oxides from combustion plants halved NO_x emissions from these sources.

EU

Sweden generates only a small proportion of the sulphur dioxide and nitrogen oxides that fall on its territory. Thus, in order to solve its acid rain problem, Sweden must seek the cooperation of neighbouring states. Initially the EU was slow to respond. However, since 1988 it has issued a number of directives which target areas such as sulphur in fuel oils, sulphur dioxide and nitrogen oxide emissions from power stations, air quality in urban areas, and so on.

Future prospects

Despite significant reductions in emissions of sulphur dioxide and nitrogen oxides within the EU between 1980 and 2000 (see Figure 4.13), the acidifi-cation of soil and water is expected to continue in Sweden. Only the rate of increase will fall. Improvements occurred in the 1990s, but complete recovery will require further reductions in the emission of sulphur and nitrogen compounds. Currently, around 7000 Swedish lakes are kept alive by liming (Figure 4.14). Only when European emissions of acidifying substances have been reduced by between 70 and 80 per cent will the damage to Swedish lakes, forests and soils be halted.

Figure 4.14

Liming Lake Övre Bergsjon, near Göteborg

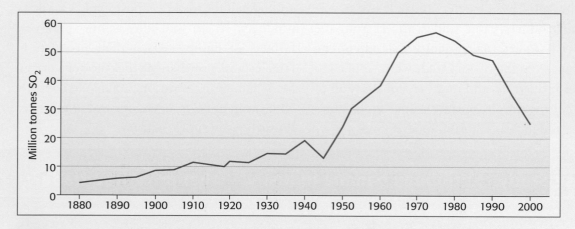

Figure 4.13

Emissions of sulphur dioxide in Europe, 1880–2000

Activity

1 Describe the distribution of acidified soils in Sweden shown in Figure 4.10.

2 Study Figure 4.12 in conjunction with an atlas and suggest how the following factors might influence the spread of sulphur dioxide and nitrogen oxides to Sweden:

   • location of the pollution sources • prevailing winds • mean annual precipitation.

   What factors appear to account for the quantity of sulphur and nitrogen oxide deposition in Sweden?

Transnational economic issues
The EU's global trading relationships

During the 1990s the EU's international trade policy for farm products became a global issue. The EU operates as a customs union, protecting its domestic market with import tariffs, and using subsidies to boost exports. Agriculture has benefited more than any other EU industry from this protectionist policy.

The World Trade Organisation

The World Trade Organisation (WTO – the successor to the General Agreement on Tariffs and Trade, or GATT) is an international organisation committed to the liberalisation of trade. In 2001 it comprised 142 member states, including all 15 EU countries. Since the formation of GATT in 1948, massive reductions in tariffs have taken place, prompting a huge expansion of world trade. Agriculture, however, has resisted these changes. In 1999 tariffs on agricultural goods still averaged 40 per cent.

The attack on EU protectionism

In the mid-1990s barriers to trade in agricultural products came under attack from the WTO. It argued that agriculture should not be exempt from the rules of trade which applied to other industries, and that the globalisation of agriculture would mean cheaper food, more trade and increased wealth for everyone.

The EU's protectionist policies were the main target, especially for major exporters of agricultural goods such as the USA and Canada. They argued that the EU's trade policies for agriculture amounted to unfair competition and that EU farmers were among the most heavily subsidised in the world. Subsidies caused overproduction and the export of surplus production depressed world prices, threatening the livelihoods of farmers worldwide. Meanwhile exporters to the EU market, such as Canadian cereal growers and Argentinian beef producers, were restricted by tariff barriers.

It was not just farmers in the USA, Canada and other more economically developed countries (MEDCs) who complained about the EU's trade policies for agricultural products. If anything, poor farmers in less economically developed countries (LEDCs) have been hit even harder. For instance, in the late 1990s exports of cheap dairy products from the EU threatened Jamaica's dairy industry. The EU spends £1.1 billion a year on export subsidies to its dairy industry – an industry that controls around half the world's export market for dairy products. These subsidies allow high-cost farmers in Europe to sell their products in Jamaica and elsewhere at rock-bottom prices. Many Jamaican producers, unable to compete with cheap imports, have gone out of business, threatening an entire industry.

Case Study: Caribbean banana industry – what price free trade?

Unlike Jamaica's dairy industry, the EU's protectionist policies have beneficially served the interests of poor farmers growing bananas in the Caribbean (Figure 4.15).

EU policies towards Caribbean growers

The EU has, until recently, given trade preference to banana growers from the Caribbean. Many of the Caribbean islands that supply bananas to the EU are former colonies of the UK and France, and they take about 20 per cent of the EU market (Figure 4.16). Owing to these historic links, Caribbean growers have received preferential treatment from the EU. The tariff on their bananas was just one-tenth of that paid by South and Central America producers. These trade concessions were critical for the economic well-being of many Caribbean islands. For example, around one-half of all export earnings for Dominica, St Lucia and St Vincent comes from bananas.

Figure 4.15

Washing and packing bananas on a small plantation, St Lucia

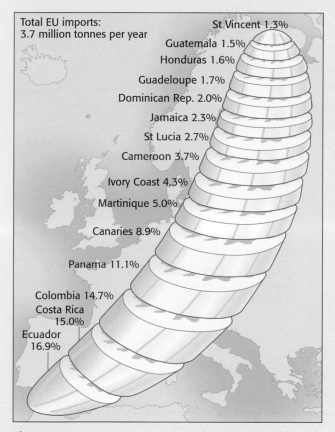

Total EU imports:
3.7 million tonnes per year

St Vincent 1.3%
Guatemala 1.5%
Honduras 1.6%
Guadeloupe 1.7%
Dominican Rep. 2.0%
Jamaica 2.3%
St Lucia 2.7%
Cameroon 3.7%
Ivory Coast 4.3%
Martinique 5.0%
Canaries 8.9%
Panama 11.1%
Colombia 14.7%
Costa Rica 15.0%
Ecuador 16.9%

Figure 4.16

The origin of EU banana imports

Opposition from large-scale growers

In South and Central America, banana production is large-scale **agribusiness** (Figure 4.17). In countries such as Ecuador and Colombia, American transnational corporations (TNCs) own and operate huge plantations. Three of them – Chiquita, Dole and Del Monte – account for two-thirds of the world's banana exports. They argue that the preference given by the EU to Caribbean growers violates the WTO's rules,

and have demanded equal access to the lucrative EU market. Without preferential trade arrangements, however, the small Caribbean growers, lacking the environmental and economic advantages of the South and Central American producers, will not survive.

Caribbean countries	South and Central American countries
Hilly or mountainous growing areas. Limited land availability.	Large flat plains. Wide land availability.
Poor soil conditions and low yields (not more than 4 tonnes/ha).	Rich soil and high yields (7–10 tonnes/ha).
Hurricanes are a hazard to growers.	Hurricanes are rare.
Majority of workers are independent, small farmers.	Plantation agriculture with plantations often owned by TNCs.
Relatively high wages.	Low wages; poor social conditions of workers.
Unit cost of inputs much higher because of small scale of production and poor soil types.	Lower unit cost of inputs because of large-scale production.
High prices because of high labour costs, small-scale production, etc.	Low prices because of low labour costs and economies of scale.
High shipping costs because of small volumes, and more port calls.	Low shipping costs because of high volumes.

Figure 4.17

A comparison of banana-growing conditions in the Caribbean and South and Central America

Outcome

This example shows how the globalisation of free trade can benefit powerful TNCs, with their headquarters in MEDCs, at the expense of small farmers in LEDCs. In the face of the WTO's demands, the EU is due to modify its tariff arrangements for banana exporters. A tariff quota system will operate until 2006, but it is not yet clear how the quotas will be allocated. One possibility is a 'first come first served' system. For example, the first 2 million tonnes of bananas supplied to the market could be eligible for a low tariff quota. Such an arrangement would favour the large-scale growers in South and Central America with their greater flexibility and more efficient transport systems. The Caribbean growers argue for the retention of guaranteed access to the EU market. The alternative, they suggest, would cause severe economic and social damage to the Caribbean.

Multifunctionality

The EU has advanced the argument of **multifunctionality** in order to justify its subsidies and protectionist policies towards agriculture. Essentially multifunctionality recognises that agriculture does more than simply produce food: agriculture is vital to the survival of rural communities throughout the EU; it has a crucial role to play in recreation and wildlife conservation; and it maintains historic cultural landscapes. Hence, it is argued, subsidies to agriculture are essential if rural life and the countryside are to be safeguarded.

However, the concept of multifunctionality is controversial, and many countries see it as a thinly veiled attempt to defend EU farmers from world competition. Many believe that agriculture should be treated like any other industry. Nevertheless there is no doubt that agriculture does have important multiple functions in the EU. The argument that agriculture is different, and therefore deserves special treatment, has credibility.

	Activity
1	Consider the arguments for and against the protection of EU agriculture from global competition, and draw up a list of pros and cons. Decide where you stand on the issue and be prepared to defend your position in a class discussion.
2	Suggest reasons why the globalisation of economic activity is regarded as a major transnational issue today.

Globalisation, FDI and the single market

The globalisation of the world economy has brought huge **foreign direct investment (FDI)** in manufacturing and service industries to the EU in the past 20 years. FDI was given renewed impetus in the early 1990s with the creation of the single market. By locating production in the EU, foreign TNCs could evade tariffs levied on imports. At the same time a location in the EU, now free of customs barriers between member states, gave unrestricted access to a market of 370 million people.

The UK attracted more than one-quarter of all FDI into the EU between 1987 and 1997. Thus in the early 1990s TNCs such as Toyota, Honda, Fujitsu, Samsung and LG built factories in the UK (Figure 4.18). From their UK manufacturing bases they exported most of their production to Europe.

Figure 4.18
The Toyota car plant at Burnaston, Derby

The issue of inward investment

FDI has advantages and disadvantages for any country or region. On the positive side it creates jobs, boosts exports and promotes new technologies and new production systems. Central Scotland was one region that benefited hugely from inward investment by foreign TNCs in the 1980s and 1990s. This investment, particularly in electronics, compensated for the job losses caused by de-industrialisation and the decline of industries such as steel, shipbuilding and coal. By the late 1990s Scotland's electronics industry was producing 30 per cent of Europe's laptops and PCs, and 15 per cent of its semiconductors. The industry, dominated by TNCs, employed 60 000 people, almost one-quarter of the region's workforce. Such was the success of FDI in the electronics sector that central Scotland was dubbed 'Silicon Glen'.

FDI, however, does have a downside which makes it controversial. The most obvious drawback is **disinvestment**, which usually involves factory closure (or partial closure) and job losses. Often TNCs close plants as part of a global strategy, transferring production overseas where costs are lower. At the turn of the century the global electronics industry suffered a sharp downturn that had serious consequences for Silicon Glen. In 2001 NEC shed 600 jobs in Livingston, Compaq cut 700 jobs in Erskine, and Motorola closed its Bathgate plant, making 3100 workers redundant. Any regional economy that depends heavily on FDI, such as that of central Scotland, is always sensitive to slumps and recessions in global manufacturing. Critics of global capitalism also argue that foreign TNCs have little attachment to an area, and weaken local firms by attracting the better-qualified workers.

FDI and monetary union in the EU

In 1999, 12 of the EU's 15 member states joined the European monetary union. This event created a two-tier system: a majority of countries in the so-called euro-zone, but with Denmark, Sweden and the UK retaining their own currencies, albeit with an option to join later.

Impact of monetary union

The UK's decision not to join the single currency in the first round could have serious implications for FDI, particularly in manufacturing industry. Toyota and Nissan are just two of many TNCs with large investments in the UK which have urged the British government to adopt the euro. Both companies export around 80 per cent of their cars – the vast majority – to euro-zone countries. The high exchange rate of the pound against the euro (which may be temporary) has made British-made cars expensive and less attractive to European buyers. Moreover, parts were more expensive and companies incurred extra costs in changing currencies. Exporters argue that if the UK remains outside the euro-zone it will be less attractive for future FDI, and some firms might even abandon manufacturing in the UK altogether.

While there seems little likelihood of a company such as Toyota, which has invested £1.5 billion in the UK since 1990, abandoning production in the UK, new investment is another matter. For example, in 2000 Toyota invested £350 million in a new assembly plant in Valenciennes in north-east France, rather than extend its existing plant at Derby.

None the less, the UK's reluctance to join the euro did not stop FDI reaching record levels in 1998 and 1999. In 1999 FDI into the UK amounted to £47 billion and created 58 000 new jobs (Figure 4.19). The bulk of this investment was in ICT and internet services, telecoms, finance and other services. Three-quarters of FDI came from countries outside the EU, with the USA by far the biggest investor. By contrast, investment in manufacturing industry, and especially in major projects, was down significantly.

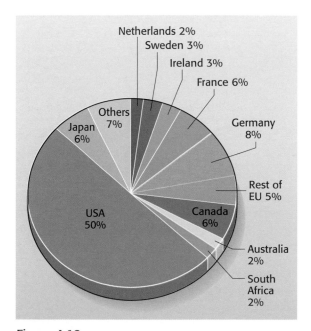

Figure 4.19
Sources of FDI in the UK, 1999–2000

Activity

Study Figures 4.19 and 4.20.

1 Calculate the proportion of FDI into the UK **a** in services **b** in manufacturing **c** from the EU.

2 Using the internet as an information source, examine *either* the issue of globalisation and FDI *or* the issue of the single currency and FDI in the UK. Prepare a class presentation which includes **a** an analysis of the relevant arguments and **b** an appropriately justified concluding statement giving your view on the issue.

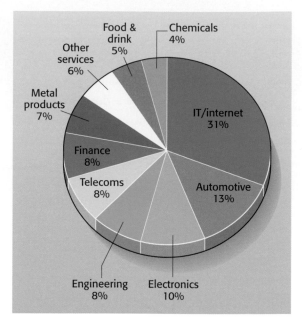

Figure 4.20

FDI in the UK by economic sector, 1999–2000

Part Two

Managing Urban Environments

Introduction

With half the world's people now living in cities (Figure 2.A), the problems of resource use, pollution, congestion, health and poverty have become distinctly urban issues. The transition from rural, farming ways of life to working for wages in a city was one of the great global social changes of the 20th century. The challenges of urban life – finding work and shelter, protecting personal health and well-being, and moving around the city – are shared by urban dwellers everywhere. Those with greater wealth are able to protect themselves from the harms posed by the city, and enjoy the comfort and freedom conferred by personal mobility. But the consequences of automobile dependence and a desire for low-density residential neighbourhoods are urban sprawl and air pollution (Figure 2.B). These conditions spoil the very environment that suburbanites seek.

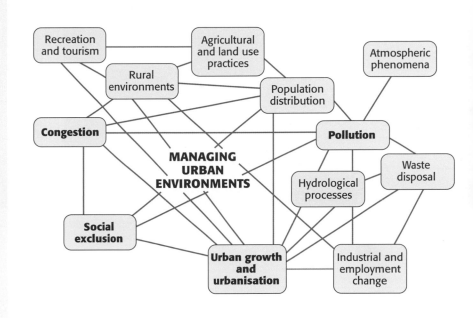

Thinking synoptically: managing urban environments

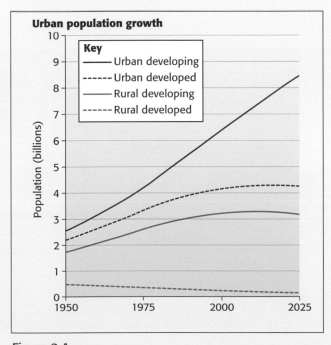

Figure 2.A

Urban population: growth and distribution, 1950–2025

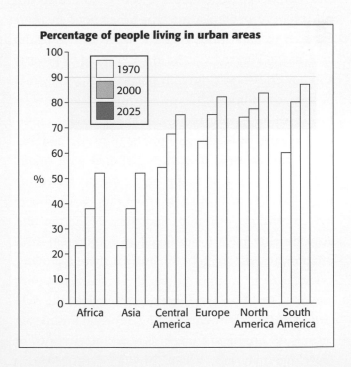

Figure 2.B

Air pollution over Prague, Czech Republic

Figure 2.C

A run-down urban district, Brooklyn, New York

Towns and cities everywhere must now face up to whether unlimited urban expansion is sustainable or desirable, or if they should search for new ways of enticing residents back to their historic centres. Social and demographic changes promise to assist this process of **re-urbanisation**. The urban poor are more exposed to conditions that are hazardous to health and safety (Figure 2.C) and are prevented by poverty and powerlessness from fully participating. They may be trapped in inner cities or informal settlements far from areas of employment, condemned to long journeys to work by inadequate public transport systems. **Social exclusion** is frequently twinned with spatial exclusion, indicating that programmes to revive and restore abandoned urban neighbourhoods are vital to overcoming poverty and inequality. None the less, governments have often failed to implement such programmes successfully. By contrast, there is growing evidence from around the world that the urban poor are fully capable of assisting themselves given the right circumstances. Through starting informal businesses, setting up credit unions, building communities or recycling materials, urban dwellers demonstrate a capacity for innovation. Managing cities successfully increasingly seems to depend on combining 'top-down' policies with popular initiatives (Figure 2.D). It also means reconciling the needs of both human and environmental health. Poverty and pollution are part of the same problem. A sustainable city is also a socially just city.

Figure 2.D

An urban regeneration scheme in Southampton

Essay questions

1 To what extent is it true to say that the problems of urban areas in LEDCs and MEDCs are essentially the same, and that they differ only in terms of scale and severity? Use examples from both LEDCs and MEDCs to support your arguments.

2 How important is it that large urban areas in MEDCs and LEDCs achieve sustainable growth in the near future?

3 Discuss the view that urban sprawl in MEDCs is hard to contain, even with the increasing use of brownfield sites.

Suggestions for further reading

D. Drakakis-Smith (2000) *Third World Cities*, 2nd edition, Routledge.

H. Girardet (1999) *Creating Sustainable Cities*, Green Books.

M. Pacione (ed.) (1997) *Britain's Cities*, Routledge.

R. Tolley and B. Turton (1995) *Transport Systems, Policy and Planning*, Longman.

United Nations Centre for Human Settlements (1996) *An Urbanizing World: Global Report on Human Settlements*, Oxford University Press.

Websites

World Bank:
www.worldbank.org/

Social Exclusion Unit:
www.cabinet-office.gov.uk/seu/

Council for the Protection of Rural England:
www.cpre.org.uk/

The Sierra Club:
www.sierraclub.org/sprawl/

London's Transport Strategy:
www.london.gov.uk/mayor/strategies/
  transport/index.htm

Texas Transportation Institute:
http://mobility.tamu.edu/

United Nations Population Data:
www.un.org/esa/population/

Global Vision Sustainable City:
www.global-vision.org/city/footprint.html

5 Urban growth

KEY THEMES

- Rapid urbanisation is now a global phenomenon, with the highest rates in some of the poorest countries.

- In LEDCs, housing provision is shifting from directly assisting poor urban dwellers to enabling them to build their own communities.

- Urban sprawl is found in MEDCs and LEDCs, but there is disagreement over whether it is harmful and whether policies should be introduced to stem the process.

- Inner urban areas in MEDCs are being regenerated through government programmes and the social changes of a new phase in demographic transition.

Urbanisation and urban growth in LEDCs

Since 1950 the majority of LEDCs have been transformed from rural to urban societies. In the space of two generations, a majority of their citizens have switched from supporting themselves through agriculture to earning a wage from factory work or service jobs. This transition from peasant farmers to urban dwellers was one of the great social upheavals of the 20th century. Although rural life is still the norm in China, India and some other large countries, the processes leading to urbanisation will also change them by the middle of this century. Rapid urban growth is not a new phenomenon, but never before has it affected so many countries. The fact that the fastest rates of urbanisation are now in some of the poorest countries adds to the challenges of managing the process.

Urbanisation is the process by which a greater proportion of a country's population lives in towns and cities. It can be distinguished from **urban growth**, which is simply the increase in the numbers living in urban areas. The urbanisation process is historically and geographically uneven, as illustrated by Figures

5.1 and 5.2. In 1950 the MEDCs were predominantly urban societies, as were a handful of countries in South America. Since then, the rate of urbanisation in MEDCs has slowed significantly, but in LEDCs it has increased dramatically. Not all LEDCs are the same, however. Whereas rates slowed down in Latin America in the 1980s, urbanisation in Asia and Africa has continued rapidly. By the year 2000 almost half the world's 2.85 billion urban dwellers lived in Asia (Figure 5.3). In terms of sheer numbers of new urban inhabitants, the leading countries are China, India and Brazil, which are among the very largest LEDCs.

The most rapid urbanisation in any period is often found in those countries that have the lowest levels of urbanisation to begin with. Countries such as Botswana, Mozambique and Laos experienced very rapid urbanisation in the 1980s and 1990s, but they are still mainly rural societies (Figure 5.4). Well-known mega-cities in LEDCs, such as Mexico City, São Paulo and Karachi, are no longer the sites of the highest rates of urban growth. Instead, smaller cities in poorer countries, such as Dhaka, Bangladesh and Kabul in Afghanistan (see Figure 5.1) rank among the fastest-growing places.

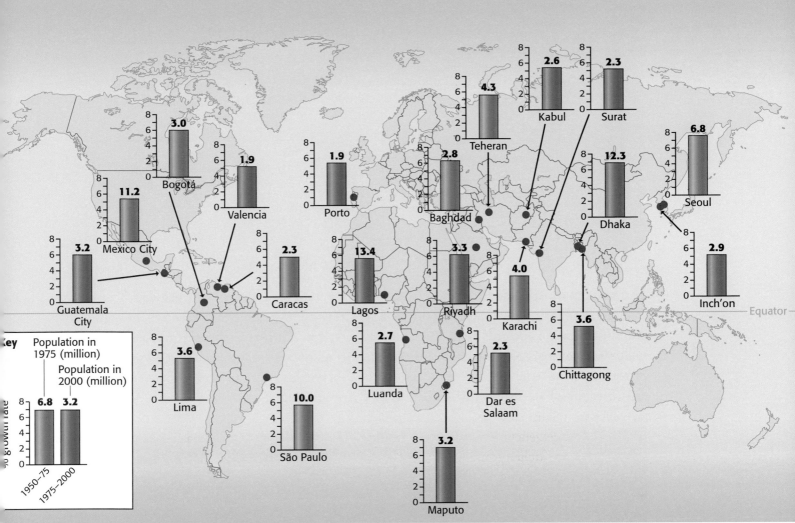

Figure 5.1

World levels of urbanisation showing fastest-growing cities 1950–75 and 1975–2000

	Percentage urban				Urbanisation rate	
	1950	1975	2000	2030	1950–2000	2000–2030
World	29.7	37.9	47.0	60.3	0.91	0.83
North America	64	74	77	84	0.4	0.3
Latin America & the Caribbean	41	61	75	83	1.2	0.3
Europe	52	67	75	83	0.7	0.3
Oceania	62	72	70	74	0.3	0.2
Africa	15	25	38	55	1.9	1.2
Asia	17	25	37	53	1.5	1.3
MEDCs	54.9	70.0	76.0	83.5	0.65	0.31
LEDCs	17.8	26.8	39.9	56.2	1.62	1.14

Figure 5.2

Levels of urbanisation by world region

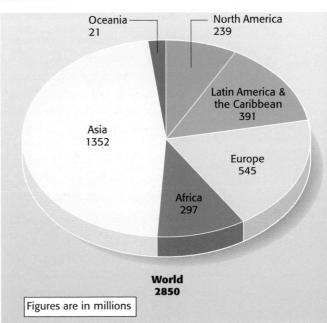

Figure 5.3

Urban population by region, 2000

Figure 5.4

Countries with the highest rates of urbanisation, 1980–99

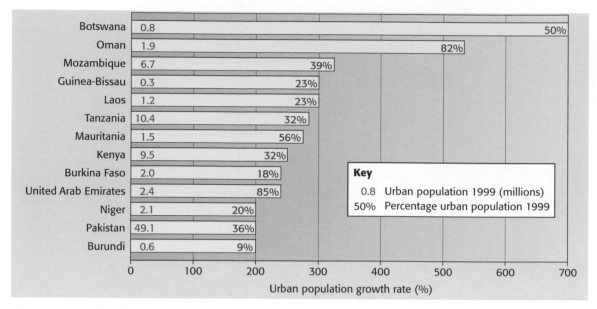

The causes of urbanisation in LEDCs

Urbanisation is broadly linked to both demographic transition and economic development, including regional economic inequalities. This process was as true in the 19th and 20th centuries for what are now the MEDCs as it is for today's LEDCs. The balance of factors changes over time and varies from region to region. Gilbert's general historical model (Figure 5.5), appropriate to Latin America, shows how urban growth passes through several stages.

Figure 5.5

Gilbert's model of urban and regional development in LEDCs

Phase 1: Dependent urbanisation, 1500–1900
- LEDCs as sources of raw materials and markets for industries in MEDCs.
- Ports act as centres for agricultural and mineral exports to MEDCs.
- Urban primacy; investment concentrated in one or a few large cities; rail networks focused on coastal ports.
- Colonial administration concentrated in one or a few large cities.
- Small national elites cooperate with foreign powers and merchants to capture profits of trade.

Example: **Argentina in the 1800s**

Phase 2: Inward-oriented industrialisation or import-substitution, 1930s–1970s
- Restrictions on imports by tariffs and quotas.
- Government support for national industries by subsidy, investment, and control over banking.
- Rapid growth in manufacturing in textiles, consumer goods, and plastics.
- Concentration of manufacturing in large cities.
- Local assembly of imported parts in coastal cities.
- Rural–urban migration in search of factory jobs, services, and construction.
- Increased importance of location near to centre of government power, i.e. large cities.
- Maintenance of urban primacy.

Example: **Mexico 1950s–1980s**

Phase 3: New international division of labour, 1970s–2000
- Governments try to attract TNCs in low-cost manufacturing and agriculture.
- Efforts to cut labour costs and reduce worker unrest.
- Subsidy of infrastructure and facilities for TNCs.
- Relocation of some economic activities to Export Processing Zones; decline in urban primacy.
- Increased use of female labour from rural migrants.
- International migration.

Example: **Philippines from 1970s onwards**

The demographic aspect of urban growth and urbanisation has two components:

- rural-to-urban migration
- natural increase.

In general, migration contributes more to growth in the early phases of rapid urbanisation. In some regions, notably the Gulf and Southeast Asia, international migration is becoming a factor in urban growth. Elsewhere, in southern and central Africa for example, civil war and environmental disasters have forced refugees into urban areas. The contribution of natural increase to the populations of cities is more important in the later stages of growth. Although demographic transition models expect fertility to fall over time, levels may remain high in cities where children's labour is important to household survival.

The general pattern of world urbanisation since 1950 is that countries with the fastest-growing economies generally show the highest rates of urbanisation. Among LEDCs, however, high rates of urbanisation are found even when economic growth is slow (see Figure 5.6), perhaps because, even in relatively poor countries, there can be huge gaps in wages and standards of living between rural and urban areas. Urbanisation cannot be understood separately from regional and social inequality.

Economic development may lead to urbanisation, but urbanisation can in turn stimulate economic growth. It is not clear which causes which. Many LEDC governments believe that investing in large cities can speed up development, by attracting **transnational corporations (TNCs)**, for example. Roads, hospitals, electricity supply and other aspects of infrastructure are improved first in cities. Often, a country's economy is heavily concentrated in one place. In 1985 for example, Nairobi was home to over half of Kenya's industrial companies but to only 7 per cent of the population.

Housing issues in LEDCs and MEDCs

Housing not only meets the human need for shelter, it is also the key to meeting other basic needs. Clean, dry and warm accommodation with adequate water and sanitation is essential for health. Housing may also provide income and savings for those who own property.

Standards of housing can be assessed worldwide in terms of:

- quantity
- quality, e.g. rooms per person, level of services
- tenure – illegal and insecure, renting or owning
- affordability.

In 1990 the United Nations Centre for Human Settlements (UNCHS) conducted a survey of housing standards in 52 cities using measures that could be applied to all kinds of cultures and societies, such as the number of rooms per person. The survey showed that housing standards were generally highest in high-income countries and lowest in low-income countries (see Figure 5.7), although it also found great variations within each income group, suggesting that wealth alone is not the

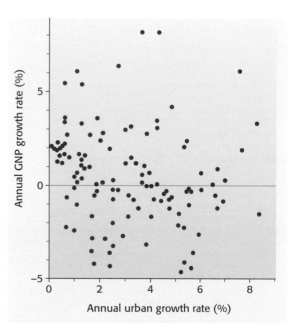

Figure 5.6

Rates of urban population growth and growth in GNP per capita

Figure 5.7

Housing quality by income grouping of countries, 1990

	Floor area per person (m²)	Persons per room	% permanent structures	% with water connection
Low-income countries	6.1	2.47	67	56
Low/mid-income countries	8.8	2.24	86	74
Middle-income countries	15.1	1.69	94	94
Mid/high-income countries	22.0	1.03	99	99
High-income countries	35.0	0.66	100	100

only variable determining standards. For example, as measured by the ratio of rent to income, Hong Kong is a more expensive city in which to rent a flat than New York. Income equality and government policy are also important, as are construction costs.

Not all individuals and households want the same kind of housing. Preferences vary within and between societies, often for cultural and historical reasons. Among MEDCs there are significant differences in the level of home-ownership, often assumed to be the most desirable form of tenure. Residents of German and Swedish cities, for instance, are just as likely to rent their home as their counterparts in LEDCs (Figure 5.8).

Such international comparisons of housing standards show that poor families generally pay a higher proportion of their income for shelter than wealthier families, in both MEDCs and LEDCs. However, whereas the main housing issues in MEDCs are quality and affordability, in LEDCs the problems are quantity, quality, tenure and affordability. In the UNCHS survey, over half the sampled dwellings had no permanent water supply and a third of them were not permanent structures.

Housing solutions in LEDCs

Figure 5.9 demonstrates that providing low-cost housing for urban residents in LEDCs involves the government ('public'), the private

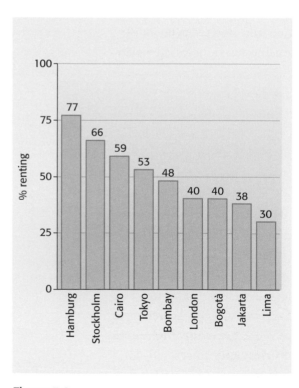

Figure 5.8

Proportion renting in MEDC and LEDC cities

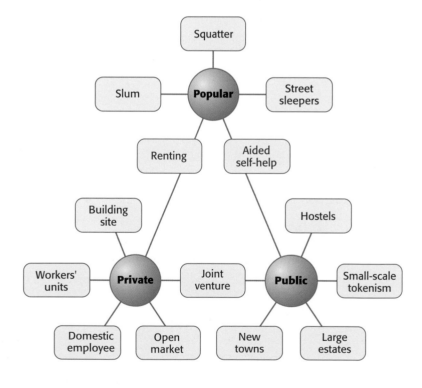

Figure 5.9

Typology of low-cost housing supply

sector and low-income residents themselves ('popular'), either alone or in cooperation.

It is important to stress that the poor often help themselves without the aid of the government or the private sector. It is often the case that most owners, renters and squatters live in housing that began as a self-built shelter, erected on land not owned or rented by the individual, and completed without proper planning permission. Such **squatter settlements**, or self-help housing, generally account for 30–60 per cent of all housing in LEDC cities. In Delhi, Ibadan and Nairobi, for example, 75 per cent of housing is illegal. Such settlements may offer the barest minimum of shelter, water, sanitation and electricity. They may be located on the most hazardous land, near rubbish dumps, toxic facilities, steep slopes or river floodplains. On the basis of his work in South America during the 1970s, American architect John Turner proposed that such settlements could improve over time.

Turner's model

Turner's model emphasises that households at different income levels have different housing needs. These needs may change over time if the household becomes better off (see Figure 5.10). He concluded that governments should allow the very poor to design and build their own housing in order to meet their immediate needs. His model recognises three kinds of individual or householder.

1 **Very low-income households or bridge-headers:** often newly-arrived in the city, their first priority is to find work, usually low-skilled. Proximity to work, often the city centre, is more important than ownership or high-quality shelter. Bridgeheaders are often single men.

2 **Low-income households or consolidators:** after establishing themselves, they can afford to travel to work and put more emphasis on housing quality and security. This is a phase when the family may join the male bridgeheader.

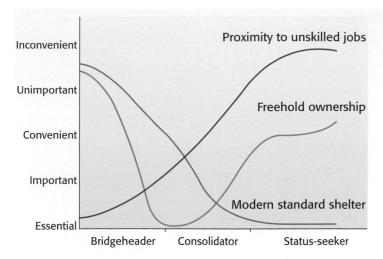

Figure 5.10

Turner's model of housing priorities

3 **Middle-income households or status-seekers:** they are settled and give higher priority to housing quality and ownership or security of tenure. Proximity to work is not so important.

Government response

National and urban governments have usually given housing a low priority in LEDCs. It is assumed that housing is not a productive investment compared with roads, bridges, ports and power stations. When funds are scarce, housing drops down the list of priorities.

There are many options available to governments wanting to provide housing, each with their advantages and disadvantages (Figure 5.11). Slum clearance and public housing projects were popular in the 1950s and 1960s in Venezuela and Hong Kong, for example. Freezing rents is another option, but is likely to be costly.

Beginning in the 1970s a new approach of Assisted Self Help (ASH) was adopted throughout LEDCs with the encouragement of the World Bank and other international organisations. ASH involved two strategies:

- upgrading existing squatter settlements, providing basic services such as water and electricity

Response	Advantages	Disadvantages
Slum clearance	• Makes land available for other uses, e.g. offices, shops, and stadiums	• Forces poor to relocate without meeting their needs
Public housing	• Higher standards of design and building	• Expensive, inflexible and often located too far away from jobs
Rent control	• Keeps rents low by law, making housing more affordable to low-income groups	• Discourages new investment in housing by landlords and the private sector
Aided self-help (sites-and-services, squatter upgrading)	• Lower cost than public housing • Makes use of poor people's time, energy and resources • Supported by international agencies	• Expensive to administer • Often located on undesirable land • Only helps the richest of the poor • Short-term fix • Lets government avoid responsibilities for good housing • Maintains status quo
Enabling	• Administrative reform • Low cost • Makes use of community resources • Supported by international agencies	• Requires community organisation • Depends on international aid • May not help the poorest or most socially excluded

Figure 5.11

Government responses to housing for the poor

• site and service schemes offering a family a plot of land, making available low-cost building materials and gradually introducing services; access to credit was also granted.

Such schemes were rapidly taken up, particularly in Chile, India, Pakistan and Turkey. There were many successes, such as in Rio de Janeiro, although they proved expensive. Three-quarters of the projects did not meet the costs of land, materials, services and administration. Many were located on the cheapest land available, far from workplaces and urban amenities.

In 1988 the United Nations launched a new Global Strategy for Shelter to the Year 2000, based on a new seven-point enabling approach outlined in Figure 5.12. The idea behind this approach is to remove legal and administrative obstacles and to enable the poor to help themselves, often by forming community organisations. The government does not provide or subsidise housing itself; instead, it reforms the land market, banks and local government to make it easier and more affordable for builders to build and families to borrow.

1 Clarify and strengthen property rights in land.

2 Reform housing and construction finance to make money and credit available for buying housing.

3 Make housing subsidy simpler and more targeted.

4 Coordinate delivery of services, and target service delivery on underused and vacant land in existing urban areas.

5 Reform land and housing development regulations to better balance costs and benefits.

6 Promote competition in the construction industry.

7 Form partnerships between government, private sectors and community groups.

Figure 5.12

Global Strategy for Shelter to the Year 2000 (United Nations)

Activity

1 Study Figure 5.2 and present the data in the form of a line graph. To what extent is the line for the world representative of MEDCs and LEDCs, and how would you account for any similarities and differences?

2 Investigate the economic development of an LEDC of your choice. Describe the extent to which your findings support or conflict with Gilbert's model of urban and regional development in LEDCs (Figure 5.5). Are there any other geographical factors that should be taken into consideration?

In 1991 almost four in every ten residents of the city of Rio de Janeiro lived in substandard housing. One million people lived in squatter settlements, known as *favelas*, 900 000 lived in slums and another 200 000 lived in unplanned settlements, mostly on the edge of the city but on land owned by the households. Despite falling levels of rural–urban migration as well as a slow urban growth rate of only 0.67 per cent a year, the city lacked 120 000 housing units at the start of the 1990s.

To meet their basic housing needs, poor residents have been building *favelas* since the 19th century. There are almost 600 scattered around the city, some on hillsides near the centre and others in semi-rural surroundings (Figure 5.13). The largest, Roçhina, houses 42 900 people, but many are much smaller. They are found on hillsides, beside waterways and lagoons, alongside roads and railways, and under bridges. These are marginal sites not demanded by commercial users or wealthier families. Floods and landslides in 1988 destroyed many of these homes,

partly because of blocked and inadequate drainage. Dumping raw sewage and industrial waste into the city's waters exposes many dwellers to infectious diseases. *Favelas* vary widely in terms of the provision of services, education and the level of overcrowding (Figure 5.14). The oldest are well-integrated into the city.

In the 1960s the government cleared the *favelas*, forcing 140 000 people to move, sometimes as far away as 40–50 km. Less than 1 per cent of public spending currently goes on housing, but since 1993 the city has introduced ASH policies to support *favela* dwellers without moving them. There are four programmes.

- 'Living without risk': relocating 18 000 families away from land liable to flooding or landslides.
- '*Favela* living': granting low-cost loans to families through micro-finance institutions.
- '*Favela Bairro*': upgrading 82 mainly medium-sized and less poor settlements, including providing better transport, flood prevention, hillslope protection and reafforestation.

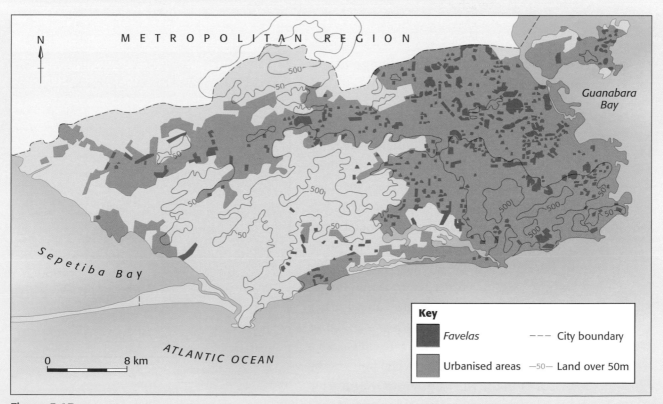

Figure 5.13

Rio de Janeiro's *favelas*

- *'Bairrinho'*: a similar programme aimed at 28 smaller *favelas*.

The programmes have helped improve the quality of life for some of the better-off *favelas*, in part thanks to a grant of $180 million from the Inter-American Development Bank. To reach many of the smaller, newer and outlying settlements will require much more funding. One disadvantage for the *favela* dwellers who have been helped is that they now have to pay taxes for their services.

	City	All *favelas*	Mangueira	Francisco de Castro	Boqueirao	Caminho do Bicho
Date of origin			1881	1961	1931	1973
No. of houses			246	24	42	38
Population			811	91	142	169
% dwellers with inadequate water	4	15	0	4	95	26
% dwellers with inadequate sewerage	9	37	0	25	100	97
% dwellers with inadequate rubbish collection	4	21	0	0	100	100
Mean no. of rooms per household	4.8	4.06	5.45	8	3.3	3.2
Mean no. of persons per household	3.5	4.0	3.2	3.8	3.4	4.5
% illiteracy of people over 15 years of age	6.1	15.4	6.4	7.6	22.6	53.4

Note: These figures are based on a survey by the city's planners, which ranked the *favelas* by overall quality of life. Mangueira and Francisco de Castro were among the highest ranked; Boqueirao and Caminho do Bicho were among the lowest ranked.

Figure 5.14

Quality of services in Rio de Janeiro's *favelas*

Housing in MEDCs – the challenge of changing demographic and social structures

In most MEDCs the size of the population is either growing slowly or declining, as described by the demographic transition model. But there is still pressure on housing from rising incomes, inter-regional migration, international migration, social change and demographic change. Declining marriage and birth rates combined with delayed marriages and increasing divorce rates have led to a second demographic transition, creating smaller families and greater numbers of smaller households – see Figures 5.15 and 5.16 for trends in the UK and Canada. Housing built for families with children may be too large or in the wrong place for the growing number of smaller households. In fact, the growth in the number of households resulting

Household type	% of all households	
	1961	2000
One person under pensionable age	4	14
One person over pensionable age	7	15
Two or more unrelated adults	5	3
Married couple, no children	26	29
Married couple, 1–2 dependent children	30	19
Married couple, 3 + dependent children	8	4
Lone parent, dependent children	2	6
Others	18	10
Total	**100**	**100**

Note: Dependent children are those under 16 or aged 16–18 and in full-time education.

Figure 5.15

Types of household in Great Britain, 1961–2000

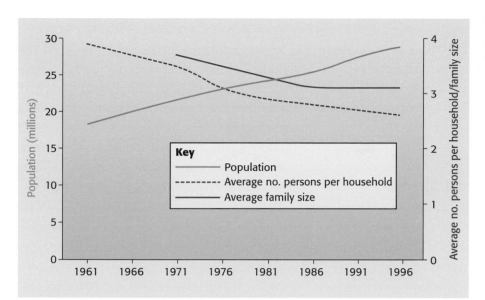

Figure 5.16
Family and household
size in Canada,
1961–96

from the decline in average household size is one of the main factors causing urban sprawl and putting pressure on the housing supply in congested cities and regions, such as London and south-east England. In addition, recent experience suggests that forecasting the effects of social and demographic change on housing demand is a difficult process (Figure 5.17).

After decades of population loss through out-migration there are signs that the centres of many cities are being repopulated. New cultural facilities, the renovation of historic districts and the demand for high-wage office workers willing to work long and unpredictable hours are among the causes of revival. In French cities (Figure 5.18) the newcomers are more likely

Figure 5.18
The repopulation
of French cities

Planning for the volume and location of future housing demand is difficult. In the space of a decade the UK government revised its predictions based on demographic information. In 1996 the Department of the Environment (DoE) announced that the country would have to accommodate 4.4 million new households from 1992 to 2017. In 1999 it revised the projection downwards to 3.8 million from 1999–2021. The reason for the new estimate was a faster than expected rise in the number of people cohabiting. As a result, the South East would have to find room for 200 000 fewer new houses than originally thought. In 1999 the government announced that it would no longer 'predict and provide', or project the demand for housing and then meet it. Instead it promised to 'monitor and manage', revising figures every five years and not automatically meeting demand. The new policy was seen as a victory for environmentalists.

But in 2000 the Office for National Statistics increased its prediction for the total UK population in the year 2021 by 1.23 million, or 500 000 extra households. This was mainly the result of increased levels of international migration. It predicted that London would increase by 1 million people in 20 years, easily overturning the benefits of the earlier downward revision.

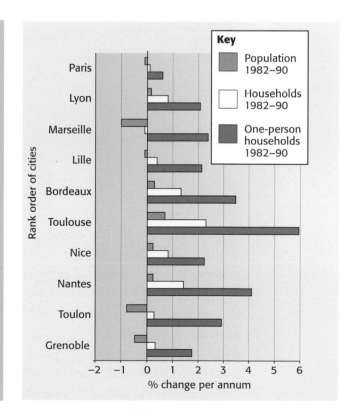

Figure 5.17
From 'Predict and provide' to 'Monitor and manage'

to be professionals and managers, and half are aged 25–29 years. In Toulouse, for example, by 1990 four out of every ten households in the centre consisted of a single person. In Paris, the number of single female professionals increased by over one-third from 1982 to 1990.

Containing urban sprawl

Urban sprawl consists of low-density settlement extending beyond the boundaries of built-up areas. It involves high dependence on private automobiles and is often the result of poorly planned or unplanned development. Although sprawl is linked to population growth, it is also caused by falling household sizes, increased demand for low-density living and a desire to escape from cities because of pollution, crime or high taxes. Urban sprawl can exceed population growth. The US population, for example, grew by 47 per cent between 1960 and 1990, but the urbanised area increased by 107 per cent in the same period.

Sprawl is blamed for the loss of farmland and natural areas, as well as environmental problems such as air pollution and flooding. Figure 5.19 summarises the problems blamed on urban sprawl in the USA, although critics argue that these problems are exaggerated by environmentalists and that many are caused by other factors such as modern farming – see Figure 5.20.

Sprawl is a particular issue in countries with few controls on development, such as Australia, Canada and the USA, where many major cities are growing rapidly. Las Vegas, for example, grew by over 80 per cent in the 1990s. Sprawl also affects European countries, which are already densely populated, and cities in LEDCs such as Cairo and São Paulo. In Southeast Asia geographers have identified a phenomenon called the **extended metropolitan region (EMR)**. These regions, as represented in Figure 5.21, occur where urban and rural differences have become blurred as a result of the increase

Figure 5.19

The problems blamed on urban sprawl in the USA

Problem	Evidence
Destruction of farmland, parks and open space	• 160 000 ha of rural land developed per year • 70% of prime or unique farmland under threat
Increased air pollution because of greater use of vehicles	• 5.4 billion kg a year of pollutants from all vehicles
Increased water pollution because of loss of wetlands and disruption of hydrology	• Over 40 000 ha of wetlands destroyed each year
Increased flood risk from building on wetlands and floodplains which used to act as sponges to soak up heavy rainfall	• Between 1992 and 2000, floods caused over $89 billion of damage and more than 850 deaths
Destruction of natural beauty	• Destruction and fragmentation of habitats in the Sonoran Desert, Arizona
Threat to heritage	• Lancaster County's historic Amish farms and villages swallowed up by sprawl
Under-use of existing public services	• Between 1970 and 1990 Minneapolis–St Paul closed 162 physically adequate schools
Waste of taxpayers' money in construction of unnecessary roads, sewerage, schools and other urban services	• Between 1970 and 1995 Maine spent over $338 million on new schools in new areas, but the number of pupils fell by 27 000
Social and spatial segregation	• Expensive low-density housing is only accessible to the rich, leaving poorer families isolated in the cities
Inner city unemployment because of the excessive time and expense of travelling from job-poor cities to job-rich suburbs	• In Boston, only 14% of entry-level jobs can be accessed within only one hour's commuting from the centre
Waste of time commuting	• Average driver spends 443 hours a year on the road

Note: Information and evidence taken from the Sierra Club, USA, and other sources

Critics of environmentalists argue that urban sprawl is nothing new and affects only a few areas. They have produced the following facts in support of their case:

- Less than 5% of the USA's land surface is built on.
- Only 0.0006% of the USA's land is developed each year.
- 75% of the population lives on just 3.5% of the land.
- The rate of suburbanisation was highest in 1920–50.
- Only a quarter of the farmland lost since 1945 has been due to urbanisation, and rates of loss were lower in the 1960s than in the 1990s.
- Land area under crops increased between 1992 and 1997.
- The amount of land in protected wildlife areas and rural parks is over 50% more than in urban areas.
- There is no clear correlation between population density, commuting and air pollution.

Figure 5.20

In defence of urban sprawl, USA

in personal mobility and the spread of urban settlements but without completely swallowing up farming areas. The result is a complex pattern of interlocking land use as industry, rice farming and housing are crammed together, usually without adequate planning controls. Often, separate villages and settlements maintain their own local government independently of the main city, making planning coordination difficult. Examples of EMRs include Bangkok, Ho Chi Minh City, Manila, Yangon and Jakarta, where the local word *desakota* (meaning 'city-village') is sometimes used.

Managing urban sprawl: green belts and new towns

There are many potential solutions to urban sprawl based on three main approaches:

- designating areas where no development is allowed
- channelling urban growth to selected towns and cities
- increasing urban residential densities and attracting residents back to the city.

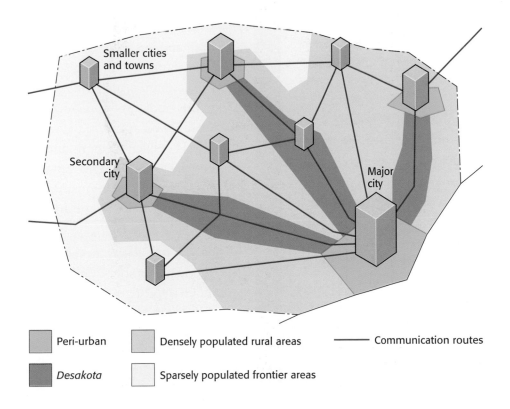

Figure 5.21

A model of the extended metropolitan region in Southeast Asia

Smaller cities and towns

Secondary city

Major city

- Peri-urban
- *Desakota*
- Densely populated rural areas
- Sparsely populated frontier areas
- Communication routes

Planning generally combines policies from each of these approaches. In the USA they are collectively termed **smart growth** solutions, and are backed by a nationwide coalition of environmental groups, community organisations and politicians (Figure 5.22).

Policy	Aim	Example
Urban growth boundaries, or green belts	To restrict physical sprawl	Portland, Oregon
Land purchase	To prevent valued land from being developed	Maryland's Smart Growth and Neighborhood Conservation Programme
Revitalisation of city centres	To attract residents back	Minneapolis
Switching transport investment from intercity highways to city transport schemes	To make cities more attractive	The US government rejected a highway near Salt Lake City
Impose fees on developers	To charge the full costs of environmental harm	Portland, Oregon
Adequate public facilities	To require roads and sewer lines to be paid for before new development	Various cities throughout the USA
Location-efficient mortgages	To provide better loan terms for dwellings near public transport or city centres	Proposed for the future

Figure 5.22

Smart growth policies, USA

Green belts

One of the first and most successful policies designed to manage urban sprawl was that of **green belts** – areas around the edge of cities where development is not normally permitted. Green belts were pioneered in London and Moscow in the 1940s, and have been adopted in the USA, for example in Portland, Oregon. Other conurbations, such as Paris and the Ruhr, have created green wedges or zones interspersed with built-up areas. In the UK, green belts have five main objectives:

- to prevent towns and cities from merging into one another, e.g. West Midlands
- to protect the countryside and farms around cities
- to provide a clear boundary between town and country so as to preserve the setting and character of historic towns, e.g. Oxford

- to provide areas of recreation and amenity near big cities
- to encourage urban regeneration by directing new development into **brownfield sites**.

Although they have been regarded as one of the country's great planning successes, the future of green belt policy is uncertain. They have been blamed for stifling development and pushing up house prices within cities, as well as blighting farmland. Development has leapfrogged beyond the boundary of the green belt, putting pressure on small towns and cities and on the under-protected countryside. They are also said to force commuters to make longer journeys to work. Lincoln and Norwich are two cities that have rejected the option of having green belts. With mounting pressure to find room for more housing, particularly in south-east England, it is likely that the policy will come under greater threat in the future.

Activity

1 Construct a 3-column, 8-row table to occupy approximately one side of A4 paper. In the top row, head the columns 'Strategy', 'Advantages' and 'Disadvantages', respectively. In each of the remaining seven rows, enter one of the elements from Figure 5.12 in the lefthand column. From what you have read in this book, and referring to other sources as appropriate, conduct an analysis of each element and enter your conclusions in the Advantages and Disadvantages columns. What is the overall outcome of your analysis?

2 Examine Figure 5.14 closely. What is the relationship, if any, between the date of origin, number of houses, population and the other indicators of quality given in the table? Would it be safe to assume that such relationships always hold true in other similar settlements in LEDCs?

Case Study: Portland, Oregon

Portland (Figure 5.23) is often ranked near the top of quality of life surveys of US cities, but in many ways it is not typical. It has some of the most stringent controls on development in the country. An urban **growth boundary** or green belt surrounds Portland and 23 nearby small settlements. The green belt protects the attractive rural landscapes of the Willamette Valley and helps invigorate the inner city. Portland managed to accommodate a 50 per cent growth in population by increasing the built-up area by only 2 per cent between 1970 and 2000. Vehicle miles increased by only 2 per cent over the same period.

Now, however, the city is running out of land. The number of residents rose by a fifth in the 1990s. Average house prices increased by 15.6 per cent between 1993 and 1996, compared with 1.8 per cent for the whole country. The return of middle-income people to city neighbourhoods is driving out poorer families. Elsewhere, residents object to using every vacant lot of land because it leads to a loss of open space within the city. To find affordable housing many families have moved further away, to the adjacent city of Vancouver on the other side of the Columbia River, from where 50 000 people commute each day.

Figure 5.23
Portland, Oregon

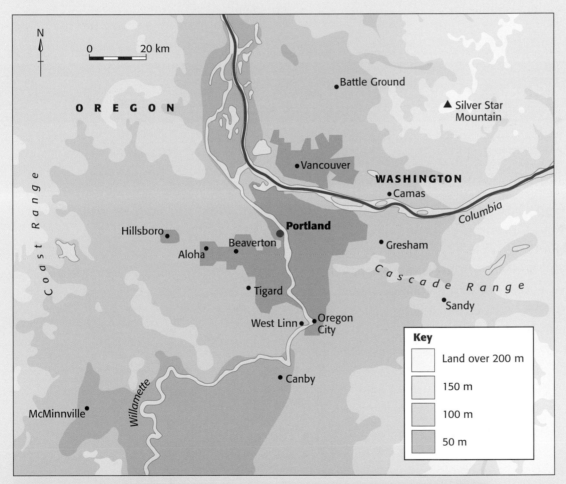

Liverpool Community College

The city of Portland in its natural setting

New towns

There are many different kinds of planned settlement designed to manage urban growth. They are called new towns, satellite cities, expanded towns, and overspill towns. In practice it is difficult to distinguish between them. **New towns** generally share four features:

- they are meant to be free-standing, not physically joined to a larger settlement
- they are designed to be self-contained, with a balance of jobs, residents and services
- they are planned as socially balanced communities with a range of housing
- they use neighbourhoods as units for planning communities.

Around 70 countries have built new towns of one kind or another, including the USA, France, Sweden, Japan and Egypt. In Paris they were placed on growth corridors in order to channel development along distinct axes. There are 31 in the United Kingdom, dating from the 1950s.

Many new towns have been successful, although balancing jobs, residents and urban services often proves difficult. New towns may encounter problems attracting people away from existing cities. Some are located too far from major centres, resulting in isolation; others are so close that they may become no more than commuter towns or 'dormitory settlements'.

Case Study: Cairo's new towns

In order to alleviate urban sprawl, protect scarce farmland and provide better living conditions for the residents of the city's overcrowded districts, the Egyptian government began planning a series of new settlements around Cairo in the 1970s. They were also designed to draw people away from the city, which contains 40 per cent of the country's urban dwellers. The city of Cairo has 3 million inhabitants in a wider metropolitan region of 10 million.

Initial plans called for:

- three satellite cities about 40 km from Cairo with up to 500 000 residents
- four new towns, further away, with up to 1 million residents
- two new settlements on the edge of existing built-up areas
- three special nature communities linked with specific aims such as desert land reclamation.

In practice the various settlements were more or less alike (Figure 5.24). They were located in five growth corridors, while Cairo itself was surrounded by a ring road to prevent outward expansion. Although some new towns such as 6 October and 10 Ramadan were successful at attracting businesses, they gained few

residents. Most workers continued to live in Cairo and commute. Head offices also stayed in Cairo. More distant towns, such as Sadat City, failed to attract jobs or residents. Others suffered from water shortages and poor public transport.

Figure 5.24

Cairo's new settlements

Developing brownfield sites

An alternative to urban sprawl is the greater use of land and buildings in existing built-up areas. This use takes two forms:

- conversion of unused buildings into new homes, e.g. warehouses into flats
- development on brownfield land.

Brownfield land consists of areas previously used for industry or commercial activity which are now derelict or unused. Sites on such land are often contrasted with those on **greenfield sites**, but the reality is that a continuum of sites with differing degrees of earlier development is often to be found.

Major cities, especially those with an industrial past, may have large amounts of brownfield land. England has over 57 000 ha of previously developed and unused land in cities, equivalent to almost 5 per cent of all developed land. In Glasgow, for example, 12 per cent of land is classified as derelict. The closure of factories, steel mills, shipyards, gasworks and coal-fired power stations leaves behind vacant sites. If left unused, there is a danger that they will reduce the desirability of neighbouring areas, leading to blight. Many governments now regard them as potential sites for redevelopment and housing.

Problems of using brownfield sites

Brownfield sites have many limitations for planners and developers. They are often contaminated with industrial chemicals or waste from factories and power stations (Figure 5.25). If the pollution dates from many years before, the current owners may not wish to pay for cleaning up the site.

An example of a brownfield development is Barking Reach on the banks of the River Thames in inner London. To make the site safe for houses, offices and schools, the developers had to bury overhead electricity cables, remove fuel ash from three power stations, and reclaim marshland by raising the ground level. Four thousand homes are planned for the site, arranged in distinct neighbourhoods and

separated by linear parks. The parks will serve as cycleways and provide water drainage.

There are also problems of location. In England, there is an abundance of brownfield sites in cities with declining populations, such as Newcastle and Liverpool, but fewer where the demand is greatest, in London. Unused land is often scattered throughout a city in small parcels, making it more expensive to develop and more difficult to access, as in the case of Baltimore in the USA (Figure 5.26). Lastly, such sites often provide valued and scarce open space within cities. They can become urban oases for wildlife, providing a home for rare plants and birds. They are often more biologically diverse than farmland.

Country	Number of sites
Ireland	1 000
Portugal	4 000
Denmark	7 000
Spain	25 000
Italy	30 000
France	100 000
UK	100 000
Netherlands	110 000
Germany	200 000

Figure 5.25

Estimated number of contaminated sites in European countries

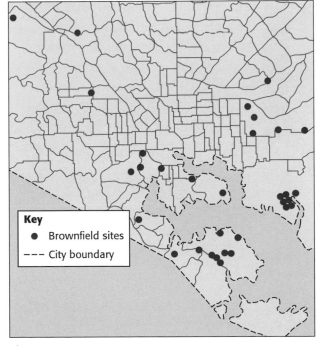

Figure 5.26

Brownfield sites in Baltimore City

Policies for brownfield sites

Two main kinds of policy are applied to re-using brownfield sites. One involves establishing public bodies responsible for identifying sites, cleaning them up and making them available to developers. The other is based on offering financial incentives directly to landowners, builders and developers. In line with this second approach, the UK government has introduced a range of tax incentives in order to help meet its target of 60 per cent of all new housing to be built on brownfield sites. As an encouragement to developers and builders, lower VAT rates are applied to the conversion of houses into flats, tax credits are paid to developers who clean up the land, no VAT is payable on houses that have been empty for 10 or more years, and 100 per cent capital allowances are available when the space above shops is converted into flats. In addition, the government has introduced a 'sequential approach' which allows local authorities to require developers to use brownfield sites before any greenfield sites can be considered.

Activity

Write a short essay evaluating the appropriateness to urban planning of the shift in philosophy from 'Predict and provide' to 'Monitor and manage'. In your essay, refer to an urban area known to you, and attempt to assess in what ways this shift might influence the nature of its development.

Revitalising the inner cities

Urban decline can be measured in terms of population loss, high unemployment, physical decay and declining environmental quality. Most large cities in MEDCs have experienced all or some of these problems since the 1960s, and in some cases before then (Figure 5.27). The root cause lay in general economic changes, particularly as national and urban economies moved away from the production and handling of goods to services – producing and distributing information and expertise. The 20 largest British cities lost 500 000 jobs in two decades. But decline was also associated with population out-migration, especially as young people of working age and families moved out to the suburbs and new towns.

Re-urbanisation

Since the 1980s there have been signs that the population fall in both cities and inner cities has slowed down or reversed, a process known as **re-urbanisation**. The central areas of once declining manufacturing cities and ports, such as Pittsburgh, Hamburg, Manchester, Barcelona and Lille, now contain new shops, offices, cultural and sports facilities and, above all, residents.

The causes of re-urbanisation lie in a combination of demographic, social and economic changes, only partly linked to government planning. Demographic and social changes include the second demo-

Figure 5.27

Population change in British cities, 1901–99

City	Population change for period (%)					
	1901–51	1951–61	1961–71	1971–81	1981–91	1991–99
Birmingham	+ 49.1	+ 1.9	−7.2	−8.3	−5.6	+ 0.6
Cardiff	+ 29.1	+ 18.4	+ 0.7	−3.4	+ 4.6	+ 10.2
Glasgow	+ 24.9	−2/9	−13.8	−22.0	−14.6	no data
Leeds	+ 19.3	+ 2.5	+ 3.6	−4.6	−3.8	+ 1.4
Liverpool	+ 10.9	−5.5	−18.2	−16.4	−10.4	−4.8
London	+ 25.9	−2.2	−6.8	−9.9	−4.5	+ 5.7
Manchester	+ 8.3	−5.9	−17.9	−17.5	−8.8	−1.8
Newcastle	+ 26.1	−2.3	−9.9	−9.9	−5.5	−1.8
Sheffield	+ 23.0	+ 0.4	−6.1	−6.1	−6.5	+ 0.4
Great Britain	+ 32.1	+ 5.0	+ 05.3	+ 0.6	+ 0.02	+ 2.9

graphic transition which has resulted in more young and single-person households on the one hand, and more 'empty nesters' – couples whose children have grown up and left home – on the other. Such people may be attracted to what cities have to offer – arts, entertainment, restaurants, nightlife. In the USA, falling crime rates have persuaded people to return. Finally, cities have plenty of jobs where hours are long or unpredictable, making commuting impractical. These occupations include financial services, media and entertainment, IT and software industries.

The prospects for central districts of large cities and suburban and outlying areas are promising. By contrast those parts of the city in between the inner suburbs and older industrial quarters – lying within the zone in transition – are missing out on new investment. The fear is that a 'doughnut-ring' effect will occur, creating an abandoned zone trapped between areas of prosperity.

Planning for urban regeneration in the UK

Government responses to urban problems in MEDCs date back to the 1930s. In the UK, policies to manage urban growth and contain sprawl were formulated in the 1940s, leading to green belts and new towns on the outside of cities and slum clearance and new housing estates on the inside (Figure 5.28). Such post-war reconstruction gave way to revitalisation and renewal from the 1960s, as the severity of poverty, inadequate schools and poor housing became more obvious. Waves of social unrest and urban riots in the mid-1970s and early 1980s convinced the government of the need for a greater planning response. Later policies can be divided into two periods.

1979–91: redevelopment

This period was characterised by schemes for reviving run-down inner cities through encouraging private sector involvement rather than

Period	Approach	Features	Programmes and policies
1945–60	Reconstruction	• Slum clearance • Masterplans for towns and cities • New housing, rebuilding after the war	1947 Town & Country Planning Act led to green belts and new towns
1960s	Revitalisation	• Social and welfare policies for disadvantaged people and areas	1968 Urban Programme Educational Priority Areas
1970s	Renewal	• Focus on the inner city, based on partnerships between central and local government • Renovation of existing dwellings	Housing Action Areas 1976 Scottish Development Agency 1976 Glasgow Eastern Area Renewal scheme 1978 Inner Urban Areas Act
1979–91	Redevelopment	• Greater role for private sector • Focus on property-led development, reducing bureaucracy • Public money 'levering in private' • Flagship developments often on waterfronts	1981–Enterprise Zones 1981–93 Urban Development Corporations City Action Teams Garden Festivals 1988 City Grant
1991–2001	Regeneration	• Greater involvement of community and local authorities • More coordination of programmes and policies • Focus on sustainable development and heritage conservation • Combined programmes on health, education, training, crime and housing • More use of brownfield sites • Access to National Lottery funding	1991 City Challenge 1993 Single Regeneration Budget 1994 English Partnerships 1998 Urban Task Force 1998 New Deal for Communities 1998 Neighbourhood Renewal Fund 2001 Urban Regeneration Companies

Figure 5.28

Approaches to urban planning in Britain, 1945–2001

government spending alone. The principle known as 'levering in' was based on public spending on reclaiming and cleaning-up land and building transport and infrastructure facilities in order to attract private investment. Thirteen Urban Development Corporations (UDCs, Figure 5.29) were established for this purpose. They were outside local authority control and were designed to speed-up the redevelopment process by taking charge of all the necessary operations in their areas. At the same time, 25 Enterprise Zones were designated in both large and medium-sized cities. These zones were generally smaller than UDCs. Firms locating in them could receive big reductions in taxes and rates, special grants and loans for buildings and machinery, and relaxed planning regulations (Figure 5.30).

Figure 5.30

Job prospects in the Dudley Enterprise Zone, 1988

An official review of urban redevelopment policies in this period found that government spending did reduce unemployment in some of the 123 areas surveyed, but not in the areas of highest unemployment and most need. Some were worse off than at the beginning. The review added to a number of weaknesses and limitations identified in the redevelopment approach:

- the value of property and investments in property varies in cycles and can result in financial losses
- local authorities and local communities were often side-lined
- there were too many poorly coordinated and overlapping different policies and programmes
- there was no coherent and strategic vision for the redevelopment
- new jobs went to commuters rather than to local people
- new housing for the well-off forced out local people
- 'new' firms were often relocations rather than start-ups.

1991–2001: regeneration

Many of these problems were addressed by new programmes introduced from 1991 onwards. From 1993 the various funds and programmes

Figure 5.29

Location of Enterprise Zones and Urban Development Corporations

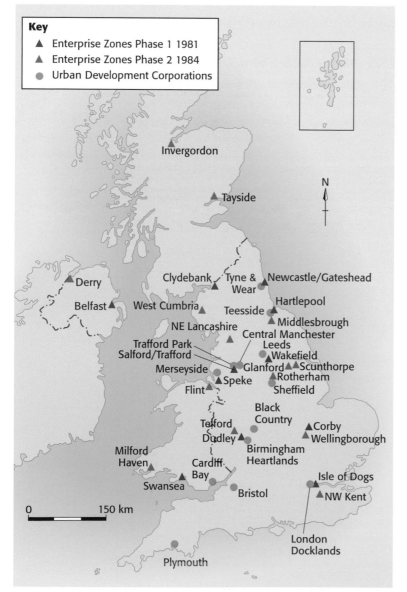

Key

▲ Enterprise Zones Phase 1 1981
▲ Enterprise Zones Phase 2 1984
● Urban Development Corporations

Invergordon

Tayside

N

Derry

Clydebank   Tyne & Wear   Newcastle/Gateshead

Belfast   West Cumbria   Hartlepool
   Teesside
NE Lancashire   Middlesbrough
   Central Manchester
Trafford Park   Leeds
Salford/Trafford   Wakefield
Merseyside   Glanford   Scunthorpe
   Speke   Rotherham
Flint   Sheffield

   Black Country
Telford
Dudley   Corby
   Wellingborough
Milford   Birmingham
Haven   Cardiff   Heartlands
   Bay
Swansea   Isle of Dogs
   Bristol   NW Kent

0   150 km

London Docklands

Plymouth

for England and Wales were brought together under a Single Regeneration Budget, now partly administered by the new Regional Development Agencies. A new scheme called City Challenge ran in the early 1990s. By inviting local authorities to devise projects themselves and to bid for funds, having consulted with local communities, it answered the complaints that existing funding was too centralised. Even so, it was criticised for forcing local authorities to spend large amounts of money competing with one another for inadequate funding. English Partnerships was created to take over the reclamation and sale of derelict land.

Two new schemes were initiated in 1998. The New Deal for Communities was allocated £1.2 billion to spend on 39 projects over three years. It focuses on the poorest areas of the country,

and is designed to tackle jointly problems of health, crime, education and unemployment. The Neighbourhood Renewal Fund has £800 million to reduce inequality. In response to the government's Urban Task Force, chaired by architect Lord Rogers, there were also new laws to encourage regeneration, including tax incentives for developing brownfield sites and provision for the formation of 12 new urban regeneration companies. If these policies are to succeed, they will have to address a number of questions:

- Can government spending create jobs in areas of high unemployment?
- Do such programmes merely displace problems to other parts of the city?
- Can well-off families and children be attracted back to cities without displacing poorer or more vulnerable households?

Case Study: Manchester – redevelopment and regeneration

The differences between redevelopment and regeneration can be illustrated by comparing two schemes in Manchester. Manchester was once the most dynamic city in the world, home of the industrial revolution. But as early as 1918 the city's cotton industry was in decline, followed by metal-working and engineering after 1945. In 1981, the time of the Moss Side riots, unemployment stood at 20 per cent and the city had lost 194 000 people in 20 years – almost one-third of the population.

In 1988 the Central Manchester Development Corporation (CMDC) was designated. It covered only 187 hectares, including large parts of the southern edge of the city centre but omitting the low-income neighbourhoods of Moss Side and Hulme (Figure 5.31). The CMDC was a 'bricks and mortar' approach, designed to recover derelict land and buildings. In eight years it achieved some of its aims:

- £373 million of private investment was 'levered in' with £82.1 million of UK government funds and £5.1 million of European Union structural funds
- 4944 jobs were created – fewer than predicted

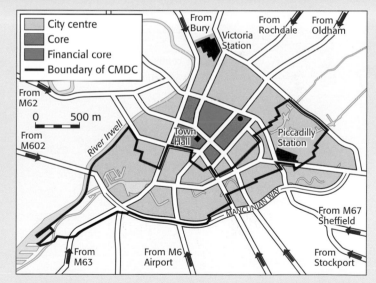

Figure 5.31
The Central Manchester Development Corporation area

- 73 per cent of new firms were start-ups or spin-offs, not relocations, mainly in financial and legal services
- 2583 dwellings were built in an area where the initial population had only been 250.

Although the CMDC was judged a success, it did result in an excess of office space and provided housing mainly for young, affluent professionals. The number of bars in central Manchester doubled between 1994 and 1998, and 85 000 people travel to the centre at weekends for the nightlife. Critics say that there are now too many bars and restaurants for them all to survive.

In 2000 the New East Manchester (NEM) plan was announced by a consortium of English Partnerships, the North West Development Agency and Manchester City Council. Together the consortium members have formed one of the new urban regeneration companies proposed by the government in 2000. It intends to build a new town in East Manchester focused on the new Commonwealth Games stadium, due to be open in 2002 (Figure 5.32). The area lies within the city's doughnut-ring of declining inner suburbs, with many social problems – depopulation, joblessness, mortality levels 50 per cent above the national average, and high levels of crime. Nevertheless, it has assets such as canals, a river, historic buildings and vacant land, as well as improved access from the M60 and ring road.

Unlike the CMDC, the NEM plan aims to address the social problems of communities alongside physical and environmental problems. It intends to:

- recover at least 30 per cent of the area's 1100 ha of derelict land
- renovate 7000 existing homes
- build 12 500 new homes
- double the population to 60 000
- create 15 000 jobs in business parks and commercial centres
- create new shopping centres to replace small, scattered shops
- create a Sportcity new town centre including the Commonwealth Games stadium, a velodrome and other sports and leisure facilities.

The NEM plan aims to include and coordinate a range of existing programmes, including the New Deal for Communities, an Education Action Zone, a Sports Action Zone, a Sure Start training programme and Ancoats Urban Village company. It proposes to obtain funds from the Single Regeneration Budget, the European Structural Fund and the National Lottery.

Figure 5.32

New East Manchester plan

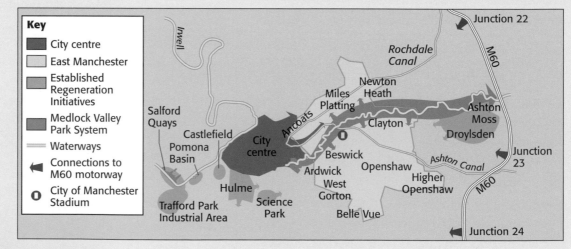

Activity

1 Compare the two Manchester schemes closely and weigh up their similarities and differences. Is there any evidence for believing that the NEM scheme will produce better results in the long term than the CMDC project?

2 Evaluate the contents of Figures 5.19 and 5.20. To what degree do you think that the same arguments might be applied to European towns and cities, including those in the UK?

6 Social exclusion

KEY THEMES

● Different explanations of urban poverty, inequality and social exclusion attach different levels of significance to individual behaviour and social conditions.

● Social exclusion has important spatial dimensions, including poverty concentration, unequal access to urban services and unequal exposure to urban harms.

● The interaction of social and neighbourhood factors can lead to multiple deprivation.

● Opinions differ about whether the role of the informal economy in LEDCs is a last resort or a seedbed for entrepreneurs.

● Informal work conditions and labour exploitation may exist even in modern export-processing zones in LEDCs.

Social and economic inequality

According to most international assessments, the number of people living in poverty in the world is increasing. In 1987, 1.2 billion people lived on less than $1 a day. In 2000 the number was 1.5 billion. As individual countries undergo urbanisation, poverty increasingly becomes an urban phenomenon. And as by 2025 the majority of city residents will live in the poorest countries of the world, it is open to question whether urbanisation makes people better off in the long run. About one in every eight urban dwellers does not have access to safe drinking water, and one in four lacks simple sanitation.

Poverty, inequality and social exclusion

Poverty can be absolute or relative. **Absolute poverty** prevails when a person's total earnings are not sufficient to provide for the basic requirements of existence – food, clothing and shelter. International comparisons use a figure of $1 a day as the standard. In most societies people need more than the basics to sustain their self-esteem, personal security and general happiness. **Relative poverty** exists when a person cannot afford what their society regards as sufficient for well-being. In societies where goods and resources are distributed unevenly between people, inequality exists. Growing inequality, when the gap between rich and poor is increasing, is often referred to as **polarisation** (Figure 6.1).

Figure 6.1

Growing inequality in the UK 1980–99: measurement of income by Gini coefficients

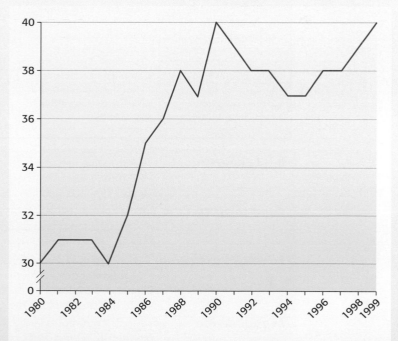

Note: The standard measure of inequality is the Gini coefficient: a score of 0 is complete equality and 100 is complete inequality.

The causes of urban poverty vary from society to society, and there is disagreement about whether individual behaviour or the functioning of social and economic systems as a whole is the root cause (see Figure 6.2). The 'culture of poverty' view was framed by an anthropologist, Oscar Lewis, based on research in India, Puerto Rico and Mexico in the 1960s. It ascribes poverty to the deviant behaviour and reduced expectations of the poor themselves. These ideas were later applied to MEDCs, such as the USA, where the poor were redefined as an 'underclass'. Critics of such views argue that poor people share the same aspirations as others, but are blocked from realising them. This view is expressed in more recent policies on the informal economic sector in LEDC cities.

Urban poverty is normally associated with low earnings, resulting from unemployment, low-wage work, illness and/or family break-down. Poverty is often the cause and consequence of these problems. Although these conditions have been ever-present in MEDCs and LEDCs, important new concepts of poverty and inequality in modern societies are now being explored. These ideas include fuel poverty, financial exclusion and the digital divide, and are summarised in Figure 6.3. When

Figure 6.2

Principal theories of urban deprivation

Theory	Basis of theory	Perceived source of the problem	Action needed to address the problem
Culture of poverty	Poverty is caused by the individual failings and inadequacies of poor people	Behaviour of individuals	Social education
Cycle of deprivation	Individual failings are passed on from one generation to the next; inappropriate attitudes persist	Relationships between individuals, families and groups	Assistance with child-rearing and education
Institutional malfunctioning	Failures of planning, management and administration cause social problems	Relationships between disadvantaged people and officialdom	Better management of governmental processes and services
Maldistribution of resources and opportunities	An unequal and unfair distribution of resources causes social problems	Relationships between under-privileged and government	Positive action on behalf of the poor, including policies targeted at selected areas, e.g. inner cities
Class conflict	Capitalist societies have in-built inequalities that give the rich advantages over the poor	The political and economic structure, especially the status of the lower socio-economic groups	Social and political transformation

Figure 6.3

New concepts of poverty

Fuel poverty	Poor people spend a higher proportion of their income on heating and lighting, but often live in less energy-efficient dwellings and cannot afford to keep warm. It affects 5 million people in the UK.
Food security	Food security exists when people have physical and economic access to sufficient, safe and nutritious food to meet their dietary needs and food preferences for an active and healthy life. 800 million people worldwide lack food security.
Financial exclusion	When banks and other financial institutions shut down their branches in poor neighbourhoods, residents may be forced to use more expensive sources of loans and credit, or be unable to afford insurance for cars, homes and property. 2.25 million people in the UK have no bank account.
Digital divide	Poorer households lack access to information technology, such as the internet. In the UK, 60 per cent of households headed by professionals and managers were online in 2000, but only 14 per cent of households headed by semi-skilled and unskilled workers were connected to the internet.

poverty is accompanied by powerlessness, such that an individual group or neighbourhood is prevented from fully participating in society and is denied the full benefits of citizenship, the result is social exclusion. Social exclusion often has a spatial dimension.

Spatial dimensions of social exclusion in cities

Poverty, inequality and social exclusion have distinct geographical patterns. Their causes are often rooted in particular places and their incidence varies between cities and rural areas, between different cities, and within cities. Six key elements are identifiable:

1 The **geographical distribution** of forms of deprivation and disadvantage is generally uneven across cities, as the four maps of Manchester in the 1990s illustrate (Figure 6.4). East Manchester stands out as an area of high mortality, illness, youth unemployment and low birth-weights – all associated with poverty.

2 Inequality and social exclusion are frequently related to **poverty clusters** or **concentrations**. Poor urban neighbourhoods rarely exist in isolation. In the UK, 244 of the poorest 284 wards in the country are grouped together in 51 poverty clusters, to be found in mainly industrial and ex-industrial areas, inner London, ex-coalmining areas and seaside towns.

3 Poverty is frequently **spatially persistent** in areas of the city for long periods. Figure 6.5 compares poor areas in London recorded by Charles Booth in 1896 with results derived from the 1991 census. There is a striking similarity in the patterns a century apart.

4 There may be close **spatial proximity between poverty and wealth**, notably in the cities of LEDCs, but also in MEDCs. By some measures Inner London is the richest urban area in Europe, but nearly half the capital's children are living below the poverty line according to the Greater London Authority.

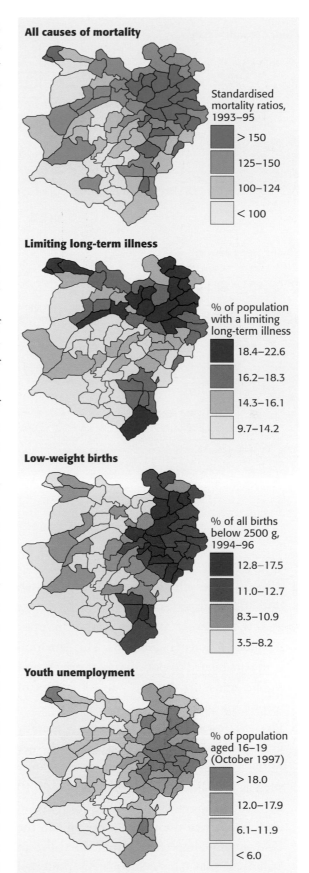

Figure 6.4

Social exclusion in Manchester in the 1990s

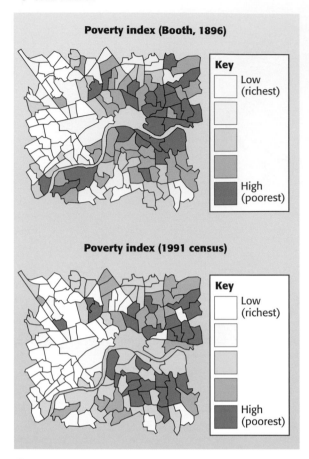

Figure 6.5

Persistence of poverty in London, 1896--1991

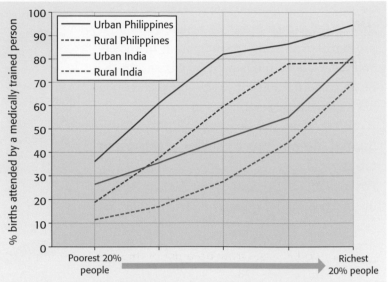

The graph shows the proportion of births attended by a doctor, nurse or midwife for different social groups, and for urban and rural areas.

Figure 6.6

Urban/rural and wealth differences in access to child healthcare: India and the Philippines

5 Physical **access to services** such as water, sanitation, surgeries, schools, parks, banks and the internet is often worse in poor neighbourhoods (Figure 6.6). This situation is in part related to poor levels of private and public transport, but also to difficulties of resourcing and staffing.

6 Physical **exposure to harm** is generally greater in poorer neighbourhoods, whether in the form of crime and violence or hazards such as landslides (Figure 6.7). In Britain, 10 per cent of inner city residents are burgled each year: twice the national average. In the USA, low-income tenants may often live in buildings that are inadequately protected against fire, in neighbourhoods where fire-fighting services have been cut back.

The Road to Trauma

by Ian Roberts

The social class gradient for child injury is steeper than for any other cause of death. Twenty years ago the risk of death for children in the lowest social class was three times that of those in the top. Today, the differential is fivefold.

Being hit by a car is a leading cause of death in childhood. Children risk pedestrian injury while crossing roads, and a key determinant of the number of roads crossed is car ownership. Children of families without a car cross an average five streets a day, compared with three streets for families with one car and two streets for families with two or more cars.

The British pedestrian injury epidemic peaked around 1930. Since then death rates have fallen – but not because roads have become safer. The most likely reasons for decline are the massive reduction in walking and the better survival chances of injured children through improvements in healthcare. In the struggle for the streets, pedestrians lost.

For most of the world, though, the war is just beginning. Eighty per cent of the world's cars are owned by 15 per cent of the world's population. Like most Western epidemics, road trauma is now being exported to the developing world. This year, about 300 000 children will die on the world's roads, with millions seriously injured. Whether in England or Ethiopia, most of those who die will be poor ... By 2020, road crashes will have moved from ninth to third place in the world disease-ranking, occupying second place in developing countries

Figure 6.7

Poverty and road traffic accidents – from *The Guardian*, 9 May 2000

<table>
<tr><td colspan="2">**Activity**</td></tr>
<tr><td>1</td><td>Examine the theories of urban deprivation given in Figure 6.2. Assess the extent to which these theories seem to be relevant to an urban area known to you, and describe the forms of evidence you would need to test their relevance. Do you think these theories overlook any key influences on urban deprivation?</td></tr>
<tr><td>2</td><td>Figure 6.6 compares access to certain services in the rural and urban areas of two LEDCs. Draw up a list of those services in your home area which you believe are not equally accessible to all members of the community for **a** spatial reasons and **b** socio-economic reasons.</td></tr>
</table>

Multiple deprivation

It is clear from the above examples that the various dimensions of social exclusion – poverty, ill-health, exposure to harm, etc. – reinforce one another. At the same time, they are concentrated spatially into deprived neighbourhoods. Being deprived in one area of life may make it more likely that a person or area is deprived in another area of life. Someone who knows few employed people will find it harder to learn about what jobs are available. If incomes in a neighbourhood fall, shops and banks may close. If families leave an area, vacant and abandoned houses push down property values and encourage crime and vandalism. All of these situations are examples of **multiple deprivation** (see Figure 6.8).

Deprived areas

One way of thinking about multiple deprivation is to consider how neighbourhood or environmental characteristics interact with social characteristics. Certain areas, such as London's East End (Figure 6.5), suffer from 'intrinsic characteristics' such as poor location and physical or environmental deterioration of the sort set out

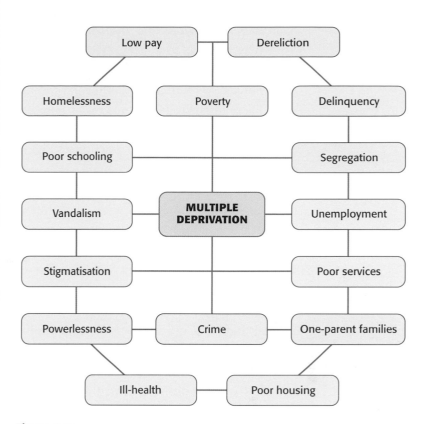

Figure 6.8

The anatomy of multiple deprivation

Intrinsic area characteristics	Condition	Outcomes
Location and transport links	Poor access	Low status
Physical style and ownership	Segregated community	Low value
Environment	Unattractive, poor quality	Low desirability
Economy	Low investment	Low mix

Acquired area characteristics	Condition	Outcomes
Population mix	Low status deters more ambitious	Concentrated poverty
Reputation and history	Image activates fear	Rejection and isolation
Standards and services	Performance is poor	Deteriorating conditions
Poor supervision	Low morale reduces incentives	Negative behaviour
Weak informal controls	Intimidation prevents action	Withdrawal

Figure 6.9

The intrinsic and acquired characteristics of poor areas

in the top half of Figure 6.9. Regardless of who lived there, they would be unattractive places. They may be close to concentrations of heavy industry, toxic facilities or waste dumps, or poorly linked by roads and other forms of transport. These intrinsic conditions may be hard to change. On the other hand, the 'acquired characteristics' of an area (lower portion of Figure 6.9) derive from the kinds of people who reside there. They may include over-concentrations of people who are vulnerable by virtue of illness, age, poverty or ethnic identity.

Pockets or clusters of disadvantaged and vulnerable individuals form in a number of ways, including:

- *in situ*, for instance following the collapse of local industry or, as in some coalmining areas, an exceptional level of work-related poor health
- by low-income individuals drifting into low-rent areas of cities, most notably the housing-poor and the homeless
- through public sector allocation of the poorest-quality housing to the most vulnerable people, leading to 'socio-tenurial polarisation', or the concentration of groups such as the infirm elderly, single parents, and the mentally ill into high-rise public housing
- by exit, when the better-off leave or abandon neighbourhoods.

These processes may occur in combination. In MEDC cities they give rise to two general types of deprived neighbourhood, suggesting that there is no single way in which areas become the sites of social exclusion.

The first type of deprived area, **inner cities**, are characterised by older, 19th-century neighbourhoods where the factories and work that once supported them have gone, leaving behind a legacy of joblessness, poor health, physical decay, low property prices and a lack of investment. Particularly in the USA, but also in Western Europe, these districts may be home to recently arrived immigrants or racially excluded groups (Figure 6.10).

The second type of neighbourhood is the **peripheral estate**, outer suburb or, as it is called in France, *la banlieue*. In many cases these areas have resulted from slum clearance policies designed to address the problems of inner cities. In Glasgow, for example, the relocation of low-income residents from the central quarters to new housing estates on the outskirts has resulted in the over-concentration of single-parent families in the latter. In France, high-rise housing known as *grands ensembles* was built on cheap land on the outside of cities (Figure 6.11). Although standards of dwelling were

Figure 6.10
Two young immigrants in Paris

Figure 6.11
A *grand ensemble* in Paris

good, such places had inadequate services and were physically isolated from both workplaces and urban amenities.

Tackling multiple deprivation

As there is no single cause of multiple deprivation in urban neighbourhoods, there is no single policy or set of policies that can guarantee success. Examples of government-led programmes for urban regeneration are given in Chapter 5. Early programmes were faulted for focusing too much on physical regeneration and not enough on the other dimensions of multiple deprivation. A more recent programme in Britain, the Neighbourhood Renewal Unit, is one attempt to resolve these problems (Figure 6.12). In preparation for this programme, the government has commissioned

Neighbourhood Renewal aims to tackle the problems of Britain's most deprived areas within 20 years, starting in 2001. It involves:

- *floor targets on employment, health, crime, education and housing, e.g. to eliminate all substandard housing by 2010*

- *£800 million neighbourhood renewal fund for the 88 most deprived areas*

- *Local Strategic Partnerships between public agencies, private businesses, charities and community groups, to give local people a greater say*

- *neighbourhood wardens or managers to act as local leaders*

- *a community empowerment fund to assist local organisations.*

Figure 6.12
Neighbourhood Renewal, 2001

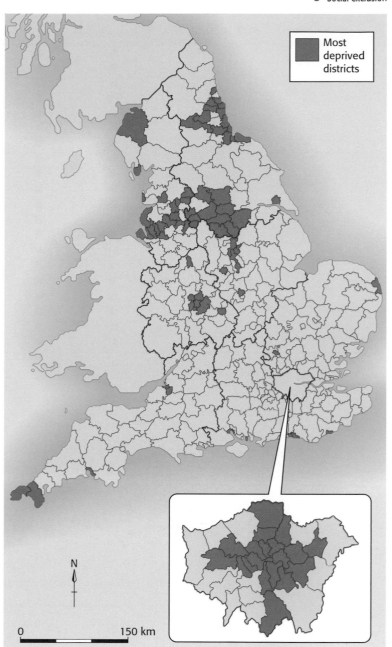

Figure 6.13
The most deprived local authority districts in England, 1998

a new index of multiple deprivation which shows that multiple deprivation is heavily concentrated in urban areas (see Figure 6.13). The index employs a range of measures and reveals how neighbourhoods that score badly on one dimension, such as employment, often also score badly on others (Figure 6.14).

Government programmes are often accused of being imposed in a top-down fashion, insensitive to local needs. Alternative responses

Ward	District	Income	Employment	Health	Education	Housing	Child poverty
Benchill	Manchester	■	■	■	■	●	■
Speke	Liverpool	■	■	■	■	●	■
Thorntree	Middlesbrough	■	■	■	■	◆	■
Everton	Liverpool	■	■	■	◆	✻	■
Pallister	Middlesbrough	■	■	◆	■	●	■
Vauxhall	Liverpool	■	■	■	◆	✻	■
St Hilda's	Middlesbrough	■	■	■	■	✻	■
Princess	Knowsley	■	■	■	●	◆	■
Grangetown	Redcar & Cleveland	■	■	◆	◆	●	■
Granby	Liverpool	■	■	■	●	◆	■
Pirrie	Liverpool	■	■	■	◆	●	■
Breckfield	Liverpool	■	■	■	◆	●	■
Longview	Knowsley	■	■	■	●	●	■
Cherryfield	Knowsley	■	■	■	◆	●	■
Portrack & Tilery	Stockton-on-Tees	■	■	◆	■	✻	■
Harpurhey	Manchester	■	■	■	◆	✻	◆
Beswick & Clayton	Manchester	■	■	■	◆	●	◆
Kirby Central	Knowsley	■	■	■	●	●	■
Regent	Great Yarmouth	■	■	◆	■	◆	◆
Northwood	Knowsley	■	■	■	◆	◆	■

This table uses data from the Index of Multiple Deprivation calculated for the DETR. A score for each element, e.g. income, health, is calculated for each of the country's 8414 wards using several indicators. Each ward is then ranked.

Key
■ = in top 1% most deprived wards
◆ = in top 5% most deprived wards
● = in top 10% most deprived wards
✻ = in top 20% most deprived wards

Figure 6.14

The most deprived wards in England, 2000

sometimes come from community organisations or non-governmental bodies such as faith groups and charitable foundations. Such bottom-up alternatives have been pioneered in the USA, including:

- community businesses owned by local people
- community development corporations that provide credit, housing, education and training
- credit unions and community development banks that tackle financial exclusion.

The idea of credit unions for low-income people was inspired by the example of the Grameen Bank, started for, and by, women in Bangladesh. By forming small 'borrowing circles', groups of five women are able, with one another's help, to raise sufficient capital to start businesses. Credit unions have also been historically important for newly-arrived immigrants overlooked by conventional banks. In the case of alternative policies, MEDCs and LEDCs may be able to share information and ideas.

Activity

Obtain or draw a simple outline map of England and Wales and, with reference to Figure 6.13, put on and name the areas of greatest deprivation. (There is no need to name all the districts individually where they are clustered together.) Which areas do not seem to fit the general pattern of association with declining industry, and why?

Hulme lies to the south of Manchester's city centre, outside the area covered by the Central Manchester Development Corporation (see Figures 5.31 and 5.32 in Chapter 5). Its high-rise housing was built between 1964 and 1972 in order to re-house people from the slums cleared in the area. Five thousand dwellings were built, mainly in 7-storey blocks, some with 13 storeys, surrounded by open space. Poor physical design and bad materials caused problems of damp and condensation, to which were added cockroach infestations. Large areas of unsupervised space encouraged vandalism, crime and drug dealing. Families left in large numbers, and Hulme acquired a poor reputation that rubbed off on the remaining residents.

In 1991 Manchester City Council decided to demolish the estate rather than repair or renovate it. The council formed a partnership with a private developer, AMEC, and successfully bid for £37.5 million City Challenge funds to regenerate the area. A new layout of denser, low-rise housing set in a grid of streets and parks has been planned. High-rise buildings are being demolished (Figure 6.15) and some houses renovated. New shops, including a supermarket, are being built.

Some local residents are not content with aspects of the scheme, including the low level of public consultation and community participation. There have been protests over the loss of trees and open spaces, the attempted closure of the local school, and the effect of the supermarket on small shops in the neighbourhood. The experience of Hulme suggests that physical regeneration cannot be completely successful without local consent.

Figure 6.15
Demolition of housing blocks in Hulme, Manchester

Under-employment in LEDC cities

Since the 1960s there have generally been more workers than jobs in the cities of the LEDCs. Unlike in MEDCs, governments and employers usually cannot provide support for unemployed workers, resulting in three forms of unemployment:

- **open unemployment**, recognised in official statistics
- **under-employment**, or the under-utilisation of workers because:
  - they are employed only on a daily, weekly or seasonal basis, for example in tourism
  - there are more workers than are needed to do a job, e.g. street vending

  - they work in family firms, where their labour is not really needed
- **misemployment** – activities that do not contribute to the good of society, such as crime and begging.

Where there are more workers than jobs, wages are low. As a consequence, many potential workers are wasted in LEDCs. But there may still be more job opportunities in cities than in rural areas.

The informal economy

An alternative to seeking work in well-paid and secure jobs is the **informal economy**. There are many definitions of informality, most of which derive from a distinction made by the

International Labour Organisation in the 1970s (see Figure 6.16). Most experts now agree that this distinction is too crude, and that it hides many linkages between the formal and informal sectors. These links include flows of materials and goods, the provision of cheap labour by informal workers which contributes to lower costs in the **formal economy**, and the fact that the same person may work in both economies at the same time or in the course of a year. It makes sense to think of a continuum from informal to formal work, as suggested by Figure 6.17. Some economists simply distinguish a

category of 'unprotected workers', who have no job security, health benefits or holiday pay, and are subject to long hours for low pay. Such workers can be found in factories as well as on the streets.

The proportion of the workforce in the informal economy of LEDCs is likely to vary from below a fifth to above a half (Figure 6.18). In cities, however, the informal sector may be much larger, accounting for 40–60 per cent of workers who may be found in a huge variety of jobs, from street vendors (Figure 6.19), taxi drivers and construction workers to garage mechanics, maids and security guards. In many cases the sector provides employment for the majority of women workers, as Figure 6.18 indicates. When times get hard, owing to economic recession, households may turn to informal work as one of their strategies for survival (Figure 6.20).

Governments once expected informal economies to shrink as countries developed. They focused their employment policies on the formal sector, but by the 1980s, and especially during the hard times which the highly indebted countries encountered in the 1990s, new policies were being introduced. The Peruvian economist Hernando de Soto championed the informal economy as a seedbed for entrepreneurs rather than a refuge for the desperate. His argument that governments should remove legal obstacles to self-employment and starting small businesses has been widely adopted. Critics argue, however, that there is a limit to the number of jobs the informal sector can provide.

Working for transnational companies

The most recent phase of urbanisation in LEDCs is linked to the emergence of a new international division of labour accompanying the change made by many LEDCs from import-substitution to export-orientation. Coincident with this change, transnational companies (TNCs) were relocating many of their manufac-

Figure 6.16

Characteristics of the formal and informal sectors

Informal	Formal
Easy job to enter	Difficult entry
Reliance on local resources	Frequent reliance on overseas resources
Family ownership of enterprises	Corporate ownership
Small scale of operation	Large scale of operation
Labour-intensive and adapted technology	Capital-intensive and often using imported technology
Skills acquired outside the formal school system	Formally acquired skills, including from overseas
Unregulated and competitive markets	Protected markets, through tariffs, quotas and trade licences
Little or no health and safety protection for workers	Some protection, higher levels of trade union membership

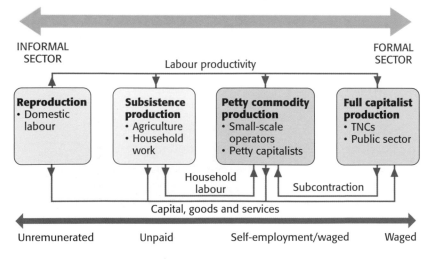

Figure 6.17

The informal/formal sector continuum

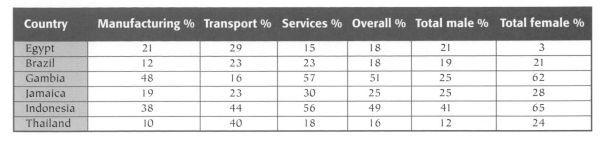

Figure 6.18

Levels of informal production and employment in LEDC countries

Country	Manufacturing %	Transport %	Services %	Overall %	Total male %	Total female %
Egypt	21	29	15	18	21	3
Brazil	12	23	23	18	19	21
Gambia	48	16	57	51	25	62
Jamaica	19	23	30	25	25	28
Indonesia	38	44	56	49	41	65
Thailand	10	40	18	16	12	24

Figure 6.19

Street vendors in Jaipur, Rajasthan, India

Responses:

- Increase the number of workers per household
  – women and young males enter the workforce on leaving school.

- Increase reliance on informal employment
  – e.g. young women enter domestic service.

- Increase household size
  – living with parents and grandparents to save money
  – adding relatives and friends to the household.

- Lower expenditure on goods and services
  – cutting back on clothes, household maintenance
  – consuming less beef and milk
  – providing goods and services at home rather than purchasing them.

- Emigration to the USA
  – more men and women journeyed to the USA.

Figure 6.20

Household response to economic crisis in Guadalajara, Mexico

turing and data-processing activities to places where wages were lower. LEDCs introduced two main geographical policies to attract TNCs:

- **Free Trade Zones (FTZs)**, usually near ports, where companies can import and export without paying duty
- **Export Processing Zones (EPZs)** comprising industrial estates where foreign companies pay few or no taxes and are subject to low levels of government regulation.

Over 70 countries established EPZs from the 1970s onwards, led by Mexico, the Philippines, India and China. The first firms to locate in these zones generally specialised in textiles and clothing. Their impact is evident in the data illustrated in Figure 6.21. Later arrivals have tended to concentrate on pharmaceuticals, power tools, vehicle components, electronics and data processing equipment. For example, Japanese companies now manufacture audio-

Figure 6.21

Changes in employment in the textile, clothing, leather and footwear industries, 1980–93

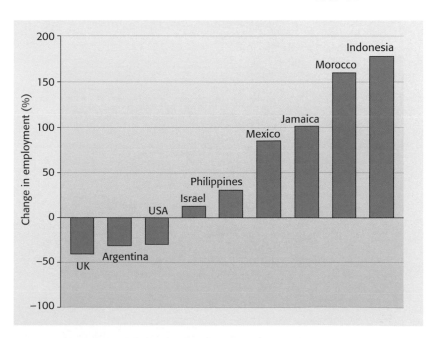

visual equipment in Indonesia, car parts in Thailand, computer hard-disk drives in the Philippines and power tools in China. Newly industrialising countries (NICs) such as Taiwan and Korea developed so successfully that their workers became too costly for foreign companies, who then moved on to new countries, such as Vietnam.

Although EPZs may appear far removed from street vendors, they are also involved with the informal labour market. The available jobs are frequently part-time or casual, with low pay, long hours and poor working conditions. Three-quarters of workers in EPZs are women, generally young and single. Employers regard these workers as less militant, although many are now organising trade unions with international help. Protestors have targeted well-known global brands such as GAP, Nike and IBM, which own or use factories in EPZs, alleging that they exploit workers. Unions in MEDCs regard the low wages paid in EPZs as unfair competition. In 1998, one survey found wages in Chinese EPZs to be as low as 13 US cents per hour, compared with the US minimum wage of $10 an hour. The firms themselves claim that their wages and conditions are usually much better than in other workplaces within the country.

Case Study: Cavite Export Processing Zone, the Philippines

There are four EPZs in the Philippines. The first opened in 1972. The largest is Cavite (Figure 6.22), about 140 km from the capital Manila, which has swallowed up several small fishing villages. It has over 200 factories and over 55 000 workers. Nike, GAP, IBM, Marks & Spencer and Intel all have goods made there. Textiles, clothing and electrical goods are the main industries.

EPZ incentives include:

- tax- and duty-free import of machinery, parts and raw materials
- four to eight years' 'tax holidays' for new firms
- only 5 per cent tax on gross income after the tax holiday period
- rents from 27 US cents per square metre per month
- no charge on sending profits overseas.

Almost 70 per cent of employees and 40 per cent of managers are female (Figure 6.23), although men outnumber women in fabricated metals. The EPZ has provided the province of Cavite with much-needed work. It has turned Rosario, once a small fishing village, into a town of 60 000 people. One in three children from local schools go straight to work in the EPZ after leaving. Teachers say that children stay in school to finish their education because they know that the factories prefer to employ educated English-speaking workers. The workers, however, sometimes paint a different picture, one of harsh conditions, low pay and serious threats to health, as illustrated by the story of Carmelita Alonso:

'Carmelita Alonzo was a worker at a Taiwanese-owned garment factory in the Philippines, who died from excessive work. The factory, V. T. Fashion, produced skirts, jackets, dresses, short pants, vests and blouses for GAP, Guess, Jones New York, Eddie Bauer, May Co, Macy, Liz Claiborne, Ellen Tracy, Head, Benetton, Ruff Hewn, LeQ, Chachi, Ralph Lauren, and Banana Republic. Carmelita died on 8 March 1997, International Women's Day, at the Andres Bonifacio Memorial Hospital in Cavite after 11 days in hospital. According to a statement released by her co-workers at V. T. Fashion, "Carmelita was killed by her 14-hour workday every day plus overtime of eight hours every Sunday." The workers denounced the system of quotas set by the company which forced them to work 12 to 14 hours per day. According to the Workers Assistance Center in Rosario, Carmelita had died because of the strict regime in V. T. Fashion and its sister company, All Asia Garment Industries, which forces workers to obey a

Figure 6.22
The location of
Cavite in the
Philippines

A worker in Cavite

compulsory 14-hour shift. Until V. T. Fashion burned down in a fire on 1 April 1997, there were 1046 workers, 90 per cent of whom were women aged between 17 and 30. Workers received only 155 pesos (US$5.96) as the daily minimum wage, and are subjected to overtime. This wage is not enough to meet the living costs of workers and rising prices. Workers were made to work from 7 am to 9 pm during weekdays, 7 am to 7 pm on Saturdays and 6 am to 2 pm on Sundays. Rest periods were usually an hour during lunchtime and 30 minutes in the afternoon. Less than half of the workers were regular workers. Most were employed on three- to four-month "apprenticeship" contracts or as contractual workers with employment contracts of only five months. Others were employed on six-month contracts.'

Source: CorpWatch (www.corpwatch.org)

| Product | Management and staff | | | | Employees | | Total | |
| | Foreign | | Filipino | | | | Number | % |
	Male	Female	Male	Female	Male	Female		
Wearing apparel	62	10	209	451	1617	8369	10 718	28.0
Athletics shoes and gloves	13	2	121	54	1425	2539	4154	10.9
Hosiery	28	1	2	44	337	889	1301	3.4
Plastic products	23	1	75	55	342	608	1104	2.8
Fabricated metals	17	1	60	42	377	82	579	1.5
Electronics and electrical goods	189	5	1283	888	2798	12 040	17 203	45.0
Other	50	5	121	127	1034	1867	3204	8.4
Total	382	25	1871	1661	7930	26 394	38 263	100

Figure 6.23
Workers in
Cavite Export
Processing Zone,
the Philippines

Activity

1 Present the information given in Figure 6.23 using the graphical technique that you consider to be most suitable. What patterns of employment are evident from the data?

2 Use the internet, or other suitable sources, to examine the distribution of favoured trading and manufacturing zones in regions of the world other than Southeast Asia. The Free Zones of the Dominican Republic comprise one example:

http://members.tripod.co.uk/DominicanRepublic/FZ.htm

7 Congestion

KEY THEMES

● Across the world urban dwellers are becoming ever more dependent on private vehicles for moving around the city.

● Traffic congestion is a problem in all kinds of cities, rich and poor, large and small, and it has both economic costs and implications for health and well-being.

● Policies to address traffic congestion include responding to demand, managing demand, and urban planning and design.

The urban transport problem

Movement in the city

Being able to travel between home and work, and to reach schools, shops, hospitals and other amenities, and to do so quickly, cheaply and safely, is vital to the well-being of urban dwellers. In addition, a tenth or more of journeys is for carrying the goods essential to urban economies. Managing urban travel successfully depends upon understanding the choices residents make between different modes of transport. There are seven main ways of moving in the city, each with its advantages and drawbacks for the individual and for society at large.

1 **Walking** may be the principal means of travel in LEDCs among the urban poor, and even in MEDCs one-third of journeys are made on foot. But despite its benefits in terms of health and fitness, the popularity of walking to work and to school is declining in most MEDCs. Pedestrians are also at risk from other forms of travel (see Figure 6.7 on page 90).

2 **Cycling** rarely accounts for more than a tenth of journeys in MEDCs, but is as high as 80 per cent in China. Certain MEDC governments, notably the Netherlands, Germany and Denmark, actively promote cycling as a cleaner and healthier alternative to the private car. For journeys under 4 km it can be the quickest form of travel door-to-door, but cyclists are exposed to vehicle traffic. Three-wheel cycles, or rickshaws, are a common form of taxi in Asian cities.

3 **Private cars** generally account for the majority of trips in MEDCs and many LEDCs. They offer flexibility of route and timing, convenience and comfort; car ownership is also widely perceived to confer status. Although the fixed costs of buying and insuring cars are relatively high, the comparatively low running costs mean that there is little incentive for owners not to use them once purchased. The major drawbacks are associated with congestion and pollution.

4 **Buses** are the cheapest form of mass or public transport, making use of existing roads and offering flexibility of routes and destinations. In India up to 40 per cent of trips are by bus, and high levels are also found in many European cities. Their major disadvantage is shared by all forms of mass transit: insufficient capacity in peak periods and excess capacity off-peak. Like cars, buses are caught in congestion but also have to stop for loading and unloading.

5 **Rail systems** are ideal for moving large numbers of passengers at high speed in densely populated urban areas. They are more energy efficient and less polluting than buses, but involve high initial building costs and generally require public subsidy to keep running. Forms of rail vary from expensive subways, only suitable for cities with at least a million inhabitants, to more modern light rail and automated systems and street trams that share road space with other vehicles.

6 **Informal buses and taxis** are a feature of many LEDCs, usually unlicensed and sometimes dangerous, but offering cheap and flexible alternatives to inadequate public transport for the urban poor. Examples include *matutus* in Nairobi and *jeepneys* in Manila.

The rise of automobile dependence

In both MEDCs and LEDCs there has been a distinct shift in the preferred mode of urban travel towards private cars and away from all other forms (Figure 7.1). In MEDCs, public transport has declined in popularity since the 1950s and, although it has recovered in many European cities, there are still significant variations between countries (Figure 7.2). While levels of car ownership in MEDCs are approaching one for every two people, they are also growing rapidly in LEDCs at 15–25 per cent a year, faster than urban population growth. Delhi (Figure 7.3) is a good example. Although in many cities half or more of journeys are by some form of public transport (Figure 7.4), in the fast-growing cities of Asia and Africa, inadequate levels of bus and rail provision are encouraging greater use of private cars.

In the world as a whole, the level of car ownership in a country generally rises with income. As a rule of thumb, when the GNP of a country reaches $3000 per capita, car ownership levels take off. Even before then, because cities are often wealthier than the rest of the country, significant vehicle use sets in. However,

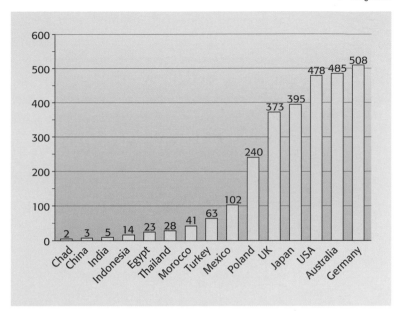

Figure 7.1

Passenger cars per thousand people, 1999

	Estimated annual travel in passenger km/person 1992–95					
	Canada	USA	Great Britain	France	Germany	Sweden
Car	18 130	17 032	10 088	11 311	8666	9202
Bus	122	681	757	736	829	1258
Rail	51	38	505	1017	753	663
People/km^2	3	28	247	106	228	20
Cars/1000 people	486	513	374	439	489	404

Figure 7.2

Travel behaviour in MEDCs, 1992–95

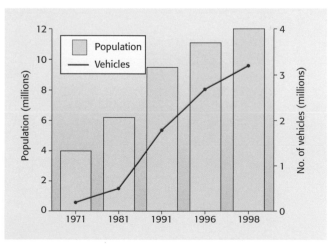

Figure 7.3

Population and vehicle growth in Delhi, 1971–98

car ownership does not automatically translate into car use. Figure 7.2 shows that in Germany and Sweden, for instance, many people own cars but travel to work by other means.

There is good evidence to show that greater access to personal cars is associated with more frequent and longer journeys (Figure 7.5).

People undertake trips in connection with work, school, and for leisure purposes that they would not have done before. Car ownership therefore confers a high degree of personal mobility and freedom, enabling people to change jobs more easily, choose an alternative place in which to live, and to enjoy the opportunities of both the city and the countryside.

When the layout of the built environment and the location of urban amenities, homes and workplaces is mainly shaped by high levels of car ownership, a city may be said to have become **automobile dependent**. In effect, alternative modes of transport become either inconvenient or impractical, such that car ownership becomes a necessity. People without a car (Figure 7.6), or who depend on public transport because of their ill-health or disability, may become socially excluded under such circumstances. Women, children, the elderly and inner city dwellers generally have lower access to private cars. When facilities that were once within walking distance, such as shops or clinics, are sited further away or are located in out-of-town sites, the transport-poor are disadvantaged. As more people opt out of public transport, those left behind generally have to pay more for the declining public services, a trap that encourages further moves into private car usage.

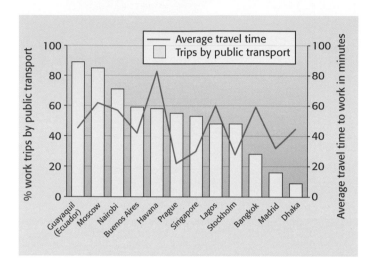

Figure 7.4

Work trips by public transport and travel time to work

Figure 7.5

Changes in travel behaviour in the UK, 1975–95

	% change 1975–95	
	All modes of transport	**By car**
Number of journeys	+ 13	+ 49
Total distance	+ 38	+ 66
Average length of journey	+ 24	+ 12
Total time	+ 19	+ 53
Average journey time	+ 5	+ 5

Figure 7.6

UK households with regular use of a car, by socio-economic group (percentage)

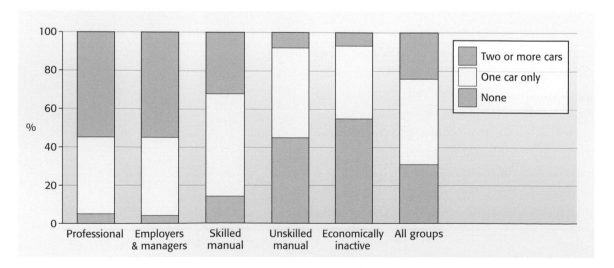

Types of congestion

There are two types of **congestion**. Vehicle or traffic congestion is the delay imposed on one vehicle by another. Person congestion or over-crowding occurs in public transport systems, particularly during peak periods. Both forms are associated with economic, social and environmental costs (Figure 7.7). These costs are incurred by individuals and businesses and may be expressed in terms of the time lost or money wasted. One survey of 68 US cities put the cost at $78 billion, 4.5 billion hours of delay and 6.8 billion US gallons of wasted fuel. In Thailand, congestion in Bangkok alone is estimated to add up to 2 per cent of the country's entire economic output. For individual drivers, the annual time lost or wasted may be longer than the average working week and the costs may reach $1000, as they do in Los Angeles (Figure 7.8). Trips during peak periods in London take almost seven times longer than normal (Figure 7.9).

Economic	Social	Environmental
• Slower movement of goods and services • Longer journeys to work • Inefficient use of road space • Delays to public transport • Discouragement of visitors, tourists and shoppers from using facilities and shops in congested areas	• Time wasted travelling not spent at work or with family • Stress • Unpleasant urban environment for pedestrians and cyclists • Difficulties of pedestrian access and mobility	• Inefficient fuel use caused by stop–start flow • Excess fuel consumption • Greater air pollution in congested areas • Noise

Figure 7.7 The impact of congestion

City	Travel Rate Index	Annual delay per driver in hours	Annual congestion cost in $ millions	Annual congestion cost per driver in $
Los Angeles	1.55	56	12 570	1000
San Francisco/Oakland	1.45	42	3055	760
Chicago	1.40	34	4605	570
Portland/Vancouver (Oregon)	1.36	34	910	610
New York region	1.32	34	9745	595
Phoenix	1.30	31	1385	540
Colorado Springs	1.15	20	145	330

Figure 7.8 Traffic congestion in US cities

Note: The Travel Rate Index shows how much longer a journey takes at peak time than during the rest of the day. A value of 1.5 indicates that the trip takes 50% longer.

Period	London	Conurbations	Large urban areas	Small urban areas
Peak	697	274	170	106
Inter-peak	643	211	133	91
Off-peak	221	104	52	33
Weekend	476	162	98	64
All periods	543	201	124	80

Figure 7.9 Time delays in different areas at different times in the UK

Note: Figures in the table are comparisons of the time delay measured per vehicle kilometre, where 100 = the national average delay for all vehicles on all types of road at all times. Peak delay in London is therefore 6.97 times the national average.

Traffic congestion affects cities large and small, high-density and sprawling, in MEDCs and in LEDCs. For example, journey times in Bangkok, Lagos and Havana may well exceed an hour (Figure 7.4). Traffic congestion is not simply caused by high levels of car ownership and driving. City streets were often clogged in the horse-drawn era. Poor management of traffic systems and inadequate mass transit facilities also contribute.

Economists recognise congestion as an example of the 'tragedy of the commons'. Rational, logical and self-interested decisions made by individuals – in this case the decision to drive – add up to irrational and inefficient consequences for society as a whole. High levels of individual car ownership result in the costs of motoring being borne by everyone in society and not the individual driver. Collectively, motorists do not pay the real costs of roads, parking, pollution damage, and health impairment. It is, therefore, not in the interest of individual drivers to switch from cars to public transport, especially if public transport itself experiences traffic delays. The advantages of driving in terms of convenience and flexibility all go to the individual, but the costs are shared equally. Hence, while some people continue not to drive or to own a car, the benefits will outweigh the individual motorist's share of the costs. Cheap motoring encourages congestion. In the UK, for example, the real cost of motoring has stayed the same since the 1970s, but the costs of public transport have risen by 80 per cent.

Congestion and sprawl

It is often thought that traffic congestion increases as a result of urban sprawl and the deconcentration and decentralisation of homes and workplaces, as discussed in Chapter 5. Low-density urban form, such as suburbs, would probably not have developed without very high rates of car ownership. The separation of jobs, homes, schools and shops over ever greater distances requires and encourages more frequent, longer journeys. In relation to employment, the data given in Figure 7.10 show the proportion of jobs found within 3 miles, within 10 miles, and beyond 10 miles of the centres of four US cities. In extreme cases in the USA, as few as one in twenty jobs is found within 3 miles of the city centre. International comparisons show a clear association between urban density and fuel consumption, although this measure, itself, is not a direct measure of congestion (Figure 7.11).

The information in Figure 7.8 shows that among US cities there is congestion in both low-density urban sprawl regions, such as Los Angeles, and in higher-density cities that practise smart growth measures, such as Portland, Oregon. Research in Britain on the impact of counter-urbanisation on fuel energy consumption between 1961 and 1991 found that sprawl had hardly any effect by itself. In fact, there is insufficient evidence of any direct relationship between settlement pattern and transport behaviour.

Figure 7.10

Employment distribution in US cities

City	Percentage within 3 miles of city centre	Percentage within 10 miles of city centre	Percentage beyond the 10 mile ring
Portland, Oregon	30	81	19
Minneapolis	13	63	37
Chicago	19	36	64
Los Angeles	5	22	78

Note: The figures show what share or percentage of all employment is found within 3 miles of the city centre, 10 miles of the city centre and over 10 miles from the centre.

Planning responses to urban transport issues

In *Great Cities and Their Traffic* (1977), Michael Thomson identified seven facets of the urban transport problem:

- traffic movement
- accidents
- peak-hour crowding on public transport
- off-peak inadequacy of public transport
- difficulties for pedestrians
- environmental impact
- parking difficulties.

Vehicle congestion is one aspect of this problem, but the policies appropriate to addressing it also affect the other aspects. Four main approaches are identifiable and are set out in Figure 7.12. Two focus on transport and one concerns urban planning and design in general. The first option, to do nothing, is based on the assumption that traffic flow and volume find a point of equilibrium by themselves. It argues that a point is reached when further drivers are discouraged from entering the system, so congestion does not spiral out of control.

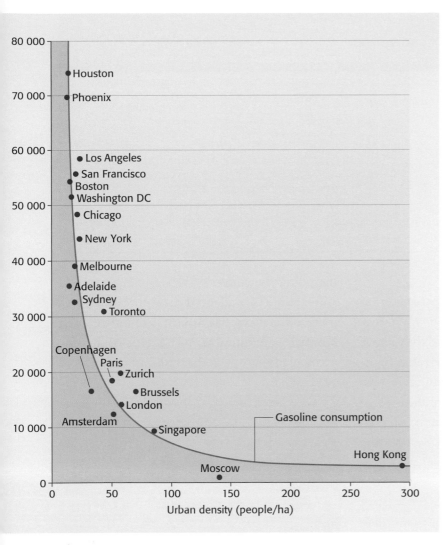

Figure 7.11

Gasoline consumption and urban densities in major world cities, 1980

	Activity
1	Examine Figure 7.2 closely for apparent relationships between the three modes of transport, the data on population density and the number of cars per 1000 people. Using different techniques, illustrate the relationships graphically and write a brief description of the greatest contrasts to be found between the six countries involved.
2	The data in Figure 7.2 are for countries as a whole. If you were trying to decide how to discourage the use of cars for **a** work purposes and **b** leisure purposes on a local scale (a single town, perhaps), what types of geographical data would you need in order to make some working proposals? Present your responses to this theme in the form of a summary table.
3	Look up the meaning of 'the tragedy of the commons'. In a few concise sentences, explain its relevance to urban congestion.

Figure 7.12

Policy responses
to congestion

Policy Responses			
Do nothing	**Respond to demand**	**Manage demand (traffic reduction)**	**Non-transport option**
	• Road building • Urban tunnels • Elevated urban highways • Double-decker highways • Fuel subsidies • Mass transit	• Improve public transport • Encourage walking and cycling • Optimise flow in existing network • Intelligent Vehicle Highway Systems • Congestion pricing • Car and van pooling • Parking restrictions • Higher fuel taxes • Traffic calming • Home zones	• Alternative work schedules • Telecommuting • Inner city revitalisation • Transport nodes and corridors • Discourage sprawl • Urban compaction

Responding to demand

In the past, the main response to congestion was to build more roads and highways, outwards, underground in tunnels, or above ground in double-decker and elevated highways. But this approach is impractical in already-developed areas because of the costs of acquiring land and the disruption to communities. Demand may also be met by building mass or rapid transit systems.

Rapid transit systems

Mass or rapid transit systems come in a variety of forms, usually based on rail transport, buses, or a combination of both (Figure 7.13). Light railway systems are becoming more widespread as viable and cheaper alternatives to subways. Vehicles for such systems travel on special roadways, elevated tracks or old and abandoned railway lines. They can remove up to 20 per cent of road traffic. Some of the latest schemes, including Vancouver's Skytrain (Figure 7.14) and London's Dockland Light Railway, are automated. Germany has almost 800 km of such networks, and most major UK cities have one, or are planning one in the near future.

Figure 7.14

Vancouver's Skytrain in a suburban district of the city

Figure 7.13

Types of urban
rail system

	Streetcars/ trams	Light rail	Suburban rail	Metro
Appropriate city size	200 000–500 000	100 000 –1 million	Over 500 000	Over 1 million
Track	On street	Fully or partly separated from street	Separated from street	Self-contained underground
Average speed (km/h)	10–20	30–40	45–60	30–40
Maximum hourly passengers	15 000	20 000	60 000	30 000
Examples	Melbourne Karlsruhe	Los Angeles Vancouver Manchester	Berlin Paris	London Moscow São Paulo

Managing demand

The alternative response to the growing demand for urban traffic is to manage it in a different way, perhaps by reducing the volume, encouraging a better mix of transport uses or by using the existing system more efficiently. Policies include the following:

- raising fuel taxes, although evidence suggests that to be effective the increase would have to be higher than is politically acceptable (Figure 7.15)
- using computers to coordinate traffic signals or, in the future, using Intelligent Vehicle Highway Systems (IVHS) to ensure efficient flow
- restricting the number, price and maximum time-period of on- and off-street parking
- charging workplaces for providing employees with parking, especially in central city areas
- calming traffic in residential areas by the use of humps and other design features, as well as creating home zones where pedestrians have priority
- constructing high-quality and safe cycle path networks – the Netherlands has led the way in encouraging cycling since the 1970s, while in the UK, Milton Keynes has a planned network of such routes
- car and van pooling, where workers share the drive to work in their own cars – this approach gained popularity in the USA in the 1970s but has declined since, and in the Netherlands, car pool car parks, with highly visible invitations to drivers to participate on an impromptu daily basis, are found on the outskirts of the larger towns and cities.

Congestion or road pricing

If congestion is caused by individual motorists not paying the full costs of their actions, then an obvious solution is to require drivers to pay more for using roads. Such **road or congestion pricing** works on the same principle as fixed-line telephone charges – callers pay more for using the network at certain times or over

Figure 7.15
UK fuel protests, 2000/2001

longer distances. Price is a way of rationing a scarce resource (phone lines or road space). Toll roads, bridges and motorways have been a feature of many MEDCs for decades or more. Experience in the USA suggests that a flow of 2200–2500 vehicles per lane per hour is ideal for smooth traffic movement. Managers could set the price of using the road at a value that would facilitate this level of flow.

An alternative is to charge motorists for entering a zone such as a city centre, a system that operates in Singapore and in Trondheim, Norway, and has been proposed for London (Figure 7.16). Such charges can be varied according to time of day, or reduced at weekends. Melbourne in Australia has a private road network for which users must pay. Singapore's electronic road pricing system (Figure 7.17) uses in-car electronic devices into which a pre-paid smart card is inserted. When the motorist enters the centre, a charge to the equivalent value of between £1 and £1.45 is automatically deducted. Critics of such schemes argue that they are designed to raise revenue rather than cut traffic, and that they impose added costs on

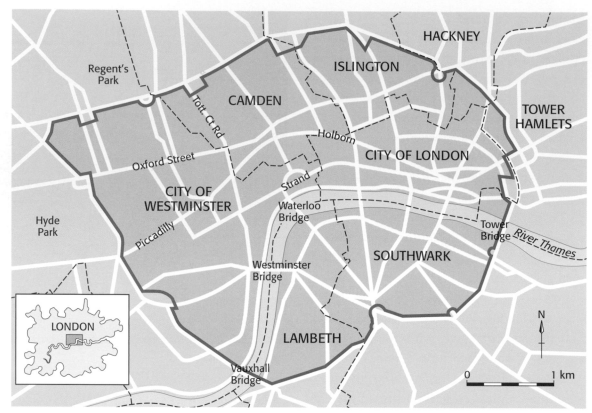

Figure 7.16
London's proposed traffic charging zone

Figure 7.17
Electronic road pricing gate in Singapore

low-income drivers. Polls suggest that such schemes are accepted more readily if the fees are used, and can be seen to be used, to improve public transport.

Park and ride

A compromise between banning cars from city centres, as in Florence for example, and free access is to intercept vehicle traffic at the outskirts and encourage travellers to switch to mass transit. Park and ride schemes, designed to persuade drivers to leave their vehicles in large car parks at the edge of the city and continue their journey by bus, are now common in the UK. Pioneered in free-standing medium-sized cities such as Nottingham and Oxford, there are now about 80 schemes around the country (Figure 7.18). Critics say that they take up valuable green belt land – a particular problem in Oxford – and encourage sprawl. They may also discourage travellers from using public transport for the whole journey.

Bus improvements

A disincentive to using buses is that they are also caught in traffic and, because they have to stop and pick up and unload passengers, they

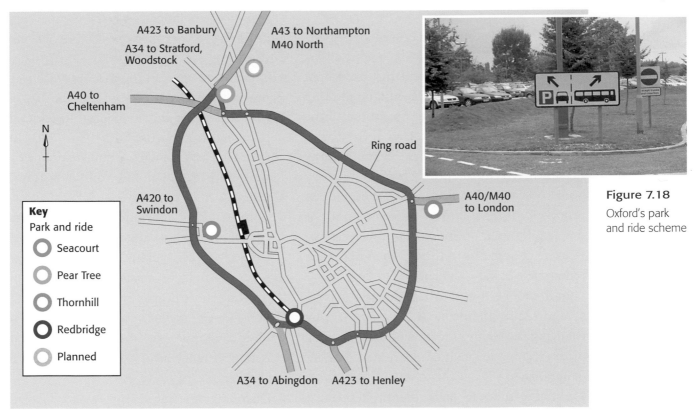

Figure 7.18

Oxford's park and ride scheme

will always be slower than private cars. A solution is to give buses priority in road use, by providing bus lanes, priority at traffic lights or driver-operated traffic lights that prevent buses from waiting. Oxford and Leeds are two cities with such schemes in operation.

A model network operates in the city of Curitiba, Brazil. In a city of 1.6 million people, the bus system (Figure 7.19) consists of 54 km of express bus arteries and nearly 500 km of feeder and inter-district routes across 65 per cent of the urban area. Despite high car ownership, the actual use of cars is low; 70 per cent of commuters use buses. Passengers are encouraged by:

- exclusive bus lanes and signal priority
- pre-boarding fare collection and a low fare equal to approximately 15 pence
- large-capacity bi-articulated buses capable of carrying 270 passengers
- level boarding from raised platforms in tube stations, taking 15–19 seconds to board
- a hierarchy of feeder mini-buses, street buses and express buses on special lanes

Figure 7.19

Boarding buses in Curitiba, Brazil

- land use planning to concentrate high-density offices and residences along transport corridors.

Non-transport options

Rush-hour congestion is caused by people going to and coming from work at more or less the same time of day, mixed in with school journeys. By staggering work shifts or allowing employees flexible working hours, the traffic peaks can be smoothed out. Half of Germany's workforce is on flexible shifts. Telecommuting, or working partly or entirely from home using home-based communications systems, is often proposed as a solution to congestion. At present, though, no more than 2 per cent of workers choose this option, even in high-tech economies such as California.

In the longer term, urban planners may be able to reduce the demand for movement by changing the relative location of homes, workplaces, shops and facilities. There are a number of options:

- Creating zones of higher-density residential areas: for example, in Britain, increasing the density of dwellings from the present average of 25/ha to 35–40/ha or more in new developments (Figure 7.20).
- Creating nodes and corridors by using major transport routes or intersections as sites of higher-density, mixed use development, as practised in Curitiba, for example. Stockholm's suburban satellite towns are based on the rail mass transit system.
- Compaction by moving towards a 'compact city' of high-density and mixed land use, well connected by public transport. Urban services would be arranged in a hierarchy, enabling most people to obtain daily goods by walking or cycling.
- Re-urbanisation, or the planned revitalisation of inner urban areas as described in Chapter 5.
- Discouraging sprawl by smart growth measures of the type discussed in Chapter 5.

Figure 7.20

Plan of a high-density mixed use neighbourhood (75 units/ha)

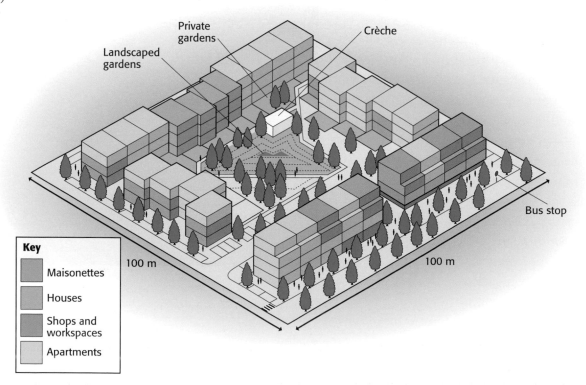

Bangkok (Figure 7.21) has a reputation for being one of the world's most congested and polluted cities. It is an example of how not to proceed. Driven by a booming economy of manufacturing and services, Bangkok has sprawled out across a wide region (Figure 7.22). Over 8 million people live in the metropolitan area, and twice that in the region as a whole. Since the 1950s the main solution to traffic problems has been to build new roads, then tollways, then double-decker expressways. The need for mass transit was recognised in 1971, but the existing suburban railway is slow, single-track and crossed by roads. Finally, in 1999, the Bangkok Transit System, an elevated railway, opened its first 24 km of line, with more planned. However, the fare is more than twice the cost of a bus, and passenger numbers have been below expectations. A subway and monorail loop around outer Bangkok are now under construction.

The various schemes have not met with much success. Over 80 per cent of journeys are made by car, but the average journey for commuters takes 60 minutes and average speeds in the centre are 6 km/h. Congestion costs $272 million a year – roughly 2 per cent of Thailand's GNP. Land use planning and transport systems are not integrated, and there has been a marked failure of coordination among the many different local governments in the wider region. In the 1980s car ownership levels more than trebled, but the economic recession of 1997–98 resulted in much lighter traffic as finance companies repossessed tens of thousands of cars and new car

purchases fell from 1000 to 300 per day. Until 1996 traffic signals were hand-operated by police officers, but a new computerised system has not worked because of inadequate electricity and telephone systems. Two new ring-roads are being built, but they may simply encourage further sprawl.

Figure 7.21

Bangkok and its elevated urban expressways

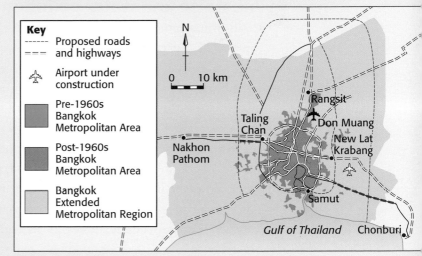

Key
- - - - - - Proposed roads and highways
= = = Proposed roads and highways
✈ Airport under construction
Pre-1960s Bangkok Metropolitan Area
Post-1960s Bangkok Metropolitan Area
Bangkok Extended Metropolitan Region

N

0   10 km

Rangsit
Taling Chan
Don Muang
New Lat Krabang
Nakhon Pathom
Samut
Gulf of Thailand   Chonburi

Figure 7.22

The Bangkok region

Activity

1 Revisit Figure 7.12. From your own experience of measures taken to address urban transport issues and problems, critically evaluate the view that the 'Do nothing' approach has much to commend it.

2 The topics addressed in Chapter 5 (on urban growth) are clearly related to problems of urban transport. However, a 'chicken and egg' situation is often evident, making it difficult to devise successful solutions to problems of congestion. Under the two headings of 'Prevention' and 'Cure', draw up a list of factors that might be used **a** to avoid congestion in the first place and **b** to stem its adverse aspects where it has become a major problem.

8 Pollution

KEY THEMES

- Urban pollution is a major cause of poor health in MEDCs and LEDCs, but cities do not necessarily become more polluted over time.
- The major challenge facing cities is how to reconcile the 'brown agenda' of health and inequality with the 'green agenda' of environmentalism.
- Informal modes of service provision in water, sanitation and waste collection may be among the solutions for LEDCs.
- A sustainable city has a more circular metabolism in which outputs become new inputs, with high levels of re-use and recycling.

Air, noise and water pollution

Pollution is generally thought of as the introduction of contaminants into the environment such that their presence or level becomes harmful to life. In urban areas pollution may also include the adverse effects of noise and excessive light. Modern cities have mostly succeeded in separating out and enclosing water, sewage, solid waste, electricity, food, and pests. However, in cities in LEDCs, as well as in poor areas of MEDC cities, the boundaries between successful and unsuccessful separation are often inadequate or break down, exposing urban dwellers to harm. Cities are concentrations of pollution-generating activities, but at the same time they provide the best conditions for reducing their impact.

The impact of pollution on urban populations partly depends on the natural features of each city. Air pollution tends to be worse in either cold or hot climates. More fuel is used for heating in cold cities, while ozone formation is higher in warm conditions. Surrounding mountains, such as in the cases of Los Angeles and Mexico City, prevent the dispersal of airborne pollutants. The severity of water pollution partly depends on the height of the local water table and the configuration of rivers, lakes and bays.

Water pollution

Water in urban areas becomes polluted from specific point sources such as factories and from non-point sources when run-off carries contaminants into storm drains and water bodies (Figure 8.1). Household waste, although relatively minor in volume, may contain many sources of pollution.

In LEDCs, a major cause of water pollution is the failure to manage sewage. Around a quarter of the residents in Latin American cities, and half or more of those in African cities, are not connected to adequate sanitation networks. In the worst cases, a single public toilet may serve hundreds or even thousands of people. Even cities with sewerage systems often fail to treat waste completely. In Buenos Aires, for example, 98 per cent of waste is untreated. Investing in sewage collection, disposal and treatment systems is expensive. Lower-cost alternatives include pour-flush latrines or ventilated improved flush latrines provided at community level. Shared or condominial sewers have been installed in Brazil and

Figure 8.1
Main sources of
water pollutants

Pollutant type	Source	Effects
Nutrients	Organic matter from garden waste, containing nitrogen and phosphates; garden fertilisers	Blue-green algae growth in water courses consumes oxygen, leading to foul smells, release of toxins and harm to aquatic life
Visible rubbish and litter	Plastic bags; take-away food containers; cigarette ends	Blocks storm drains; unsightly environment
Suspended solids	Dirt, dust and mud washed off streets; construction; ash; airborne pollutants	Eutrophication; discolours water courses; pathogens and toxins stick to particles
Pathogens	Untreated or poorly treated sewage; leaking septic tanks, latrines and cesspits; household waste; pet waste; medical waste	Viruses, bacteria, fungi and parasites cause diseases such as cholera, hepatitis, gastro-enteritis and diarrhoea
Toxicants	Industrial and household wastes; pesticides and weedkillers; car oil and antifreeze; paints containing heavy metals; detergents; car emissions containing lead and zinc	Heavy metals may be related to cancers, blood disorders and diseases of the nervous system

Pakistan, saving on the cost of connecting each house to the main sewer (Figure 8.2). Improved maintenance of septic tanks can have positive effects. Ecological methods, such as sedimentation ponds, reed beds or artificial wetlands, can remove harmful nutrients. In Calcutta, wetlands treat sewage and provide fish.

Failure to separate waste from water is a major cause of disease in LEDCs. Perhaps 10 per cent of the total disease burden comes from diarrhoea and intestinal worm infections associated with contaminated water.

Air pollution

Urban air pollution comes from three main sources: domestic heating, industry, and transport. The contribution from transport sources, notably private cars, is generally increasing everywhere, as illustrated for Delhi in Figure 8.3. The main effects of air pollutants are:

- increased respiratory diseases such as asthma and bronchitis from sulphur dioxide (SO_2), nitrogen oxides (NO_x), ozone and particulates such as smoke, ash and exhaust emissions

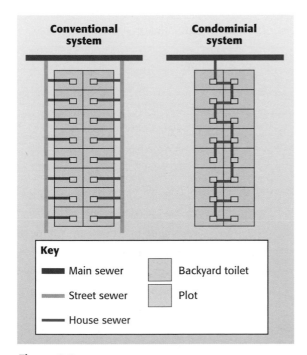

Figure 8.2

Conventional and condominial wastewater collection systems

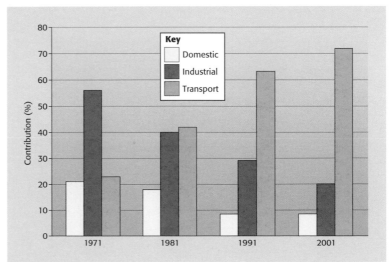

Figure 8.3

Contributions to air pollution in Delhi, 1971–2001

- acid deposition from SO_2 and NO_x
- toxic contamination from lead and carbon monoxide (CO)
- cancer from particulates and volatile organic compounds (VOCs).

Vehicles are the major source of CO and NO_x, and a significant source of particulates and VOCs (Figure 8.4). In MEDCs, a combination of pollution control measures, and the closure of many heavy industries, has resulted in long-term declines in lead, smoke and SO_2 pollution (Figure 8.5). But ozone, particulates and NO_x

may still be above recommended levels for health. The most serious air pollution is found in LEDCs, particularly in major Asian cities such as Bangkok and Beijing. The worst conditions arise from a combination of inefficient two-stroke engines, burning coal with a high sulphur content, use of leaded petrol, traffic congestion and climate.

At least 500 000 premature deaths and 4–5 million new cases of chronic bronchitis each year can be attributed to particulate pollution. Studies suggest that cutting particulate emissions has the biggest single impact of any pollution control. It has been estimated that a $10\,\mu g/m^3$ reduction in Bangkok's particulate load would cut premature deaths by 700–2000 a year, reduce hospital emissions by 3000–9000 a year, and save between 2.9 and 9.1 million working days lost because of respiratory diseases.

Pollution controls can be placed on industry and traffic (Figure 8.6). Changing the location of the source by better urban planning or traffic management is one option, but preventing pollution through the better inspection and maintenance of vehicles or the encouragement of cleaner fuels and technologies is preferable.

Figure 8.4

Sources of particulate emissions in Manila

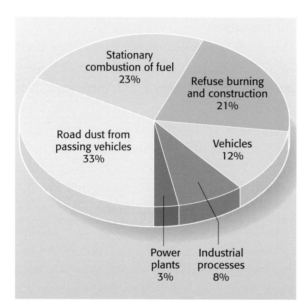

Figure 8.5

Pollution levels for major cities

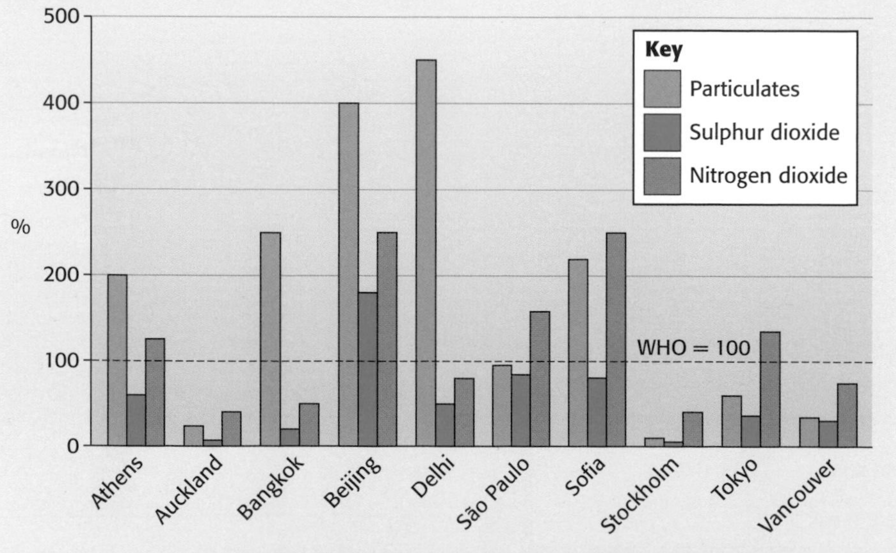

Note: 100 = World Health Organisation guideline for safe annual mean emissions. The graph shows how far each city is above or below the guideline in percentage terms. For example, Athens has double the recommended level for particulates (200%) but only 60% of the level for sulphur dioxide.

Figure 8.6
The most effective measures for reducing pollution at source

	Industry and energy					Households: Fuels	Traffic				
	Location	Fuels	Maintenance	Clean technology	End-of-pipe		Location	Fuels	Maintenance	Clean technology	End-of-pipe
Particulate matter	■	■	■	■	■	■	■	■	■	■	
Lead			■		■			■		■	
Sulphur dioxide		■	■	■	■	■		■		■	
Volatile organic compounds							■		■	■	■
Nitrogen oxides	■	■		■			■			■	■
Carbon monoxide							■		■	■	■

Case Study: Air pollution in Delhi

Delhi, in India, is reckoned to be the fourth most polluted city in the world in terms of air quality (Figure 8.7). The World Health Organisation calculates that air pollution causes 7500 premature deaths and almost 4 million hospital visits a year. Delhi's growing population is rapidly becoming motorised (see Chapter 7, Figure 7.3), and two-thirds of all air pollutants in the city come from transport (Figure 8.3). Too many vehicles run on two-stroke engines, which burn fuel inefficiently, and the city lacks a mass transit system to compare with that in Calcutta or Mumbai (Bombay). Two-thirds of vehicles are two-wheelers, including motorcycles and autorickshaws, making independent travel affordable to the poor but at high cost to health.

The Indian government has been accused of responding too slowly to the worsening conditions, leaving the country's courts to order action. The Supreme Court has ordered both changes to vehicle technology and the introduction of new standards for emissions, together with a strict timetable. These measures include:

- all buses must eventually switch to cleaner compressed natural gas (CNG)
- the Gas Authority must create a network of CNG refuelling stations
- the number of buses must increase to 10 000

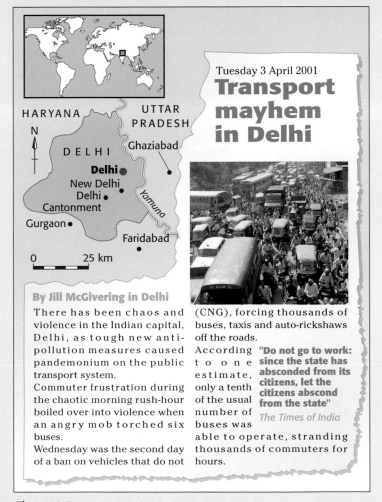

Tuesday 3 April 2001

Transport mayhem in Delhi

By Jill McGivering in Delhi

There has been chaos and violence in the Indian capital, Delhi, as tough new anti-pollution measures caused pandemonium on the public transport system.

Commuter frustration during the chaotic morning rush-hour boiled over into violence when an angry mob torched six buses.

Wednesday was the second day of a ban on vehicles that do not use compressed natural gas (CNG), forcing thousands of buses, taxis and auto-rickshaws off the roads.

According to one estimate, only a tenth of the usual number of buses was able to operate, stranding thousands of commuters for hours.

"Do not go to work: since the state has absconded from its citizens, let the citizens abscond from the state"
The Times of India

Figure 8.7
Unpopular anti-pollution measures in Delhi

- a total ban on two-wheelers over 15 years old, commercial vehicles over 12 years old and buses over 8 years old
- only low-sulphur fuel must be used, and leaded petrol will be phased out.

The policy has problems and has met obstacles. Only 1 per cent of the city's vehicles are covered by the CNG order, and there are long queues at the few stations selling it. The country's refineries cannot yet produce ultra-low-sulphur fuel which, in consequence, has to be imported. Finally, the city lacks an adequate monitoring system to assess whether the policies are working, leading to quarrels between environmentalists and the government. Few observers expect any sign of real improvement until 2004.

Noise pollution

Cities are becoming noisier. In the 1990s the proportion of European city residents exposed to an undesirable level of noise rose from 15 to 26 per cent, and in the USA over 30 million people are exposed to hazardous sound levels – defined as over 70 decibels – each day. Figure 8.8 shows the noise profile for Barcelona and compares it with complete silence and the level at which damage is caused to hearing. There are three main sources of noise pollution:

- traffic – road, air and rail
- domestic noise – car alarms, burglar alarms, DIY, car stereos, barking dogs
- noise from workplaces or incompatible land uses – discos, factories, etc.

Constant exposure to excessive noise has been linked to sleep loss, stress, anxiety, heart disease, decreased learning ability, poor work performance and interference with communication. Neighbourhood surveys frequently identify noise from fellow residents as a major nuisance. Noise levels may be increasing not just because of heavier traffic, but also because the day's noisy periods are getting longer as shops, bars and clubs stay open for longer. In rapidly growing cities in Asia and Latin America, low-income settlements are often forced into locations with high noise levels on land near airports and motorways. In MEDCs also, the pressure on land in certain sought-after areas may often result in new housing being built near excessively noisy locations. The use of brownfield sites may also increase exposure to noise.

Noise reduction takes several forms. Technologies such as 'hush kits' for aeroplanes

Figure 8.8

Noise sources in urban areas, Barcelona

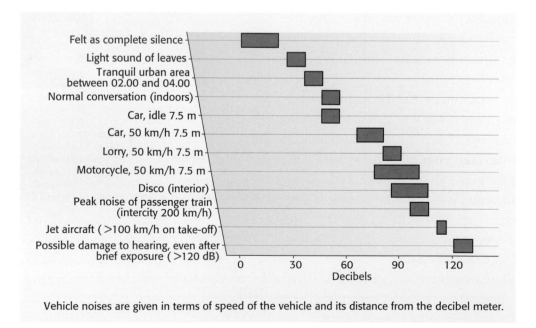

Vehicle noises are given in terms of speed of the vehicle and its distance from the decibel meter.

can drastically cut airport noise. The use of quieter materials for road surfaces and highway noise barriers reduce traffic disturbance (Figure 8.9). Trees alongside roads, railways and airports can also provide relief.

Figure 8.9

A noise reduction barrier on the M25 motorway in Surrey

	LEDCs	MEDCs
Waste per person (kg per year)	100–220 kg	300–1000 kg
Composition by weight (%):		
Paper	1–10	15–50
Glass and ceramics	1–10	4–12
Metals	1–5	3–13
Plastics	1–5	2–10
Leather and rubber	1–5	–
Wood, bones and straw	1–5	–
Textiles	1–5	–
Vegetable matter	40–85	20–50
Miscellaneous inert materials	1–40	1–20

Figure 8.10

Municipal waste characteristics for LEDCs and MEDCs

Waste disposal

The major challenge of solid waste management in LEDCs is extending formal collection and disposal services to the whole city population. Often half the city's residents are without services – usually the poor and those in outlying areas and squatter settlements. In MEDCs the major problem is the high volume of waste and the pressure to deal with it without harming the environment.

Citizens in MEDCs typically produce three to five times more waste per person than in LEDCs, and more of it consists of paper products such as packaging (Figure 8.10). The main methods of disposal are landfill, incineration and recycling, although small amounts are also composted for use as fertilisers. Canada and the UK depend on landfill sites, but these are a potential source of groundwater contamination and environmental blight (Figure 8.11). In 1996 the UK introduced a landfill tax, now worth £11 a tonne in 2001, in order to discourage burial. Critics argue that it has failed to encourage recycling and has led to millions of tonnes being

Figure 8.11

A landfill site at Hempsted near Gloucester

dumped illegally. Japan and Denmark favour incineration, which also generates electricity, although improperly maintained plants are known to produce cancer-causing dioxins. Recycling levels vary considerably between MEDCs, suggesting that government regulation is an important factor in encouraging the re-use of materials (Figure 8.12). There are often considerable variations between local authorities within the same country; Figure 8.13 shows the marked differences for recycling rates across London. Local-level policies for recycling include separate bins for different waste products and provision of local collection centres. National policies include returnable deposits on

Figure 8.12

Recycling rates, 1995

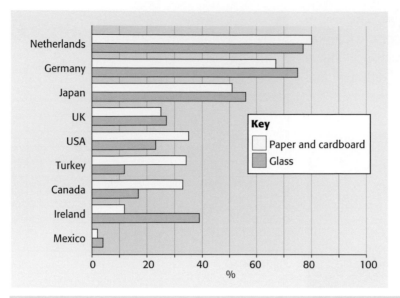

Figure 8.13

Recycling rates for the London boroughs, 2000

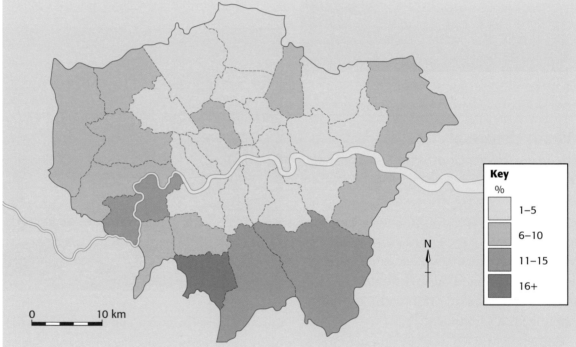

plastic bottles – compulsory in Sweden – packaging taxes, and requiring manufacturers to take responsibility for recovering materials from their products once their working life is over.

In LEDCs a significant proportion of waste may be collected and disposed of in the informal economy, especially in Asia. Figure 8.14 compares Bangalore in India with London. Waste-pickers save resources through recycling, and reduce the costs of municipal waste disposal. In Bangalore, informal workers collect nearly ten times as much as formal employees, and as many as 40 000 people earn a living from the city's waste economy. As a result, LEDC cities are sometimes more efficient at re-using materials such as paper, glass and plastics than those in MEDCs – their residents simply cannot afford to throw things away. Nevertheless, waste pickers are generally forced into their occupation by poverty. People who handle waste are often the most despised or lowly-regarded in society, sometimes living in marginal sites or even on the waste dumps. The informal 'waste economy' is therefore a combination of environmental benefit, economic efficiency and social exclusion.

London Inhabitants: 7.6 million	Bangalore Inhabitants: 4.1 million
• 500 waste collection vehicles, including barges • 17 municipal solid waste transfer stations • 45 civic amenity collection sites • 2 incinerators • 15 small recycling centres • 2 compost sites • 18 landfill sites • 2 energy-from-waste plants processing over 1 million tonnes per year	**Informal** • 25 000 waste-pickers (mainly women & children) • Hundreds of farmers collecting waste for compost • 3000–4000 itinerant waste-buyers of newspaper, plastic and glass • 800 small dealers in waste products • 50 wholesale dealers • 300–350 plastics factories using recycled waste • Hundreds of small workshops recycling material **Formal** • 7600 municipal street-sweepers and garbage collectors • 2 glass and 4 paper recycling plants
• 3.45 million tonnes of municipal solid waste • 76% exported from the city (and 70% of that travels over 120 km) • 69% landfill • 18% converted into energy • 10% recycled • 3% composted	• Street pickers collect 15% of waste on streets, 300 tonnes a day • Municipal workers collect 37 tonnes a day • 210 tonnes of cow dung collected each year for fuel • 400 000–500 000 tonnes of materials recovered and recycled

Activity

1 Figure 8.5 illustrates pollution levels for ten major cities. For Athens, Beijing, São Paulo and Stockholm, look up their general economic and urban geographical characteristics in a suitable reference work (e.g. Encarta, Encyclopaedia Britannica etc.) and attempt to explain the differences between them.

2 Plot the data given in Figure 8.10 using a suitable comparative technique or techniques. (Use the middle value of the data ranges.) What explanation would you suggest for the differences between LEDCs and MEDCs?

Sustainable cities

Cities are often regarded as parasites by environmentalists because they consume vast amounts of resources, including land, water and energy, and generate huge volumes of waste in the form of pollution. Urban growth is one of the major environmental problems facing the world. However, at the same time, cities present the best opportunities for more energy and resource-efficient lifestyles. By concentrating so many people in small areas they make the provision of services such as sanitation and waste collection easier; they provide more opportunity for generating power from solid waste; they make mass transit more affordable and desirable; and they reduce the demand for land. Turning urbanisation from a threat into an asset represents a significant challenge in both LEDCs and MEDCs.

Ecological footprints

The view of cities as parasites can be illustrated by the concept of the **ecological footprint**, developed by William Rees. This term relates to the amount of productive land required to provide a city with wood, water and food, as well as the disposal of its waste. One calculation for London suggests that an area 125 times as large as the city itself is required to support it (Figure 8.15). The impacts of urban consumption are often hidden from city dwellers, displaced into the countryside or, increasingly, to other parts of the world. Johannesburg, for example, draws its water from 600 km away. Over half of London's waste is sent more than 120 km away for disposal in landfill sites.

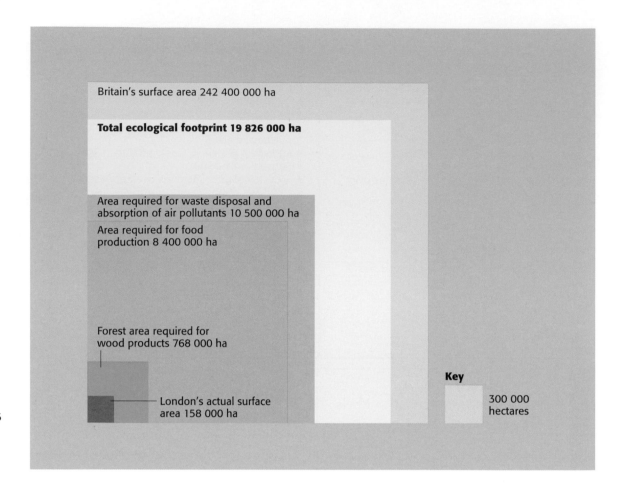

Britain's surface area 242 400 000 ha

Total ecological footprint 19 826 000 ha

Area required for waste disposal and absorption of air pollutants 10 500 000 ha

Area required for food production 8 400 000 ha

Forest area required for wood products 768 000 ha

London's actual surface area 158 000 ha

Key

300 000 hectares

Figure 8.15

London's ecological footprint

In MEDCs, in particular, people are now more remote from the ecological consequences of urban dwelling than in the past. Two generations ago British families burned coal in their fireplaces and could see how much coal they were using and how smoke affected the environment. Now, with electric heating and light, the impact of burning coal (and other fossil fuels) in power stations is not so readily seen, and neither is the impact of acid deposition from pollutants projected into the upper air by chimneys. Furthermore, many products such as the steel used to make cars and the chemicals in the batteries of personal stereos, are increasingly produced overseas, where the harmful environmental effects are also located.

Ecological footprints can be minimised in a number of ways:

- by increasing biomass production in the city, through urban farming
- by reducing or recycling waste through composting, re-use of waste water and recycling materials, including building materials
- through campaigns to buy more locally-made produce.

Chinese cities are often highly self-sufficient in meat and vegetables. Two-thirds of Kenyan urban dwellers grow at least some of their own food, and half keep livestock. In New York, over 1000 vacant city lots have been reclaimed as community gardens.

Must things get worse?

It is often assumed that environmental conditions progressively worsen, and that rapid urbanisation will inevitably cause greater damage. In MEDCs, noise and light pollution are on the increase, while in LEDCs the number of urban dwellers without adequate sanitation is growing. There are, however, examples of environmental amelioration. Air quality in some Chinese cities has been improved

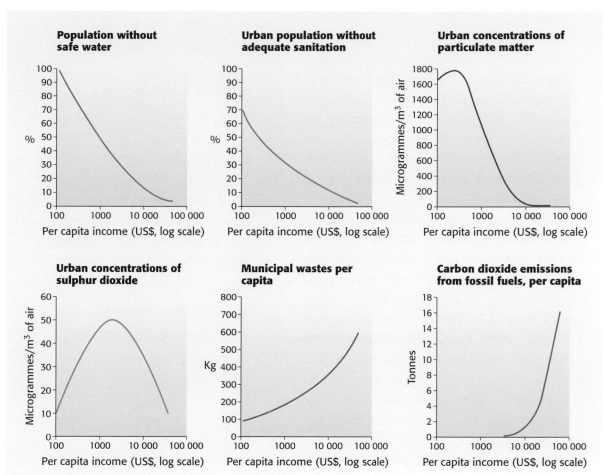

Figure 8.16

Environmental
indicators at
different
income levels

through concerted efforts to cut sulphur dioxide emissions, and London's River Thames, declared biologically dead in 1950, now supports 118 species of fish. Overall, though, it is reasonable to conclude that the mix of environmental harms will undergo change in step with development (Figure 8.16). The urban poor in LEDCs are exposed to the problems of inadequate water and sanitation, associated with illness and disease. In more developed cities, for example Bangkok, the problems of air pollution increase in importance. In MEDCs by contrast, contamination from waste or polluted water occurs rarely, but the health and environmental effects of ozone, particulates and solid waste grow in significance. This sequence suggests that development can lead to cleaner environments, but only if the environmental damage is not being exported and hidden in the form of ever-wider ecological footprints.

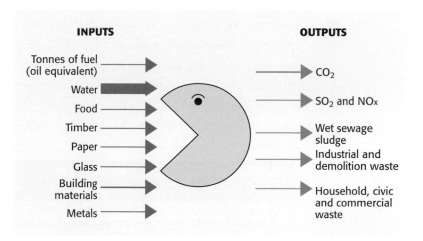

Figure 8.17

Typical
consumption of
resources and
production of
waste for a UK
city of 100 000
people

Urban sustainability

One way of thinking about urban sustainability is to envisage cities as systems that consume resources and produce waste, and to compare them with ecosystems (Figure 8.17). The difference is that natural ecosystems re-use, or recycle, many of the resources that flow through them, notably nutrients, energy, and water. Greater re-use and recycling of a city's own products – energy from waste, composting, recovered paper and glass – would shift conditions more towards sustainability. In other words, some waste products can be thought of as resources, or as the start of new processes rather than the end-point of completed ones.

Herbert Girardet has stated that a sustainable city 'is organised so as to enable all its citizens to meet their own needs and to enhance their well-being without damaging the natural world or endangering the living conditions of other people, now or in the future'. Perversely, it is generally easier to recognise unsustainable urban processes and conditions than it is to detect sustainable ones. Cities are complex systems, and improvements made in one area can sometimes cause problems in others. For example, better water services may create new problems of wastewater treatment simply because of the extra water involved.

The four principal approaches to establishing greater sustainability are summarised in Figure 8.18. As might be expected, they reflect policies associated with managing urban growth, reducing congestion and raising the quality of life in urban areas. Government regulation through laws, standards, targets and fines is significant but enforcement is often

Q: What would you do if the cost of petrol doubled over 10 years?

Might use car even more	1%
Might use car a little less	31%
Might use car quite a bit less	23%
Might give up using car	5%
Makes no difference	38%

Q: What would you do if all motorists were charged around £2 each time they enter or drive through a city or town centre at peak times?

Might use car even more	0%
Might use car a little less	23%
Might use car quite a bit less	21%
Might give up using car	7%
Makes no difference	45%

Figure 8.19

British attitudes to higher charges for motoring

expensive and unpopular. Particularly in MEDCs, policies are becoming increasingly economic. People and firms are regarded as rational consumers who will respond to price signals. Landfill taxes, congestion pricing and higher duty on leaded petrol are examples. Public surveys suggest, however, that charges will have to be high if they are to alter behaviour significantly (Figure 8.19).

Regulation	Planning and design	Economic instruments	Technological innovations
• Green belt • Growth boundary • Ban on leaded petrol • Emission controls • Parking restrictions • Vehicle inspection and maintenance	• Integrated transport and land-use planning • Urban compaction • Mixed-use planning • Higher density • Nodes and corridors • Traffic calming • Cycle path networks • Reedbeds for sewage treatment	• Congestion pricing • Landfill tax • Fuel taxes • Returnable deposits • Carbon tax • Employee parking charges • Reduced VAT on house conversions • Tax credits for clearing contaminated land	• Zero emission vehicles • Cleaner fuels • Fuel cells • Intelligent Vehicle Highway Systems • Smart buildings • Solar panels

Figure 8.18

Main approaches to sustainable urban development

	The 'brown' environmental health agenda	The 'green' sustainability agenda
Characteristic features of problems high on the agenda:		
Key impact	Human health	Ecosystem health
Timing	Immediate	Delayed
Scale	Local	Regional and global
Worst affected	Lower-income groups	Future generations
Characteristic attitude to:		
Nature	Manipulate to serve human needs	Protect and work with
People	Work with	Educate
Environmental services	Provide more	Use less
Aspects emphasised in relation to:		
Water	Inadequate access and poor quality	Overuse; need to protect water sources
Air	High human exposure to hazardous pollutants	Acid precipitation and greenhouse gas emissions
Solid waste	Inadequate provision for collection and removal	Excessive generation
Land	Inadequate access for low-income groups to housing	Loss of natural habitats and agricultural land to urban development
Human waste	Inadequate provision for safely removing faecal material (and waste water) from living environment	Loss of nutrients in sewage and damage to water bodies from release of sewage into waterways
Typical proponent	**Urbanist**	**Environmentalist**

Figure 8.20

Stereotyping the brown and green agendas for urban environmental improvement

Reconciling green and brown agendas

Environmentalists have called for many policies to make cities more sustainable, including preventing urban sprawl ('smart growth'), reducing energy and water consumption, and restricting private vehicle use. These calls tend to overlook their impact on different groups of people. The urban poor often have pressing needs for water, power and transport in order to overcome social exclusion and improve their health. Policies that recognise these needs are collectively known as the 'brown agenda', in contrast to the 'green agenda' (Figure 8.20).

The urban poor are most often the victims of urban harms and hazards. Their dwellings are usually the most vulnerable to natural hazards, they reside in the most polluted inner cities (see Figure 8.21 for predictions of air quality in London) and they are the group most at risk from traffic accidents (Chapter 6, Figure 6.7). The urban poor have the least access to public services, which may result in injustice. For

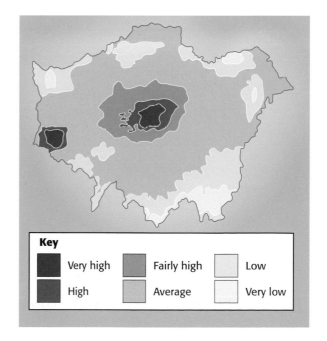

Key

■ Very high   ■ Fairly high   □ Low

■ High   ▨ Average   □ Very low

Figure 8.21

Projected average concentrations of nitrogen dioxide (NO_2) across London in 2005 example, because the residents of squatter settlements in LEDC cities commonly rely on private vendors for bottled water, they have to pay 5–10 times more than better-off families with piped supplies.

The challenge facing urban management is to reconcile the green and brown agendas. Policies for one do not necessarily meet the needs of the other. On the one hand, improved public water supplies subsidised by city governments may result in high levels of waste and inefficiency. Municipal refuse collection can put informal waste-pickers out of work. On the other hand, higher fuel taxes designed to curb driving and reduce congestion and pollution have a greater impact on low-income families, who spend a higher proportion of their budget on travel and domestic heating. Nevertheless, some innovative policies to supply water and sanitation by involving communities directly, do demonstrate that it is possible to achieve both social justice and sustainability.

Activity

1 Write a critique of the 'ecological footprint' idea (Figure 8.15), supporting your views and conclusions by reference to other areas of geography that you have studied.

2 Revisit Figure 8.16 which shows how certain environmental indicators change with rising per capita income, i.e. how they change over time as incomes rise. For one MEDC city and one LEDC city of your choice, attempt to produce graphs to show how the same indicators might vary spatially with distance from the centre. You will need to choose a single direction from the centre of each city, and to refer to a generalised map of land use or economic activity.

Part Three

Managing Rural Environments

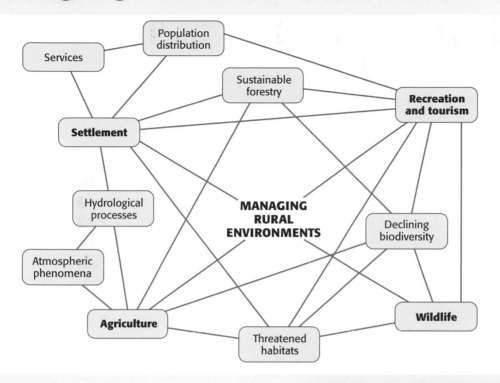

MANAGING RURAL ENVIRONMENTS

Services

Population distribution

Sustainable forestry

Recreation and tourism

Settlement

Hydrological processes

Declining biodiversity

Atmospheric phenomena

Agriculture

Threatened habitats

Wildlife

Thinking synoptically: managing rural environments

Introduction

The countryside is a contested space. This situation has become increasingly apparent since the mid-1980s, when it became clear that farming was coming into conflict more and more with other activities. For centuries, farmers' activities were seen as consistent with the interests of society at large. Their role was to produce food, and it was in everybody's interests that production was sustainable. Farmers thus 'husbanded' the land, and 'agriculture' was synonymous with 'the countryside'. There were lots of incidental benefits:

> 'Farming has always delivered more than just food and fibre. It has given us attractive landscapes, wildlife habitats, income for local people ... and a setting for many forms of outdoor recreation.' – Countryside Agency

This view has changed dramatically in the last 40 years. The interests of farmers have become less and less in tune with the wider interests of the countryside (Figure 3.A). Rural areas are no longer only, or even primarily, places where food is produced. They are the spaces used for housing by commuters, **recreation** and

Figure 3.A

Farmers in crisis

tourism, and increasingly varied economic activities. Such uses are unsympathetic with modern farming practices. At the same time, there has been pressure to conserve the less spoilt areas of the countryside. By the mid-1990s over 25 per cent of England and Wales had some sort of protected status.

Conflicting views and contested images

The intensity of the current debate about the country-side reflects the overlapping and contradictory nature of the demands competing for the same rural space:

- farming
- recreation/tourism
- conservation
- the local economy.

Amongst other factors, the conflict of rural interests was thrown into sharp relief by the foot-and-mouth crisis of 2001(Figure 3.B). Problems in one sector reverberated throughout the rural economy. Small farmers, in particular, were pushed further into crisis, while the closure of the countryside affected tourism and recreation, leading to further job losses and decline of local services.

Farmers angry over move to protect last 'wild' lands

BY SEVERIN CARRELL

Ministers are facing further anger from farmers over plans to introduce laws to stem the conversion of Britain's dwindling wild land to agriculture.

Margaret Beckett, Secretary of State for the Environment, Farming and Rural Affairs, is drafting plans to make farmers carry out environmental impact assessments (EIAs) if they wish to cultivate wild or semi-wild land. Her department believes up to 1000 farmers a year will be affected by the measures designed to protect archaeological sites and rare plants and animals. And farmers requiring EIAs could pay up to £15 000 for their assessments.

The law, bringing Britain into line with EU directives, is being resisted by farmers' leaders, who claim the proposals will add further financial costs and red tape to an industry already reeling from BSE, foot-and-mouth disease, and last winter's bad weather.

Andrew Clark, of the National Farmers' Union, called for the legislation to be as limited as possible, since Britain's rarest and most valuable environmental sites were already protected by law.

But environmentalists welcomed the proposals. Mark Southgate, adviser to the Royal Society for the Protection of Birds, said the restrictions would be minimal and increase farmers' knowledge of the land.

Wild land is being lost in the UK at a rate of 10 000 hectares a year. Grasslands alone have been reduced by up to 18 per cent since 1991.

Figure 3.B

From *The Independent on Sunday*, 26 August 2001

In most developed countries, less than a quarter of the population actually lives in the countryside. England and Wales ceased to be 'rural' in 1851, when the census recorded that more than 50 per cent of the population lived in urban areas. However, what happens in the countryside matters to us all. Rural issues cannot be ignored by the urban majority.

Why do rural areas remain important?

- Many people living in 'towns' consider that they are rural: the fastest-growing settlements in Britain are small towns deeply rooted in rural settings.
- Most of the land area is taken up by rural activities and land uses (Figure 3.C). Activities such as farming are extensive, and impinge on us because they take up so much space.
- Abiding national imagery: England is perceived through a lens that is pre-eminently pastoral. Favoured poets (Wordsworth), novelists (Hardy), painters (Constable) and composers (Elgar) are associated strongly with rural settings (Figure 3.D). This is perhaps best summed up by William Blake's poem 'Jerusalem', which stands as England's unofficial national anthem and sets a pastoral idyll

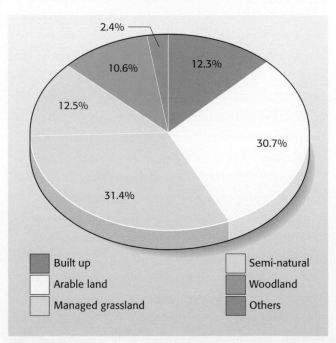

Figure 3.C

Land use in England

Figure 3.D

A rural idyll: Thomas Hardy's birthplace in Dorset

(a 'green and pleasant land') against a harsh urban reality ('dark Satanic mills').

Today, most people perceive the countryside to be in crisis. Yet rural areas are, on average, more prosperous than urban ones, despite the decline in farming and the recent foot-and-mouth crisis. The apparent paradox is easily explained: most people in the countryside are no longer associated with farming.

Essay questions

1 Consider the view that the physical environment is the dominant influence on economic activities in rural areas in MEDCs.
2 'In rural areas in MEDCs a car is a necessity, not a luxury.' Discuss.
3 Should governments in MEDCs subsidise farming in order to protect rural communities?

Suggestions for further reading

Countryside Agency (2001) *The State of the Countryside.*

V. Gardiner and H. Matthews (2000) *The Changing Geography of the United Kingdom,* Routledge.

A. Goudie (1993) *The Human Impact on the Natural Environment,* Blackwell.

K. Hoggart, H. Buller and R. Black (1995) *Rural Europe,* Arnold.

National Farmers' Union (2001) *A Strategy for UK Agriculture.*

M. Shoard (1999) *A Right to Roam,* Oxford.

M. Sissons (ed.) (2001) *A Countryside for All,* Vintage.

Websites

Recent surveys of changes in the countryside

Countryside Agency research:
www.cs2000.org.uk/report.htm

England Rural Development Programme:
www.defra.gov.uk/erdp

UK government departments and agencies

Dept of the Environment, Food and Rural Affairs:
www.defra.gov.uk/

European LEADER Initiative for Rural Development:
www.rural-europe.aeidl.be/rural-en/index.html

Countryside Agency:
www.countryside.gov.uk/information/default.htm

Forestry Commission:
www.forestry.gov.uk/

National Parks

Canadian National Parks:
http://parkscanada.pch.gc.ca/

Peak National Park: www.peakdistrict.org/

Agriculture

National Farmers' Union: www.nfu.org.uk

Farming & Wildlife Advisory Group:
www.fwag.org.uk

Soil Association: www.soilassociation.org

Environment

Campaign for the Preservation of Rural England:
www.cpre.org.uk/

Friends of the Earth: www.foe.org.uk/

9 Agriculture

KEY THEMES

- Attitudes towards farming have undergone a major change in recent years.
- The role of the farmer is changing from producer of food to manager of the countryside.
- Increased production in agriculture has led to environmental degradation.
- Farmers are increasingly being encouraged to reduce the intensity of their operations and to diversify their activities.

Countryside management – the role of farmers

Changing farming regimes

The original aims of the Common Agricultural Policy (CAP) were to increase productivity and self-sufficiency, to maintain agricultural employment and incomes, and to stabilise prices (above international levels). These aims were met by guaranteeing prices for agricultural products (through intervention-buying in order to keep grain and beef prices above a prescribed minimum and guaranteed quotas for milk production), levies on imported food, and direct subsidies to farmers in Less Favoured Areas. In effect, farmers were given every possible encouragement to increase food supply. State-sponsored intensification after the Second World War revolutionised agriculture and the rural environment, and gave rise to a completely new form of farming regime known as *productivism* (Figure 9.1). As a result wheat output rose from 1 672 000 tonnes in 1939 to 15 130 000 tonnes in 1997, while yields grew from 2.0 to 7.4 tonnes per hectare. Changes in the pattern of production were reflected in changes in land use (Figure 9.2).

From the 1980s the productivist system attracted growing criticism:

1945–85: Productivism	1985 to present: Post-productivism
State support to maximise output by rational means: • intensification (increasing yields per hectare) • concentration (increasing farm and field size) • specialisation (economies of scale)	Reduced state support (direct production subsidies cut back) Increased environmental controls (second pillar added to CAP – funds for agri-environmental programmes)
Emphasis on production/rationalisation	Emphasis on diversification/conservation

Figure 9.1

Changing farming regimes

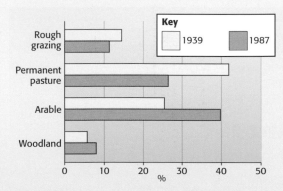

Figure 9.2

Change in land use: England and Wales 1939 and 1987 (%)

- The CAP was absorbing more and more of the EU budget and overproduction had created huge surpluses. By 1992 there were over 19 million tonnes of cereals in intervention

128

storage. Today, support for farming costs every UK taxpayer £4 a week.

- Other countries (especially the USA and other large-scale food exporters, the so-called **Cairns Group**) attacked Europe's protectionist policies, demanding a reduction in tariff barriers for food imports.

- There was mounting concern about the impact of intensive farming on the environment and health (not least the BSE crisis) and on the growing power of **agribusiness**. In England, the largest 1 per cent of arable farms control 43 per cent of wheat production. There was concern too about the impact of mechanisation on the landscape (Figure 9.3).

- The CAP had failed to keep people in farming. Mechanisation and rationalisation led to a steep decline in employment. In 1939 there were 803 000 full-time farm workers in the UK; by 1998 there were 300 000 – see Figure 9.4.

- Farmers themselves were increasingly unhappy. Incomes fell by 60 per cent between 1995 and 1999. Hill-farmers in 1998–99 were earning on average only £8000 a year (and 60 per cent of that was in the form of subsidies) even before the foot-and-mouth crisis (Figure 9.5). Factors included reduced subsidies, the high value of the pound, competition from other producers in Europe and beyond, changing consumer preferences (themselves related to food health scares),and the increasing dominance of large supermarket chains in setting prices. In 1995 the top six retailing firms controlled 86 per cent of the grocery market. Farmers accused supermarkets of profiteering at their expense. For example, while a savoy cabbage costs 13p to produce, farmers can sell it for only 11p and yet on the supermarket shelf the cabbage costs 47p.

From the mid-1980s attempts were made to cut back subsidies to farming, largely with the intention of reducing the size of the food surplus. In the 1990s more fundamental reforms were intro-

Figure 9.3

The farming landscape under a productivist regime: mechanisation and large fields

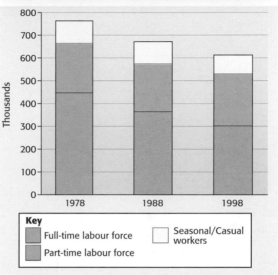

Key

- Full-time labour force
- Part-time labour force
- Seasonal/Casual workers

Figure 9.4

Trends in the agricultural labour force of the UK

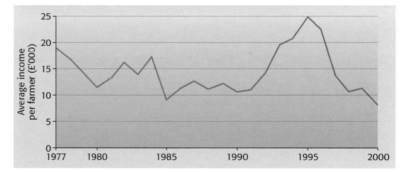

Figure 9.5

Trends in farm incomes, 1977–2000

duced aimed at reducing state intervention in the market (cereal and beef support prices and milk quotas were cut, and barriers to trade were reduced) and encouraging more environmentally-sensitive farming practices. The emphasis was now on the **sustainability** of farming.

Agenda 2000

In the latest round of reforms, a second pillar has been added to the CAP – the Rural Development Regulation – through which support is given to

Figure 9.6

Changes in nitrogen use in Great Britain, 1985–98

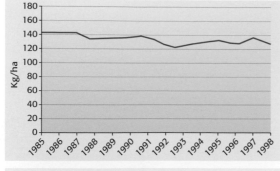

Figure 9.7

Changes in grazing intensity, UK 1988 and 1997

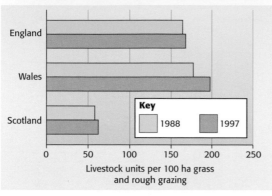

Figure 9.8

State support for UK farming, 1998–99

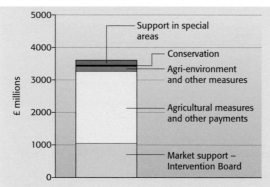

Figure 9.9

Favoured and less favoured farming areas in Europe

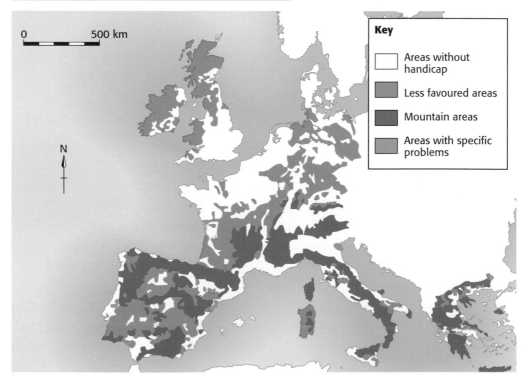

enhance environmentally beneficial farming, and to broaden the economic base of rural areas through programmes of diversification. For example, under the scheme, £1.6 billion has been allocated to the England Rural Development Plan, an umbrella for the separate schemes promoted by various government agencies. The overall aim is for 10 per cent of agricultural funds to be spent on programmes designed to enhance the environmental benefits of farming.

Since the early 1990s there have been some positive signs of a reversal of previous trends. Fertiliser inputs have fallen (Figure 9.6), agri-chemical use is no longer rising rapidly, the area under crops has fallen, and the area of woodland has increased. There is evidence to suggest that individual farms are increasingly diversified, with reductions in specialisation, although stocking densities actually increased during the 1990s (Figure 9.7). However, only 2 per cent of total agricultural spending currently goes on environmental projects (Figure 9.8). Agricultural policy is now seen as part of rural environmental management, with payments for beneficial environmental action rather than just for production. However, many schemes are voluntary, and regional take-up varies.

Large-scale farming is becoming increasingly concentrated in core farming regions. In the EU as a whole, 80 per cent of agricultural production is concentrated on less than 20 per cent of farms, particularly in 'hot-spots' like East Anglia and the Paris Basin. The remaining 80 per cent of farms are increasingly marginal to the global agri-food system – see Figure 9.9. Conservation efforts have tended to focus on encouraging low-input farming and alternative activities in these more marginal areas. The future might therefore point to a regionally-differentiated pattern. In the UK, commercial farming might be confined to core areas where large farms operate economies of scale under contract to multinational food companies, while farming in more marginal areas focuses on specialist products and becomes integrated with recreation, tourism and conservation.

The most recent crisis in the UK, the foot-and-mouth outbreak of 2001, is likely to reinforce these pre-existing trends (Figure 9.10). By highlighting the potential conflict between farming and wider interests, not least tourism, the crisis has underlined the importance of integrated planning. In addition, the foot-and-mouth crisis, like BSE before it, had an uneven impact, hitting the west and north hardest. Elsewhere, in the core cereal region of central and eastern England, farming was relatively unaffected.

A government adviser has predicted that up to 50 per cent of Britain's farms will disappear in the next 20 years (Figure 9.11), suggesting that 'farms will get bigger and that's a good thing'. In the next five years it is likely that production-related subsidies will be drastically cut and farmers outside the core regions will thus need to adjust to a new role. As geographer Hugh Clout says: 'Policies to promote ecologically sympathetic farming have led to many farmers complaining that they are being reduced to the status of park-keepers who are paid to manicure the landscape into a kind of stage-set for urban visitors to gaze upon.' Many who see the countryside as a cultural, rather than a natural, creation, oppose the idea of stopping farming and letting nature take over.

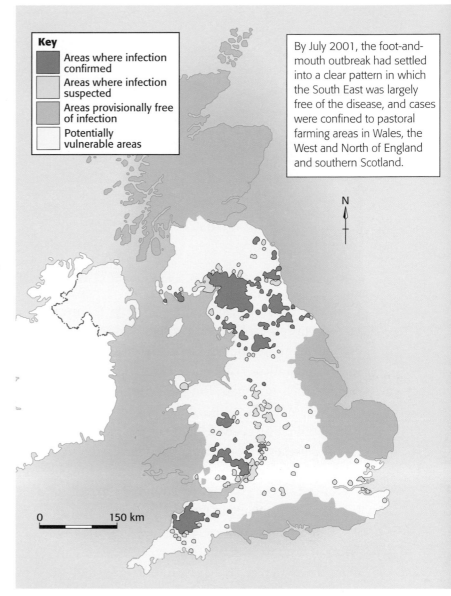

Key

- Areas where infection confirmed
- Areas where infection suspected
- Areas provisionally free of infection
- Potentially vulnerable areas

By July 2001, the foot-and-mouth outbreak had settled into a clear pattern in which the South East was largely free of the disease, and cases were confined to pastoral farming areas in Wales, the West and North of England and southern Scotland.

N

0   150 km

Figure 9.10
Foot-and-mouth outbreaks in the UK as at July 2001

Figure 9.11
A disused farm building

Figure 9.12
A former state farm in Poland now housing a privatised chicken and egg farm

Under Communism, agriculture in eastern Europe was organised around state farms ('model' units created out of previously private estates) and agricultural cooperatives (collectives theoretically run by, and for, their members, but in reality controlled by the state), see Figure 9.12. Members were given small household plots (around half a hectare) for vegetables and livestock. In Bulgaria, 1000 large collectives replaced more than a million private farms.

In practice the system proved inefficient: collectives were poorly-run and lacked capital investment. Nevertheless, agriculture remained important in terms of both its contribution to GDP and employment. There were periodic attempts to make individual collectives more autonomous, and to encourage private production. Change was fastest in Hungary, where the 12 per cent of land in private hands accounted for 37 per cent of total output. The household plots became a vital source of supply of fruit, vegetables, milk and eggs.

With the dismantling of the Iron Curtain in 1989, many countries rushed into the new era, cutting farm subsidies and privatising the land. However, large numbers of farm collective members resisted this development, preferring to remain in cooperative units rather than risk uncertainty in a free market. In Hungary, the new policies caused a temporary collapse, with lower production, higher prices and more food imports. Although output has now regained its previous levels, livestock numbers are still half the pre-1989 totals. Medium-sized commercial farms have begun to emerge, but small private farms still account for 60 per cent of output, and only 5 per cent of these are full-time holdings.

The EU set up a programme to assist eastern countries seeking to join the Union. SAPARD (Special Accession Programme for Agriculture and Rural Development) aims to provide financial assistance and technical help in order to increase efficiency and quality in agriculture, maintain jobs and protect the environment. None the less, the accession of these countries to the EU will put great strain on the system. To the existing EU grain surplus of 30 million tonnes would be added the projected eastern surplus of 8 million tonnes. Enlargement would more than double the number of farm workers in the EU and the countries themselves will experience massive structural adjustment. Productivity is only 11 per cent of the EU level, and improving productivity to just 50 per cent of the EU level would cause job losses amounting to 4 million. There is, therefore, an urgent need for rural diversification in the countries of eastern Europe.

Ironically, the de-intensification of farming is creating undesirable landscape and habitat changes in Hungary where the maintenance of valued ecosystems depended on agriculture. The alkaline grassland communities are being damaged by the abandonment of farming and the consequent reduction in grazing.

Activity

1 Write a forecast describing how the current trends in UK agriculture are likely to alter the regional pattern of farming in the future.

2 Predict the likely effects of accession to the EU by eastern European countries on:
   a farming in those countries
   b the wider human and physical environment of those countries
   c farming in current EU countries.

The impact of intensive farming

Forty years of intensive farming, supported by massive state subsidy, succeeded in its initial aims. The UK became self-sufficient in many food products. In addition, rural communities were supported indirectly through subsidies to farming, and in a wider context society gained (at least initially) from cheaper, more plentiful food, and reduced incidence of diet-related diseases, such as rickets.

These changes came at a cost that was not restricted to the taxpayers' pockets. To a great extent, these costs have been external – that is, not borne by the farmers themselves (Figure 9.13).

Consequences
Contamination of waters

Fertiliser applications increased by 800 per cent between 1945 and 1985. Bigger herds on dairy farms produced increasing amounts of animal waste in the form of slurry, which cannot safely be spread on fields. Over 90 per cent of serious UK pollution incidents are due to seepage or run-off of slurry and silage liquid.

Nitrate levels in English rivers are now between 50 and 400 per cent higher than they were in 1980, a situation that has led to problems associated with **eutrophication**. There may also be human health implications, although so far there is no proven link between excess nitrate in drinking water and incidence of 'blue baby' syndrome and stomach cancers. None the less, 5 million people in the UK live in areas where the nitrate level exceeds the EU limit. A 1991 EU directive requires governments to limit nitrate concentrations in water sources that might be used for drinking, but the cost of treating such sources would be prohibitive.

Soil erosion

A recent US study suggested that 90 per cent of cropland is losing soil above the sustainable rate. The average rate of erosion is eight times faster than the rate of soil formation. Rivers discharge 4 billion tonnes of soil every year, while wind removes another 1 billion tonnes. In England and Wales, 37 per cent of arable land is vulnerable to erosion, especially intensively farmed sandy soils on steep slopes (Figure 9.14). Soil losses have reached 250 tonnes per hectare on the South Downs, where sheep pastures, even on very steep slopes, have been ploughed up. Since the mid-1970s vulnerability has increased as a result of a switch to winter crops, with cereals being sown in the autumn. This practice

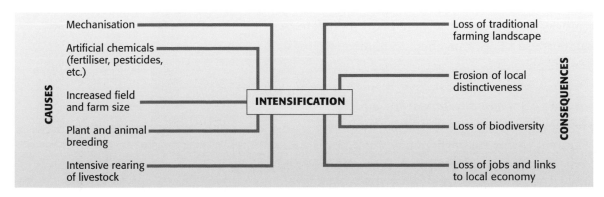

Figure 9.13

Causes and consequences of agricultural intensification

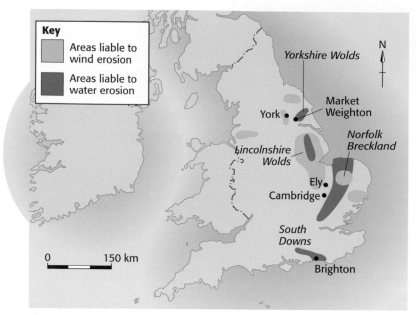

Figure 9.14

Areas in England that are vulnerable to soil erosion

Figure 9.15

State support for production led to even steeper and less productive areas being intensively farmed

provides a longer growing season and generates higher yields, but seedbeds are exposed with little vegetation cover during the period of winter rainfall. Other factors include hedgerow removal, field enlargement and the use of heavy machinery (which compacts the soil and provides channels for accelerated run-off). The reliance on inorganic fertiliser, with a consequent reduction in the humus content, has the effect of breaking up the soil structure and making it less permeable. The external, off-farm costs have been explicit in some cases. For example, in 1987 a massive flood carried soil into homes in Rottingdean, near Brighton, leading to threats of legal action against farmers.

Habitat loss

Changing land management practices (e.g. spraying of chemicals) and the direct destruction of natural environments (e.g. hedgerow removal) have a significant effect on natural habitats, and a knock-on effect on **biodiversity** (see Chapter 12).

Loss of visual amenity/landscape quality

The emergence of 'prairie'-style landscapes (Figure 9.15) in areas where fields and farms have been progressively amalgamated, and **monoculture** established, is the extreme end of

the spectrum. However, all over the country the rural patchwork has been rendered more uniform by specialisation, hedgerow and copse removal, the in-filling of ponds (Figure 9.16), and the planting of coniferous woodlands. The Countryside Agency recognises that intensive farming has tended to cause the loss of traditional farming landscapes as well as the erosion of local variation and distinctiveness, adding to a sense of 'sameness' from place to place.

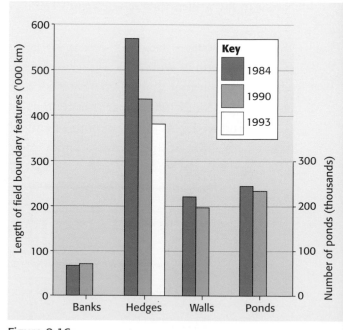

Figure 9.16

The decline of farm landscape features

The Fens were originally wetlands (reed and sedge beds inundated in winter), but systematic attempts to drain them, especially in the 17th century, have left very few examples of natural fen environment. Almost the whole of the Fenland is Class 1 agricultural land. It is an intensively-farmed, geometrical, man-made landscape: very flat, but with elevated roads and rivers. Drainage and cultivation have caused the peat to oxidise and shrink and the land surface to fall, leaving rivers up to 4 metres above the level of surrounding farmland. The area lacks hedgerows or walls: fields are divided by drainage dykes, which give the whole area an open aspect (Figure 9.17). There has never been much woodland or unimproved land in this valuable agricultural area. Traditionally, isolated pollarded willows occur in the Fens.

When Holme Fen was drained in 1848, an iron column 22 feet long was driven into the soil. Subsequent shrinkage had exposed almost 12 feet of it by 1978 (Figure 9.18). A study of changes since 1980 highlighted a number of indicators of continued intensification.

- **Land use** – increased concentration on cereals with a limited range of crops focusing on wheat and sugar beet; the number of livestock fell dramatically with the loss of grazing land.
- **Farm size** – a decreasing number of farms, and increasing average farm size. Polarisation was occurring with some large units owned by institutions, and several smallholdings farmed part-time.
- **Field size** – fields have been amalgamated, with the loss of boundaries (Figure 9.19). A quarter of the dykes have been filled in, and droveways have fallen into disuse. The broad grass verges found between dykes and droves have been ploughed up. Average field size doubled from 5.5 hectares in 1945 to 11.5 hectares in 1994.
- **Woodland** – loss of willows, no longer used for **pollarding**. However, several lines of poplars have been planted along field boundaries, changing the landscape significantly.

Figure 9.18
The post at Holme Fen

Figure 9.17
Aerial view of the Fens: note the lack of trees, and the large geometric fields

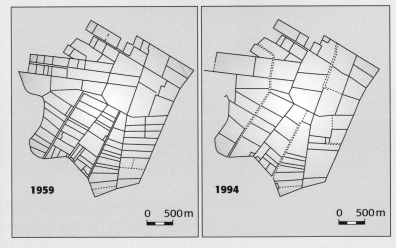

1959

1994

0   500 m

0   500 m

Figure 9.19
Progressive loss of dykes as fields are enlarged in a part of the Cambridgeshire Fens

Impact on wildlife

Drainage on a large scale led to the disappearance of fenland ecosystems from all but a few isolated protected areas. Five species of moth and butterfly disappeared. The loss of dykes, droves, grassland borders and willows has reduced the natural cover available for wildlife. Until recently, dykes were kept clear by regular application of herbicides, and willows were felled to make mechanical clearance easier. However, less intensive management of the dykes (Figure 9.20) has created opportunities for habitat renewal along verges and in washes.

Soil erosion and sustainability

Soil losses are greatest during high-wind events in the context of prolonged dry spells. On 4 May 1955, a 48-hour-long gale (locally they are called 'Fen blows') created a dust storm which whipped up soil and reduced visibility to less than 300 metres. There is some evidence that the incidence of serious dust storms is on the increase. Soil losses can reach more than 17 tonnes per hectare on bare soil, compared with 0.68 tonnes on grass and 0.012 tonnes under woodland.

Figure 9.20
Fenland drainage dyke

The peat cover was once up to 5 metres deep, but in places it is now less than a metre. With shrinkage and soil loss, the depth of peat has diminished to such an extent that farmers in some places are ploughing into the underlying clay. As fertility falls rapidly, there will come a time when the value of the land and its produce can no longer justify the high cost of keeping the area drained.

Activity

1. **a** Explain what is meant by 'external' costs in farming.

   b List and describe those farming costs that are external and for one such cost, suggest how it might be reduced.

2. Prepare an explanation of why rates of soil erosion vary so much from place to place.

Alternatives to intensive farming

Intensive farming is unsustainable because it relies on huge inputs from outside the farm system (often themselves derived from non-renewable resources), and produces large amounts of waste that cannot be disposed of safely on the farm itself. The challenge is to find an alternative that satisfies several aspects of the sustainability criterion, namely:

- **environmental** – the capacity of a farming system to carry on in the future without unacceptable pollution, depletion or destruction of its natural resources
- **socio-economic** – the capacity of the system to provide an acceptable economic return to those employed in it
- **productive** – the capacity to supply sufficient food to support the non-farm population.

The de-intensification of agriculture

Under EU directives farmers are now encouraged to reduce output, and they are compensated for the loss of earnings. Many of these schemes, introduced in the 1990s, are aimed primarily at conservation (see Chapter 12).

Set-aside schemes

Figure 9.21
A set-aside strip

The main aim of set-aside was to reduce food production, but a side-effect has been the possibility of conservation and return of natural habitats (Figure 9.21). Under these schemes, farmers are required to set aside a prescribed proportion of their land (e.g. 15 per cent in 1992–93) in return for grant aid, but the impact has not been as great as anticipated for the following reasons:

- Eighty per cent has been rotational set-aside, whereby farmers set aside a different area each year over a six-year cycle. Thus land was not left permanently uncultivated.
- Farmers tended to set aside their least productive land and compensated by intensifying production on the rest of the farm.
- Farmers tended to participate in order to receive payments for changes they would have made anyway.

Nevertheless, the scheme has contributed to a decline in the area sown with crops (down 5 per cent between 1995 and 1999) and to the small increase in woodland. Under new EU regulations, farmers are encouraged to take land out of cultivation for at least 20 years.

Nitrate Vulnerable Zones

What started as a voluntary scheme to encourage farmers in nitrate sensitive areas to restrict fertiliser input became a compulsory programme in the 1990s. Farmers are now obliged to implement action plans in areas where nitrate levels are at, or near, EU limits, and where water sources are used for public consumption (see Figure 9.22).

Environmentally Sensitive Areas (ESAs)

These areas – **ESAs** – were introduced in the late 1980s and one-sixth of the total agricultural area is now covered by ESA schemes. Farmers are compensated for using traditional practices that will maintain the character of a region. In ESAs farmers are being encouraged to adopt soil conservation techniques and not to depend so much on the addition of chemical

Figure 9.22
Environmentally Sensitive Areas (ESAs) and Nitrate Vulnerable Zones, England and Wales

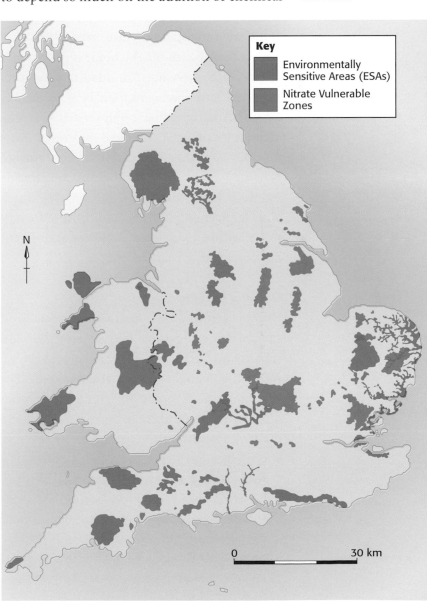

Key

Environmentally Sensitive Areas (ESAs)

Nitrate Vulnerable Zones

N

0   30 km

inputs to maintain fertility. In the South Downs ESA, for example, recommended practices include:

- limiting the energy of erosive agents, for example by restoring hedges, especially across slopes, and ploughing along contours rather than up and down slopes
- increasing soil protection by covering the soil with crop residues like straw, increasing the percentage of spring-sown crops, leaving stubble unploughed over the winter, and returning to permanent grass on steeper slopes
- improving the soil's resistance to erosion, e.g. by organic rather than inorganic applications, maintaining a coarse soil texture (tilth), and avoiding compaction by machinery.

One criticism of the ESA scheme is that it tends to attract conservation-minded farmers who may well have managed their land sensitively anyway. Another is that it only applies in certain areas, an issue that has been addressed more recently by the Countryside Stewardship Scheme (Chapter 12) and by the Countryside Agency's Land Management Initiative which aims to promote projects that incorporate new practices in a representative range of different environments.

Organic farming

Organic farming aims to practise humane and sustainable agriculture by placing maximum reliance on farm-derived renewable resources, rather than bought-in synthetic resources. The key challenge is how to maintain long-term fertility without the use of agri-chemicals. The main means currently in use are:

- **crop rotation** – such as following cereals with crops of legumes and carrots, which helps to prevent a build-up of species-specific diseases, and reduces the depletion of particular soil nutrients
- **organic fertilisers** – using farmyard manure and green manure (e.g. growing clover and then ploughing it in) – these fertilisers

release nutrients slowly and prevent excessive leaching as well as improving soil structure and water retention

- **natural pest and weed control** – by encouraging predators (e.g. ladybirds which eat aphids), and by inter-cropping (e.g. the smell of onions puts off the carrot root fly); weeds are physically uprooted and buried.

The core problem with organic farming is that yields are lower and there are fewer economies of scale. Some studies have shown that the higher price of organic food might compensate by producing higher returns than conventional farming, but the take-up of organic methods is slow. Currently organic farms cover only 0.3 per cent of the agricultural area (see Figure 9.23). Although under the Organic Aid Scheme grants are offered to help farmers convert, there are many uncertainties about future returns. The dominance of big supermarket chains and lack of experience and expertise have put off many potential organic farmers, as has the high cost of converting a farm to organic production, which requires a two-year fallow period. To date, organic enterprises tend to be concentrated on small farms in west Wales, the Vale of Evesham, Sussex, and scattered around East Anglia.

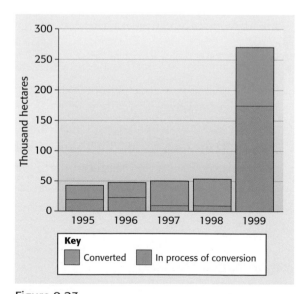

Figure 9.23

Area of UK land converted, or in the process of conversion, to organic farming, 1995–99

Diversification

Under the Farm Diversification Grant Scheme and the Rural Enterprise Scheme, the government offers incentives for farmers to move into other areas of economic activity (Figure 9.24). **Pluriactivity** is becoming increasingly common as farmers search for ways to supplement their declining farming income. Figure 9.25 shows how the proportion of farms involved in diversification has increased as farm income has declined. Pluriactivity can take several forms:

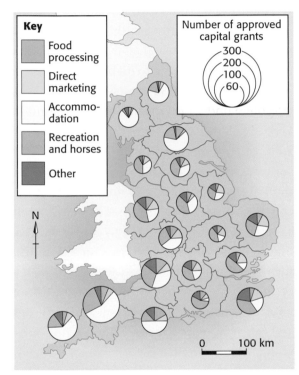

Figure 9.24

Uptake of the Farm Diversification Scheme in England in the late 1980s

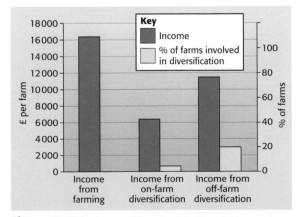

Figure 9.25

Non-farming income in England, 1997–98

1 **Farm diversification** (Figure 9.26), perhaps involving one or more of the following approaches:
   - different crops (linseed) or livestock (deer) or woodland
   - producing distinctive farm products (yoghurt, cheese)
   - direct marketing (farm shops and restaurants)
   - recreation (riding, golf centres, zoos)
   - accommodation (bed and breakfast, holiday cottages, camping)
   - use of converted barns for special events (weddings).

   It is estimated that 20 per cent of farms are involved in such activities, mostly near to cities or in tourist areas.

2 **Off-farm income generation:**
   - setting up own businesses (wine merchants, saddlery)
   - paid employment (bank, shop, teaching). A half of small farms have other, off-farm, sources of income.

Niche markets and regional speciality foods

De-intensified production, combined with exposure to competition from cheaper food from abroad, makes it difficult for anyone other than large-scale farmers in core regions to continue to farm profitably. As with organic initiatives, many farmers have realised that increasing numbers of consumers are prepared to pay premium prices for non-standardised food. Farmers can exploit a niche market if they

Holiday homes

Children's adventure playground

Figure 9.26

On-farm diversification strategies

can create an association between their product and a desirable geographical image, possibly evoking old-fashioned production processes and higher-quality standards. The EU supports such initiatives by awarding special designations to 'local' products, for instance Stilton cheese made wholly from local raw materials. The aim is to prevent other producers in other areas from 'pirating' names like Stilton or Newcastle Brown. The UK Government also encourages local speciality marketing through six regional food and drink groups (for example, 'Taste of the West'). These groups advise producers on marketing, promotion, trade fairs and funding. These schemes have also been supported by the Countryside Agency's 'Eat the View' initiative, aimed at encouraging people to buy more local produce (Figure 9.27). In Lanchester, a village in the Durham dales, a Local Foods Initiative brought together local farmers, an abattoir, butchers and five cooperative stores to promote local produce.

Figure 9.27

Promoting local produce: a farmers' market in a small country town

Genetically modified food

Despite the attractions of organic farming, there is no early prospect that it could replace conventional farming and still produce sufficient food. Many people believe that genetically modified (GM) foods offer a more realistic prospect of increased output without large inputs of chemicals. In 1999 the government spent only £1.7 million promoting organic farming, compared with £52 million on the development of GM crops (Figure 9.28), and a further £13 million on promoting the biotechnology industry.

Selective breeding and cross-pollination have been practised for millennia. What is new is the ability to transfer genes from one species to another. For example, strawberry plants have been made frost-resistant by implanting them with genes from a fish that can survive in cold water. GM offers the advantages of increased yields, longer shelf-life, better taste, greater resistance to disease (with less need for pesticides), and potentially healthier food, such as potatoes with a greater starch content that absorb less fat on frying to make chips.

However, opposition is very strong, not least among conservationists, who fear that GM species will out-compete natural species in the wild. In addition, medical experts have raised concerns over the impact on human health. In the longer term, genes can mutate during the copying process, while modification itself exposes genes to nature and to evolution with unforeseeable consequences. In economic terms, there is concern that farmers will be at the mercy of huge biotechnology firms which can both hold the patents on the genetic structure of crops and sell at monopoly prices. 'Terminator technology' also means that farmers cannot use seeds for the following year's planting.

Whether adoption of GM foods would represent a shift to more or less intensive agriculture, depends on your point of view.

Figure 9.28

A genetically modified rapeseed crop in Oxfordshire

In 1960, all 33 households in the village of Sevenhampton, near Swindon, worked on an estate of seven tenanted farms. By 1998 all the farms had been sold. One is now a golf course and two are farmed by contractors: one farm is owned by an advertising executive, the other by a helicopter pilot. The last farm worker in the village retired in 1999.

Roves Farm (Figure 9.29)covers 62 hectares, and traditionally concentrated on sheep and cereals. Subsidies, including woodland and environmental payments, now account for about 50 per cent of farming income; in 1996 they accounted for only 30 per cent. Between 1998 and 2001, the number of sheep fell from 1120 to 750, driven largely by EU regulations on **stocking densities.** Lower yields have resulted from reduced density of livestock, reduced fertiliser input, and other environmental initiatives. Throughout the 1990s, the farm responded to the EU initiatives aimed at **agri-environmental programmes**. Biodiversity has been encouraged by the establishment of new ponds and trees, and by better management of hedgerows. Some of the land is used to grow a fast-growing willow crop for use as a fuel on the farm itself which, in turn, has become a national demonstration site for biomass technology. Losses of about £20 000 a year have been experienced, so other sources of income had to be found.

Diversification has principally involved the creation of a Farm Visitor and Education Centre and a bed and breakfast business, which together now contribute 40 per cent of the total income. Over time the Centre has

Figure 9.29
Aerial view of Roves Farm

grown and its uses have been extended to include barn dances, wedding receptions and corporate entertainment events. Although it has created extra employment for the area, planners and some local people have objected to the resulting traffic on local roads, and the Centre has been forced to cut back its operations with a subsequent loss of income estimated to be in the order of £200 000 since 1997. Roves Farm has two full-time farm staff (the owners), and the Visitor Centre currently employs one full-time manager and six part-time or seasonal workers.

Activity

1 Compare the opportunities provided by organic and GM production, and suggest why neither is likely to provide a simple solution to agricultural problems in MEDCs.

2 Draw up a list of the criticisms that have been made of set-aside and ESA schemes.

3 Round off this study of agriculture by investigating the history and current operations of an organic farm. You can locate examples of these farms by contacting:
- the Soil Association in Bristol, or by consulting their website:
  www.soilassociation.org
- the organisation known as LEAF (Linking Environment And Farming) on:
  www.leafuk.org

Recreation and tourism

KEY THEMES

- Increasing proportions of land in MEDCs are being designated for protection as National Parks.
- True wilderness is increasingly rare in MEDCs.
- The twin aims of conservation and recreation tend to produce conflicts that need to be resolved through management plans.

Protecting the landscape

Across the more developed world, great emphasis is placed on preserving 'wilderness' areas. These areas are generally defined as those in which humans have not had a significant impact on the landscape, usually by virtue of being remote, with low population densities and apparently limited economic potential. In areas of relatively recent colonisation by Europeans, such as the western USA, Canada and Australia, substantial areas were designated as National Parks before any significant settlement took place. This practice became a major political issue in the USA at the end of the 19th century once the frontier was closed. The idea of a wilderness to be tamed and exploited gave way to a consensus on the need to protect surviving wild places.

The value of wilderness areas is generally regarded as threefold:

1 **Aesthetic value:** 18th- and 19th-century romanticism tended to idealise natural landscapes (seen in the work of the English 'Lakeland poets').

2 **Recreational opportunities:** 'getting back to nature' (which presupposed a nature to get back to).

3 **Biodiversity:** wildernesses provide a natural laboratory for the scientific study of ecosystems, and allow a varied gene pool to be maintained.

The world's first protected area, Yellowstone National Park in the USA, was designated in 1872. The 1964 US Wilderness Act defined wilderness as 'an area where the earth and its community of life are untrammelled by man'. Currently, more than 50 000 km² in the USA are covered by the Act. National Parks were created in England and Wales under a 1949 Act of Parliament. However, in Britain very few areas can be realistically defined as 'wilderness'. Where American National Parks are, by definition, largely uninhabited and natural, British National Parks are cultural creations, representing working landscapes (Figure 10.1). A total of 260 000 people live in the National Parks of

Figure 10.1

The landscape of the Lake District is essentially a cultural rather than a natural one

England and Wales, and almost half the land is farmed. Another contrast is in land ownership. Most of the land in British National Parks is in private hands; only a little is owned by bodies such as the National Trust.

The International Union for the Conservation of Nature (IUCN) defines National Parks as large areas where ecosystems have not been materially altered by human activity; and where there has been no exploitation or occupation. In Europe as a whole, 12 per cent of the land area is protected in some way, but 'National Park' areas as defined by the IUCN occupy only 1 per cent.

However 'wild' they may be (see Figure 10.2), the motivation for protecting such landscapes represents a precarious balance between conservation (landscape, wildlife, ways of life) and recreation (making these areas accessible for the enjoyment of all). In England and Wales, there are two types of protection: National Parks, and Areas of Outstanding Natural Beauty (AONBs).

National Parks

Twelve per cent of the land area is covered by National Park status (Figure 10.3) and comes under the authority of the National Park Authorities which are responsible for:

- **planning**, i.e. granting planning permission for changes of land use, new building, etc.
- **park management**, including maintaining footpaths, liaising with farmers, planting woodland
- **visitor services**, e.g. information centres, signposting, car parks, publications.

The network is expanding, however. The Norfolk and Suffolk Broads have a status equivalent to the National Parks; and the New Forest and the South Downs will soon be given National Park status. Scotland has no National Parks at present, although moves are afoot to designate Loch Lomond and the Trossachs, and the Cairngorms.

The 'new generation' National Parks in England are very different from the earlier ones.

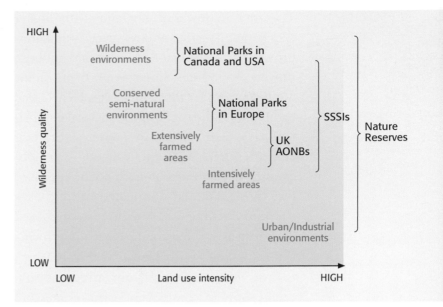

Figure 10.2

The continuum of landscapes, from natural to artificial

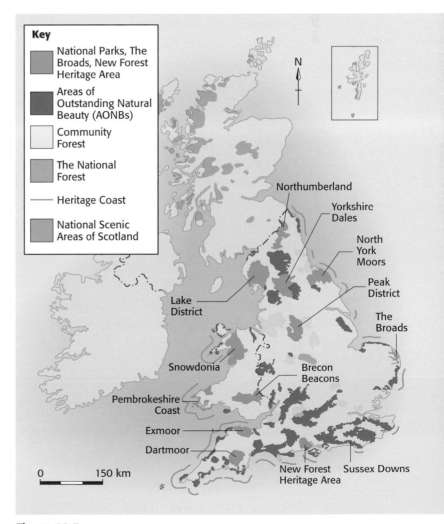

Figure 10.3

National Parks and other designated areas in England, Wales and Scotland

They are in lowland England, with higher population densities and relatively little unimproved land. National Park status has not been universally popular. Some people living on the South Downs fear that a higher profile will lead to a flood of tourists, while most local authorities view with alarm the removal of their control. There is some concern that job-creating developments might not be approved by a conservationist-dominated National Park Authority. Others feel that a strengthened authority is needed to stave off the growing threats to the South Downs – threats which today come not so much from farming as from roads, shopping centres, industrial estates and utilities. The principal issue for many is that of access: only 3 per cent of land in the South Downs, for example, is open to the public.

In Scotland, opposition to National Park status has come from owners of large estates who fear a loss of control over their land. Scottish Natural Heritage applied to the Scottish Executive in August 2001 for the Cairngorms to be designated a National Park. If the plan is accepted, the Park will become Britain's largest, twice the size of the Lake District. But in order to avoid conflict with landowners and local authorities, the new National Park Authority is not to be given planning powers, a development that has frustrated conservationists. In the past, planners have given the go-ahead to high-profile, but environmentally harmful, schemes such as the funicular railway currently being built up to the summit of Cairn Gorm.

Areas of Outstanding Natural Beauty

These are areas of the highest scenic quality, but they do not qualify as National Parks because opportunities for extensive outdoor recreation are lacking, largely because most of the land is intensively farmed.

There are 41 AONBs in England and Wales, covering roughly 15 per cent of the land area. Currently these Areas are run by the local authorities which, under new legislation, are required to draw up Management Plans, much like National Parks. Planning authorities in AONBs seek to restrain building development in open country, and tend to refuse permission to land uses that prejudice important wildlife habitats and landscapes. Buildings that serve community needs are likely to be allowed, although the site may have to be chosen with sensitivity (Figure 10.4).

Figure 10.4
A new health centre within the Chilterns AONB

Case Study: Protecting wild environments – the Canadian North

There are 39 National Parks in Canada, and more are planned. Each represents one of Canada's natural regions, defined in terms of distinctive landforms and habitats. The National Parks, presently covering 2 per cent of the country, are dedicated to the public for benefit and education, being maintained in an undamaged state for future generations.

Strict zoning operates in the parks. Some areas are designated for visitor facilities and services, usually focused on existing settlements, while others, being accessible by vehicle, are set aside for a range of outdoor pursuits. Overall, 95 per cent of the area in the National Parks is designated as 'wilderness' or 'special preservation' zones, to be conserved with minimum human interference. Recreational activities are permitted within the capacity of the ecosystems and are limited to those needing few support services. These areas do not have motorised access.

Since 1976, 10 new National Parks have been set up in the northern territories (Figure 10.5). Designation was spurred on by imminent threats being posed by resource exploitation, including:
- oil exploration in the Beaufort Sea
- oil/gas pipelines in the Yukon
- mining in the Northwest Territories.

Several are located in Nunavut, a new territory with an area of almost 2 million km^2 but a population of only 27 300. The whole territory has only 21 km of highway.

Sirmilik, or 'Place of Glaciers', in the north of Baffin Island (Figure 10.6), officially became a National Park in February 2001. It was designated partly to protect it from the effects of the increased use of the shipping route by bulk tankers. Covering more than 22 200 km^2, it has no visitor facilities at all, and no motorised access. A land of dramatic fjords, ice-fields, glaciers, tundra and wetlands, and only sparsely vegetated, it provides a habitat for caribou, arctic foxes, lemmings, seals and polar bears.

Access is by boat or snowmobile (depending on the season) from Pond Inlet, a settlement of 1200 people which lies outside the Park. In 1997 Pond Inlet received only 250 tourists by air, although a further 320 tourists passed through on cruises. A new hotel has recently been built, and tourism is expected to play a rapidly growing role in future. Indeed, it is seen as a vital economic opportunity for the Inuit, the native people.

All visitors to Sirmilik are required to register and undertake an orientation at Pond Inlet, and then to de-register when they leave. Between February and July 2001, the National Park received 82 visitors, all in or after May. Visitors to the Park come to climb, fish and watch wildlife. Polar bears are a big attraction, but they represent a serious issue in terms of the impact of tourism. Polar bears have low reproductive potential, and threats from hunting have been met by agreements with the Inuit people on quotas for 'harvesting'. Current practices are sustainable, but

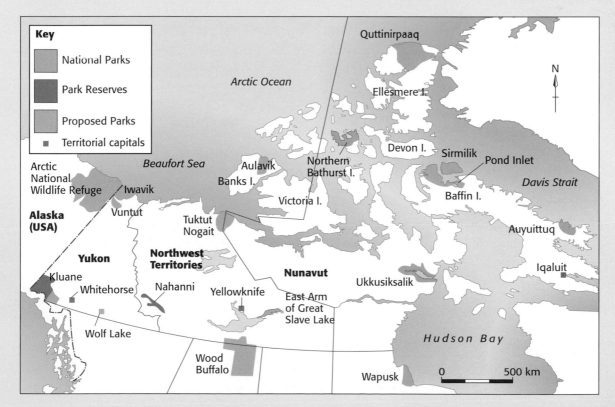

Figure 10.5
National Parks in the Canadian Arctic

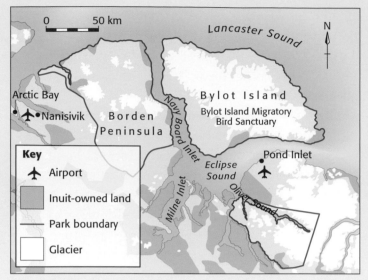

Figure 10.6
Sirmilik National Park, Canada

increased tourist numbers are a cause for concern. Polar bears can pose a threat to humans, while tourist activity tends to disrupt polar bear habitats.

Visitors are warned to be very cautious in spring when females with cubs are emerging from their dens, and in summer when the sea ice is gone and the bears are forced ashore. Inexperienced hikers are advised to hire a guide who is experienced in polar bear avoidance. As Parks Canada stresses: 'Bears and people can co-exist in parks, but this means that bears should be as little influenced by people as possible.'

The area is characterised by a very short growing season, and the impact of tourism on such a fragile environment is a cause for concern. Poorly chosen campsites can disrupt wildlife and destroy vegetated areas (particularly grass/sedge meadows). Fires can cause extensive damage, soap can enter water bodies and pollute them, and leftover food and litter can be a danger to wildlife. Visitors are given detailed advice, and reminded that it is illegal to disturb wildlife in a National Park.

Pressure, conflicts and issues

Problems arise in preserved landscapes because the three priorities of conservation, recreation, and support for local communities are likely to come into conflict, as illustrated in Figure 10.7.

Over time, pressures have increased (Figure 10.8), including:

- increased numbers of visitors (a reflection of wider car ownership, increased incomes, greater amounts of leisure time)
- a wider variety of leisure activities (as well as traditional rambling, more adventurous

Figure 10.7
Potential conflicts in National Parks

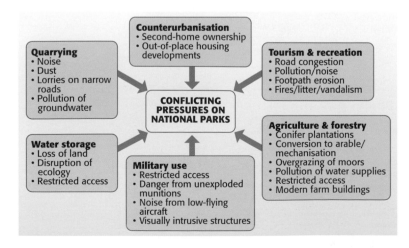

Figure 10.8
Pressures on National Parks

Water storage

Quarrying

pursuits from white-water rafting to off-road driving)

- increased rural population.

Tourism and recreation are, of course, not the only threats to conservation. Perhaps recreation is seen as the greatest issue, given that it is increasingly regarded as a solution to economic problems, yet it represents a threat to the very environment that people come to enjoy. Hence management of tourism and recreation is now essential.

An important concept in visitor management is that of **carrying capacity**. Carrying capacity does not just depend on numbers: other factors include length of stay, concentration in time and space, and type of activity. Pressures in British National Parks have become so great (more than 100 million visitors per year) that in 1997 the Countryside Commission proposed downgrading the recreational role, and making conservation the top priority.

Access to the countryside: a political issue

Britain is criss-crossed by innumerable public rights of way which are protected by law. Yet vast tracts of open country remain inaccessible because the law of trespass (at least in England and Wales) supports the right of private landowners to prevent people from walking over it.

For more than a hundred years, ramblers and landowners have clashed over rights to walk over open country – especially upland moors. In 1927 when large areas of privately-owned grouse moor in Derbyshire were put up for sale, local people raised funds to buy 300 hectares. In 1932, 400 ramblers staged a mass trespass on Kinder Scout in the Peak District. They were opposed by gamekeepers and police, and five ramblers were imprisoned. The resulting outcry helped to pave the way for the creation of the Peak District National Park in 1951. One of the consequences of the 2001 foot-and-mouth epidemic was the closure of the rights of way in most rural areas. Almost immediately, tourism felt the impact of the widely held perception that the countryside was 'closed'. The Lake District, hit very hard by the disease, was hit still harder by a severe reduction in tourist numbers.

The situation will change under the provisions of the Countryside and Rights of Way Act 2000. By 2005 walkers will have a statutory right of access to mountain, moor, heath, down and common land. Many landowners and farmers opposed this legislation, citing the potential threats of damage to property and livestock even though the Act strictly restricts access:

- People must be on foot.
- Landowners can still close land for up to 28 days a year.
- No rights of free access exist on cultivated land or parkland.

The legislation brings England and Wales into line with conditions in Sweden, where a Right of Public Access gives everyone the right to cross another person's land on foot, provided that no damage or disturbance is caused.

In the USA the vast areas of federally-owned land in the west (Figure 10.9) constitute largely unspoilt reserves which have increasingly become the focus of clashes over access. Traditionally there have been few restrictions on access, but ramblers and hikers have been increasingly replaced by off-road vehicles, 1500 of which are bought in the USA every day. These vehicles are responsible for the proliferation of unauthorised trails, habitat fragmentation, reduction in air and water quality, and conflicts with other land uses.

The impact of recreation and tourism on England's countryside

Visitors to the English countryside spend a total of £11.5 billion per year. However, 75 per cent of all visitors are home-based day visitors, so the economic benefits for rural areas are not as great as they might be. Nevertheless, recreation and tourism are major job-creators, as Figure 10.10 suggests.

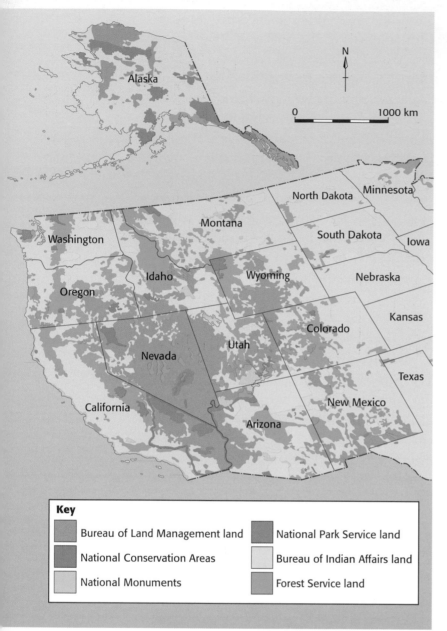

Key

▨ Bureau of Land Management land	▨ National Park Service land
▨ National Conservation Areas	▨ Bureau of Indian Affairs land
▨ National Monuments	▨ Forest Service land

Figure 10.9

Publicly owned land in the western USA

- **289 000 direct jobs:**
131 000	catering
54 000	accommodation
60 000	attractions, entertainment
23 000	shops
21 000	transport
- **49 000 indirect (multiplier) jobs:**
33 000	linkages with other firms
16 000	spending by those employed in tourism

Note: These figures are limited to employment in small settlements and do not include market towns; their inclusion would bring the total to 803 000. However, many of the jobs are part-time and seasonal, and often relatively low-paid.

Figure 10.10

Jobs in tourism and recreation in England

The economic impact on small settlements is generally seen as beneficial. In Abbotsbury, a village in Dorset with a population of 461 (Figure 10.11), visitors attracted to the Swannery, tithe barn and tropical gardens have tended to increase the range and viability of local shops, ensuring the survival of food shops such as a butcher and a bakery in the village.

The geography of leisure: visitors to National Parks

The average duration of a day trip out to the countryside is three hours in total, including one hour in transit. The average distance travelled is 42 miles (68 km). This suggests that the vast majority of trips are local, and helps to explain why National Parks such as the Peak District are much more heavily used, given that more than 20 million people live within one hour's drive (Figure 10.12).

Figure 10.11

Abbotsbury, Dorset

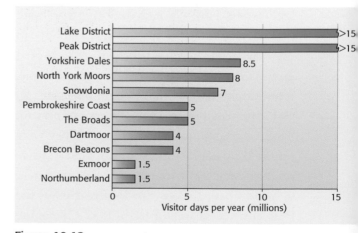

Figure 10.12

Visits to National Parks in England and Wales, 1995

Dedham Vale (Figure 10.13) is a lowland river valley, characterised by water meadows that are rich in wild flowers, and immortalised by John Constable's watercolour paintings. It is a relatively undeveloped tourist destination, but problems have arisen at two **honeypot** sites – Dedham village and Flatford Mill – and have been highlighted in the local press (Figure 10.14).

Figure 10.13

Dedham Vale, Suffolk

Figure 10.14

A newspaper headline

Pressures and responses

- **Tourism/recreation:** 72 per cent of visitors come by car (Figure 10.15). High visitor numbers tend to cause congestion and erosion, adversely affecting the local quality of life and damaging the 'pastoral' atmosphere (Figure 10.16). Local response to the commercial opportunities presented by visitor numbers has led to a proliferation of advertising signs. The National Trust has acted to limit the capacity of car parks, and to encourage dispersal from heavily-used sites by building and signposting footpaths.

- **Growth of population:** influx of commuters, working in Ipswich and Colchester. While the number of new houses has fallen, there is a problem with inappropriate extensions to existing houses.

- **Agricultural change:** field amalgamation, drainage of meadows, conversion of pasture to arable land. This process has been reversed since ESA status was granted in 1988. The National Trust has also bought land to protect it from further development.

- **Telecommunications masts:** the visual impact of masts erected by mobile phone companies is a major issue. There was local concern over a proposal by Orange to build a 30 metre high mast on a hill within sight of the Vale.

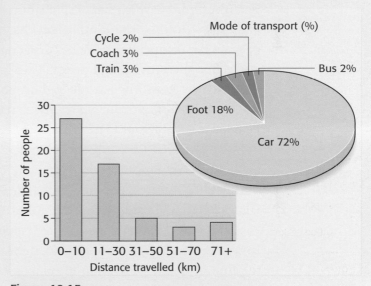

Figure 10.15

Dedham Vale visitor survey, conducted on an August Saturday in 1999

Figure 10.16

Footpath erosion along the Stour at Dedham

	Activity
1	In what ways are the landscapes of Britain's National Parks 'cultural' rather than 'natural'?
2	Prepare a table of bullet points setting out the arguments for and against extending National Park status to more lowland AONBs.
3	Prepare an explanation of how pressures on National Parks in North America differ from those in western Europe.

Management plans in National Parks

Each National Park in England and Wales is run by an Authority which has responsibility for planning control. The Authorities have to balance the competing needs of conservation and economic activity, and over the years the Peak District Authority has rejected proposals for landfill sites, electricity pylons, a trans-Pennine motorway and a race-track.

Every National Park in England and Wales has a duty to prepare a management plan setting out its strategy for the future. The Peak District National Park, Britain's first National Park and now the second most visited National Park in the world (after Mount Fuji), published the first of a new generation of management plans in April 2000 (Figure 10.17).

The Strategy Document retains a commitment to balancing the needs of conservation and recreation, but stresses the principles of sustainability and partnership.

- **Sustainability:** While the needs of conservation and recreation might create conflicts, it is recognised that one cannot exist without the other. Development must therefore meet today's needs without damage to the National Park, or to the enjoyment of future generations.

- **Partnership:** The purposes of the National Park can only be met with the agreement of the various interest groups, including visitors, landowners and local people.

The Strategy itself recognises that tourism is a double-edged sword. Tourism brings in £137 million a year, but with 22 million visitors a year, 90 per cent of whom come by car, there is immense and growing pressure on the roads and on parking capacity. There has been a 60 per cent growth in road traffic in the park since 1980. Ironically, the answer seems to lie in persuading visitors to stay longer, rather than visit for a day. This approach might increase income in an area where 52 per cent of the population already work in services, most of them tourist-related.

Figure 10.17

Management plan structure

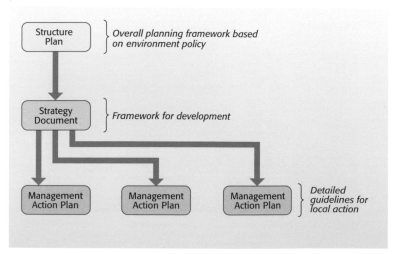

Figure 10.18

Typical farmscape in the Peak District National Park

In terms of farming, intensification has been damaging, with 75 per cent of flower-rich hay meadows being lost since 1980 (Figure 10.18), leading to a dangerous decline in the number of curlews. But the current trend from production to countryside management in agriculture is seen as a way of reducing friction between land uses: 'Conservation can ... provide new economic opportunities.'

Quarrying, agriculture and tourism have together put pressure on wildlife. The Peak District National Park is recognised as an internationally important area for three species of bird: golden plover, merlin and short-eared owl (see Chapter 12). The Dark Peak in the north is home to the only remaining English population of mountain hare.

During the course of the five years of the management plan, action plans will be drawn up with detailed guidelines for local schemes. These action plans will conform to the principles laid down in the Strategy, and should:

- encourage activities that enhance landscape and wildlife qualities
- encourage access, but discourage dependence on cars
- generate an economy that is diverse and sustainable.

Local plans might take a form similar to earlier schemes, such as the Peak Tourism Partnership of 1992–95 which focused on projects designed to manage visits to pressure points. It was based on community involvement, with efforts to raise money from visitors in order to pay for conservation measures. One outcome of the project was to encourage the use of the Hope Valley railway line, with visitors parking at a station and exploring the rest of the area by train and on foot.

Earlier plans for the Peak District Park had introduced a zoning system intended to reconcile conservation needs with the pressure of recreation, and to protect the most valued and sensitive areas (Figure 10.19). Zoning seeks to limit recreational activities in sensitive areas, while accommodating mass numbers of car-bound visitors within designated areas. It is likely that the new generation of action plans will be informed by the same zoning principles.

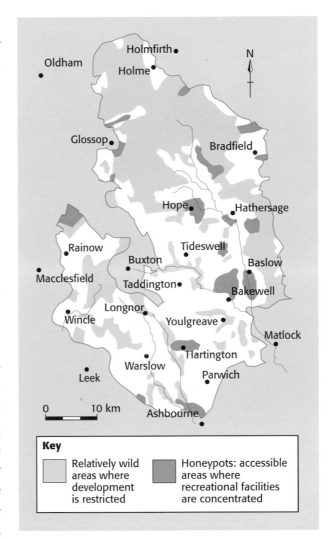

Figure 10.19

Zoning for recreational development in the Peak District National Park

Case Study: Local management at Dovedale

Dovedale, at the southern end of the Peak District, is the perfect example of a honeypot (Figures 10.20 and 10.21). It is a picturesque and stunning gorge cut deep into limestone; it is also highly accessible, and very popular for day visits. It receives more than 2 million visitors a year, 750 000 of whom walk the Dovedale footpath. At peak times, the Stepping Stones are used by 2000 people per hour. Concern had been evident about the impact of such pressure from as early as the 1970s. Cars were crowded into a highly visible (and therefore very intrusive) car park with heavy traffic congestion in the approaching roads.

Figure 10.20

Dovedale in the Peak District: reduced extract of the OS 1:25 000 map

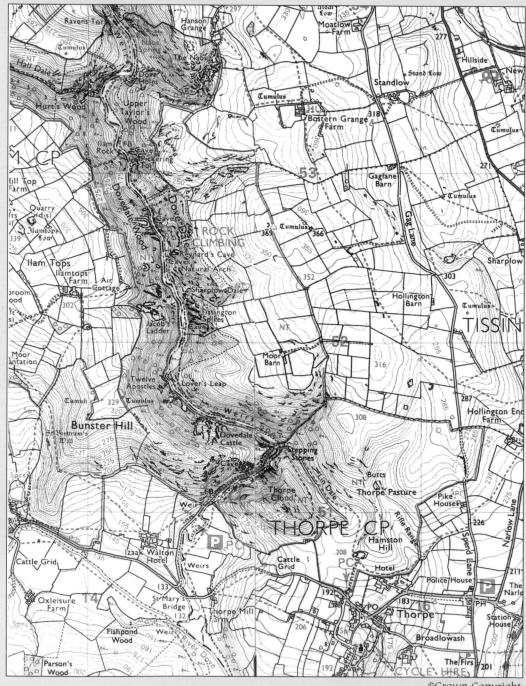

Natural scenery

Dovedale car park

Pedestrian congestion at the Stepping Stones

Figure 10.21
Dovedale scenes

Footpaths were badly eroded, as were hillsides. Local farmers complained of damage caused by trespassers, with disturbance to sheep and litter left behind. From the visitors' point of view, the area lacked good facilities.

By any measure, the carrying capacity had been exceeded. A management plan involving all interested groups was implemented from the 1980s, and it recognised three main priorities:

1 Reduce the pressure on landscape and wildlife.
2 Enhance visitor facilities.
3 Help the local community.

By 1991, the following measures had been taken:

- Car park capacity within the dale had been reduced from 750 to 400 spaces.
- Smaller, landscaped car parks were established within 3 km of the dale.
- Cars were banned from some roads at the busiest times.
- Better facilities, including a visitor centre and toilets, were built.
- Improved ranger services were introduced.
- A 10-year scheme of footpath restoration involved laying limestone flags to prevent wear and tear. Thorpe Cloud was fenced to stop visitors from scrambling up and scarring the hillside.

The results were encouraging. The number of visitors was reduced while the capacity of the main footpaths was increased. Congestion on roads and paths was also reduced.

Activity	
1	Using the information provided in Figure 10.22, describe the likely pressures on the Peak District National Park.
2	Outline the advantages and disadvantages of 'zoning' in planning recreational uses in National Parks.
3	How would you judge the success of the various measures taken by planners to reconcile conflicting pressures in National Parks?

a Origin of visitors (% of visits)

	Peak District	Lake District
Day visitors	65	26
Holiday visitors staying outside the Park	13	13
Holiday visitors staying inside the Park	22	62

b Employment structure (%)

Farming	12
Quarrying	12
Manufacture	19
Services (incl. tourism)	57

c Land ownership, 1990 (%)

Private	72.3
Forestry Commission	0.5
Ministry of Defence	0.3
Water companies	13.0
National Trust	9.6
English Nature	0.1
National Park Authority	4.2

Figure 10.22

Database: the Peak District National Park (Lake District data for comparison)

11 Settlement

KEY THEMES

- Trends in population distribution are becoming increasingly complex and diverse.
- Service provision has declined even in rural areas where population is increasing.
- Government responses have focused on initiatives to regenerate country towns and improve accessibility for the disadvantaged.

Changing population patterns in MEDC rural settlements
The changing nature of counter-urbanisation

The process of de-concentration of population involves both a shift out of core areas, and a movement down the urban hierarchy. The result has been a population revival in many rural areas, and particularly in small towns and large villages.

By the 1970s long-standing preferences for lower-density living had become less constrained by technological and institutional barriers. Changes in the nature of employment (including spatial divisions of labour and the shift to service employment and **teleworking**), rising incomes, and better transport and communications all contributed to the process of population growth in rural areas.

Counterurbanisation in the 1970s seemed to represent a dramatic reversal of the well-established trend of rural **depopulation**. However, in the 1980s, counterurbanisation slowed down. In some countries (e.g. Ireland, USA, Australia) metropolitan areas started gaining at the expense of rural areas. Even in the UK, where rural areas continued to grow (albeit more slowly) and cities continued to lose people, there were many exceptions.

The 1990s saw a renewed rural revival in most MEDCs, suggesting that counterurbanisa-tion is more than just an aberration. However, the process is now much more complex and uneven, with:

- continued decline in some remote areas that still depend on land-based activities and fishing
- decline in areas of traditional rural industry, e.g. coalfields
- decline in smaller settlements and those with a less diverse economic base
- recovery of some favoured cities.

In Brittany, for example, rural change has divided the region into two clear zones, with rapid growth in the accessible coastal areas close to the bigger towns, and continued depopulation in the remote interior.

In most MEDCs, the fastest growth is in the more accessible rural areas, and within those areas growth is focused on service centres. In the UK, rural population growth is increasingly concentrated on a 100 km belt in the South East (Figure 11.1). Indeed the UK has few genuinely remote areas, and almost all parts are within 100 km of a major city. Current growth is fastest in Cambridgeshire, Buckinghamshire and Wiltshire.

The impact of population growth has been magnified by the tendency for average household size to fall – a consequence of later marriage, more frequent divorce, and longer life expectancy. A given population will therefore create more households and consequently require more houses. The population of the UK is only growing slowly, yet more than 4 million additional homes will be needed by 2016. In the 1990s in Breckland, Norfolk, 19 per cent of parishes (mostly the smaller ones) continued to lose population, but only 8 per cent failed to grow in terms of the number of households. It is estimated that between 1991 and 2011, there will be an increase of 1 million homes in rural areas of the UK, a growth of 25 per cent.

Notwithstanding the continued process of rural recovery, that process needs to be placed in context. Between 1984 and 1998, the proportion of people living in England's rural districts increased from 26.8 per cent to 28.1 per cent. In many ways, population turnaround (the revival in the number of people) is less significant than population turnover (the replacement of one group of people by another).

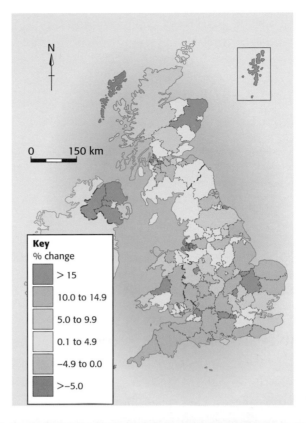

Figure 11.1

Population change in the UK, 1981–97

Key
% change

- \> 15
- 10.0 to 14.9
- 5.0 to 9.9
- 0.1 to 4.9
- −4.9 to 0.0
- \>−5.0

0   150 km

Case Study: Population rebound in the USA

The 1980s saw a net loss of population from rural districts in the USA. Although rural growth resumed in the 1990s, it was at a slower pace, and did not reach the more fragile farming economies in the mid-West, or the coalfield communities of the Appalachians. Rural areas close to cities, especially those in the south and west, grew rapidly (see Figure 11.2).

Figure 11.2

Population change across the USA, 1990–2000

Key
% change in total population

- 50.0 to 191.0
- 25.0 to 49.9
- 13.2 to 24.9
- 0.0 to 13.1
- −9.9 to −0.1
- −42.3 to −10.0

0   800 km

The 1990s saw the revival of many US metropolitan areas, and over the decade the proportion of people living in cities actually increased. As one scholar has said of the USA, 'although many people do not prefer to live in big cities, few want to live far from one' (Figure 11.3).

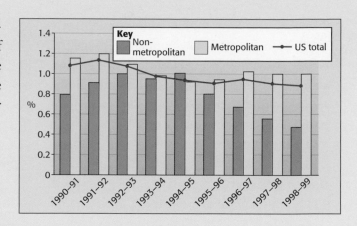

Figure 11.3

Annual population growth USA, 1990–99. Since the mid-1990s, growth in non-metropolitan counties has slowed dramatically.

Case Study: Norfolk, East Anglia

East Anglia is one of the UK's fastest-growing regions. In Norfolk, growth has been highest in the market towns and rural areas close to Norwich. Around a quarter of parishes have lost population, especially the smaller and less accessible ones.

Government plans call for large increases in new housing provision in East Anglia as a whole. This proposal reflects the increasing accessibility of the region, with electrification and increased frequency of trains on the London commuter line leading to a 10 per cent rise in passenger volume between 1998 and 1999.

Counterurbanisation has been very uneven in its impact on Norfolk. The most rapid growth has been in market towns, and to a much lesser extent larger rural parishes. While Norwich city itself has lost population, the major urban areas (including adjoin-ing 'rural' but well built-up parishes) have grown. By contrast, the smallest parishes have seen almost no growth, and many individual villages have experienced depopulation (see Figure 11.4).

	1981	1999	% growth
Major towns* and adjoining built-up parishes	273 821	299 690	9.5
Market towns	120 468	158 145	31.3
Rural parishes (> 200 people)	296 473	326 165	10.0
Smaller parishes (< 200 people)	12 111	12 500	3.2
Total	702 873	796 500	13.3

* Norwich, King's Lynn, Great Yarmouth

Figure 11.4

Population change in Norfolk, 1981–99

Population turnover and social change in the countryside

Counterurbanisation does not simply involve increasing population, or even households. It also involves population turnover (the combined effect of in-migration and out-migration), a process that is significant because migration is selective. As a result, counterurbanisation has resulted in the changed social and demographic composition of rural communities. In general, incomers tend to be relatively wealthy families and retirement migrants, while the leavers tend to be young and less well-off.

In many instances, incomers bid up the price of houses, and in making improvements to them they tend to reduce still further the stock of 'affordable' homes (Figure 11.5). In the Peak District National Park, a shortage of rented and local authority housing has been made worse by the upward trend of house prices, reflecting the area's popularity with second-home owners and commuters (Figure 11.6). It was estimated

Figure 11.5

A gentrified farmhouse in the Oxfordshire countryside

Figure 11.6

Desirable rural housing in a Derbyshire village

that England needed 80 000 new affordable homes between 1990 and 1995, but only 16 000 new units were actually built.

Population turnover also tends to reduce the demand for local services (since incomers tend to shop elsewhere), with the result that less mobile inhabitants suffer, and local jobs are lost. Some studies have shown that local landowners tend to support wealthy incomers in their opposition to proposed developments in the name of conservation, thereby reducing the prospect of new job opportunities. In addition, second-home ownership tends to contribute to population turnover by replacing permanent households with households that are resident only at particular times of year. In Brittany, for example, population losses in inland communes are associated with the buying-up of houses for second homes (Figure 11.7).

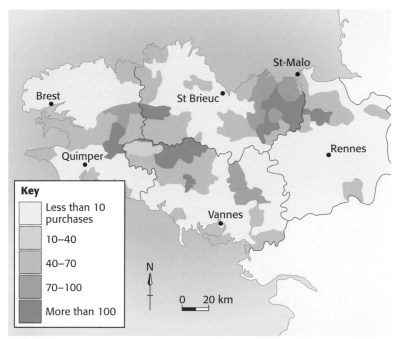

Key

	Less than 10 purchases
	10–40
	40–70
	70–100
	More than 100

N

0   20 km

Figure 11.7

The purchase of second homes in Brittany, 1988–92

Activity

1. Compare Figure 11.2 with an atlas map of the USA. On a copy of Figure 11.2, insert the names of the cities associated with areas of greatest population change.

2. Using the data given in Figure 11.8, describe the main social and demographic changes evident in east Northamptonshire villages.

3. Describe and attempt to explain the significance of village size on the extent of such changes.

	Large villages Movers*	Stayers	Small villages Movers*	Stayers
Age				
Families with children 0–14	35.2	23.8	19.1	16.6
OAPs	30.7	26.2	22.2	28.4
Social class				
I/II Professional	42.3	34.2	40.2	25.2
III Skilled, non-manual	26.5	24.6	23.1	24.1
III Skilled manual	23.0	31.3	27.2	32.4
IV/V Semi-skilled and unskilled	8.2	10.1	9.5	18.2

*Movers – moved in since 1991

Figure 11.8

Changing age and social class composition in east Northamptonshire villages (%)

Second-home ownership

Census figures on population tend to understate the extent of counterurbanisation in that they ignore second homes and holiday homes. In north Norfolk such homes represent more than 10 per cent of the total while in some districts of Wales they reach 19 per cent. The in-migration of wealthy families, often on a seasonal basis, is evident on a large scale in Brittany, coastal Spain and Portugal, and southern France (Figure 11.9).

In the village of Grimaud, west of St Tropez, 40 per cent of houses are occupied only seasonally or at weekends (Figure 11.10). Owners travel from Britain, Germany, Switzerland, or from the larger French cities. The impact on the local community can be seen in three ways:

- **Morphology:** second homes are either concentrated in a sector of the village close to the main services, or in a low-density fringe belt beyond the built-up area (Figure 11.11).
- **House prices:** these have risen rapidly, and have contributed to the out-migration of local people. Two-thirds of local households have had at least one member leave the village in recent years.

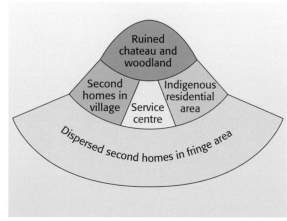

Figure 11.11

A model of residential structure in Grimaud

- **Employment:** the spin-off effect is not particularly noticeable, with less than a quarter of local households recording any direct employment benefit from incomers.

In Britain, holiday-home ownership is concentrated in the most accessible areas of attractive countryside, such as the Lake District and the Peak District. In England, there are estimated to be more than 200 000 second homes (see Figure 11.12). The Exmoor National Park Authority has recently announced intentions to ban outsiders from buying second homes in the Park. As many as 85 per cent of house sales are to outside buyers and prices have risen by one-third in three years. Exmoor prices are now 52 per cent higher than the regional average and 61 per cent greater than the UK national average. In contrast, local workers earn about three-quarters of the average national wage.

Figure 11.9

Second and holiday homes dot the hills of the Sierra de Tejeda, southern Spain

Figure 11.10

Houses in the 'indigenous' quarter of Grimaud

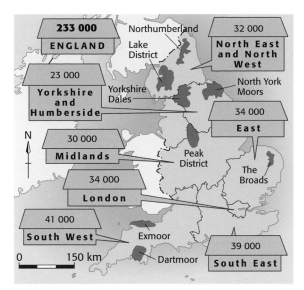

Figure 11.12
Second homes in England

The legality of the Park Authority's proposal is, however, questionable and it may not come to fruition, leaving the issue of affordable housing as a burning one in the National Parks of England and Wales.

There are both positive and negative impacts of second-home ownership:

Advantages:
- Revival of population
- Physical restoration of houses
- Owners pay council tax but impose few demands on services
- Local employment opportunities, e.g. builders

Disadavantages:
- House price inflation
- Loss of community spirit
- Lack of demand for schools and transport facilities
- Little money spent in the area
- Out-migration

Cultural erosion

The gradual erosion of cultural traditions is also felt to be a consequence of population turnover. Wales offers an interesting example: in 1997 across the country as a whole, 59 000 people moved in but 54 000 moved out. The general problems of population turnover are compounded by the threat that in-migration poses to Welsh-speaking rural communities in the far west and north-west (Figure 11.13). Holiday areas like Ynys Mon (Anglesey) experience a substantial in-migration of English-speaking people and there is concern that it is diluting Welsh culture. Studies suggest a strong cultural split between the indigenous community and the incomers.

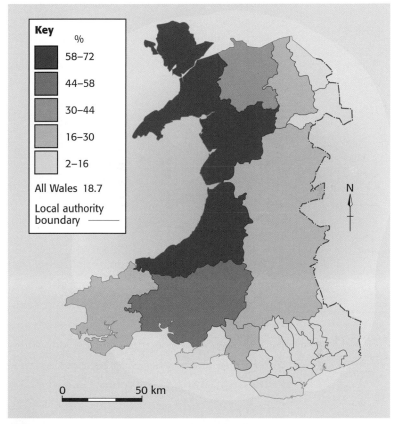

Key
%
58–72
44–58
30–44
16–30
2–16
All Wales 18.7
Local authority boundary

Figure 11.13
The proportion of Welsh-speaking people in Wales, 1991

Activity

1 Describe the impact of population turnover on rural communities in terms of **a** employment **b** services and **c** social cohesion.

2 Identify and describe the 'cultural' problems that have arisen as a result of population turnover in some areas.

3 Analyse the balance of the arguments for and against second-home ownership in rural areas. Is there a good case for different policies in different parts of the country?

The impact of change
The rural labour market

Average figures suggest that rural Britain is wealthier than urban Britain (Figure 11.14). Despite declining real incomes in farming, the average income of rural areas is inflated by the presence of commuters and new business start-ups. According to the headline of an article that appeared in the *Financial Times* in October 2000, 'Wealth is found far from the madding crowd'.

Figure 11.14

Comparing rural and urban incomes

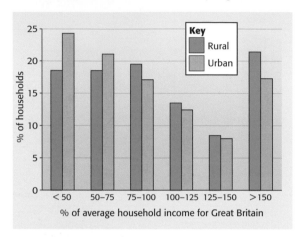

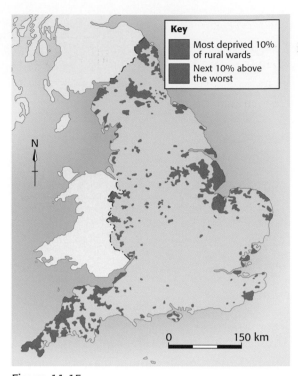

Figure 11.15

The most deprived rural wards in England

Counterurbanisation has had beneficial effects on employment in rural areas. Traditionally, rural areas have suffered from seasonal, casual and low-wage jobs as well as a limited range of job opportunities. Many new migrants to the countryside have set up new businesses, adding to the volume and diversity of employment. In addition, newcomers often increase demand for local services such as builders. However, the rate of expansion of jobs in remote areas has not kept pace with population growth, with the result that counterurbanisation has increased the volume of commuting to cities.

A quarter of the population of rural areas is in poverty; Figure 11.15 shows the distribution of the most deprived rural wards in England. The problem is not so much straight unemployment as low wages and the fact that work in traditional rural occupations is often casual in nature with no long-term contract and little job security. The growth in home-based teleworking in rural areas reflects these conditions. Areas with a high proportion of people employed in teleworking tend to be marked by high qualifications and low unemployment rates, but low average wages (Figure 11.16). Rural poverty manifests itself in

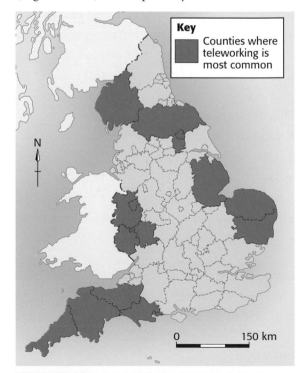

Figure 11.16

Teleworking in England

different ways. In County Durham, for example, there are pockets of rural deprivation in the ex-coalmining areas of the east, and extensive areas of more agrarian rural poverty in the remote west Durham dales (Figure 11.17).

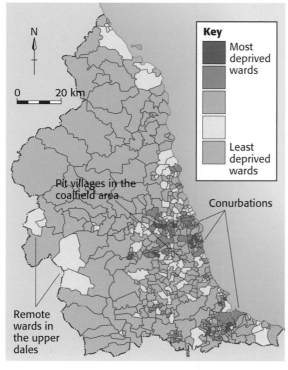

Figure 11.17

Patterns of deprivation in the North East of England

Rural service provision

Rural services continue to decline (Figure 11.18), and several examples have hit the headlines. The withdrawal of banking facilities has been widely publicised (Figure 11.19), especially in April 2000 when Barclays Bank came under strong criticism for closing 171 of its smaller rural branches in a cost-cutting exercise. At the same time, inadequate rural policing has been blamed

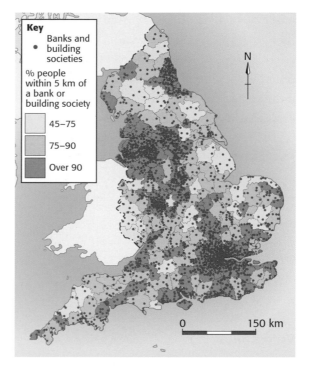

Figure 11.19

Access to banks and building societies in England

for increasing fears of crime feeding off rural isolation. In West Berkshire, an area of over 70 000 hectares and with a population of 144 000 people, there are only 22 officers on duty at any one time, and most villages are served only by the occasional passing patrol car. In England as a whole, an increasing proportion of villages is without a permanent police presence.

The proportion of villages without a post office remains at around 43 per cent, and 42 per cent of parishes are without a permanent shop. Studies suggest that when a post office closes, the village shop that housed it will lose up to 25 per cent of its turnover, and other local shops lose 15 per cent. Access to primary healthcare also remains a problem, with only 16 per cent of parishes having a GP. In general terms, the later 1990s saw a slowdown of the long-term decline

Figure 11.18

The Ex-Files

An ex-school

An ex-pub

An ex-railway

in service provision, but figures on shops show that pressures remain, particularly in the smallest size categories (see Figure 11.20). The true economic resource cost of closure is even greater if the cost of travel to post office and other facilities elsewhere is added in.

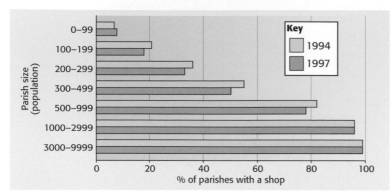

Figure 11.20

Rural shop provision

Accessibility

For communities without their own services, access to other locations is crucial. Even so, the 1990s saw the proportion of parishes without a bus service rise from 14 per cent to more than 22 per cent, while the percentage of those with a single daily bus service dropped from 28 per cent to 25 per cent. Figure 11.21 shows what happened in north Powys, Wales, after the deregulation of bus services. Access to basic services may be substantially reduced (Figure 11.22), and for many families rural disadvantage will be compounded by a lack of access to alternative jobs, all of which amounts to **travel poverty**. These are the people hit hardest by long-term declines in the provision of rural transport.

Impact on the environment

Counterurbanisation and continued urban sprawl have led to progressive encroachment onto rural land. In addition to loss of farming and recreational land, urban development has resulted in a reduction in 'tranquillity' (defined as 'outside the influence of urban areas, motorways, power stations, etc.'). Since the 1960s England has lost over 20 per cent of its tranquil areas to urban sprawl, traffic and light pollution. The average size of our tranquil areas has been reduced by 73 per cent (see Figure 11.23).

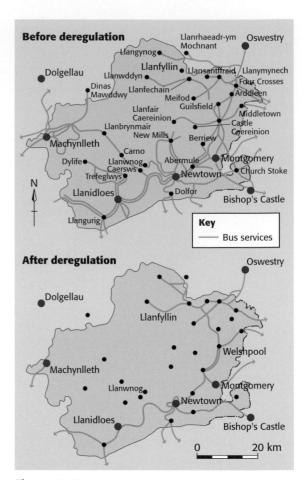

Figure 11.21

Declining bus services in north Powys, Wales

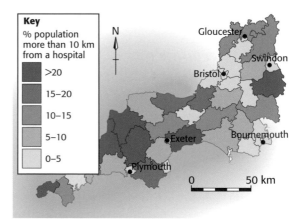

Figure 11.22

Travel poverty: access to hospitals in south-west England

The impact of urban sprawl on wildlife is seen at its most extreme in southern California, largely because, alone among megacities in the developed world, it is bordered by, and in some cases completely enfolds, desert and mountain wilderness areas. These fringe areas include major wildlife redoubts that are home to coyotes,

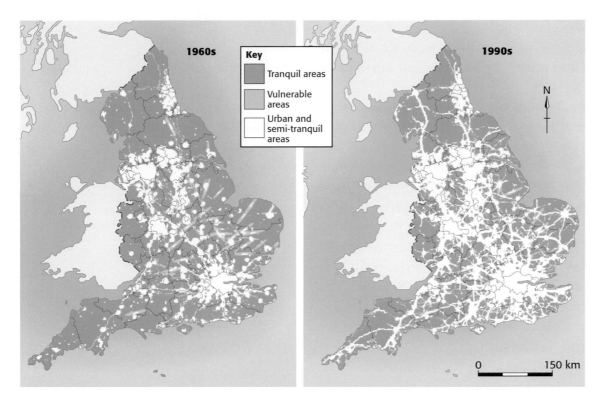

Figure 11.23
Tranquil areas of
England in the
1960s and
1990s

black bears and mountain lions (cougars), and yet are also used intensively for recreation and, increasingly, for suburban development. As a result, the number of incidents involving mountain lions has increased, leading on occasion to hysteria. As Mike Davis has written, 'As white flight and an anti-urban ethos drive the tract house frontier deeper into rugged foothills and interior valleys, suburbanites have acquired wild carnivores as unexpected and capricious neighbours. The result is a greater intimacy with nature than many had bargained for when purchasing their view lots or country estates.'

Responses to the rural challenge

In November 2000, the British Government published its Rural White Paper, setting out a strategy that has been adopted in subsequent legislation. It recognised that whether rural communities were experiencing population growth or decline, the underlying problems were often the same.

- **Housing:** there is a lack of affordable houses for local people. The White Paper called for planners to be given the right both to insist that new developments include a proportion of cheaper units, and to levy the full council tax on second-home owners.
- **Village services:** these will be protected by further rate relief on shops, pubs and garages, with financial help continuing through the Village Shop Development Scheme. The network of post offices will be retained, and the range of their services extended, enabling them to offer one-stop access to banking and a variety of government services. Rural schools will be safeguarded from closure.
- **Rural transport:** subsidies for existing services will be increased, and new initiatives encouraged. The Countryside Agency administers grants for new rural transport initiatives.
- **Economic activities:** funds will be increased for agri-environment schemes, and farmers will be encouraged to diversify. Grants will be available for other small business start-ups.

The strategy made much of the need to extend the opportunities provided by information communications technology (ICT), with the possibility of internet learning and access points in rural areas. It also stressed the need to target market towns, which were seen as the key to rural prosperity through their provision of employment and services.

In England, state support for rural regeneration represents a complex web of overlapping initiatives and responsibilities. Under a recent reorganisation, most rural issues are dealt with by the Department for the Environment, Food and Rural Affairs (DEFRA), although wider regeneration issues are increasingly being handled by the Regional Development Agencies (RDAs – Figure 11.24). Rural Priority Areas in England are shown in Figure 11.25.

Individual private organisations have also become involved. Sainsbury's, the supermarket chain, has launched the SAVE scheme – Sainsbury's Assisting Village Enterprises. The supermarket company has recognised the difficulties created for rural communities by the decline in village shops, and has responded by allowing village shops and post offices to buy non-perishable goods directly from its stores and then to resell them. The conditions for membership of SAVE are that the shops must:

- be located in a village in a rural area
- act as a focus for the provision of essential services
- be independently owned and not part of a bulk-buying group such as SPAR shops.

The scheme has been endorsed by The Post Office, ACRE (Action with Rural Communities in England) and ViRSA, the Village Retail Services Association.

Figure 11.24

Government policy in the countryside

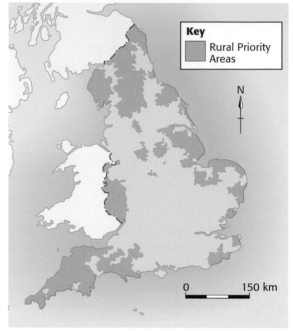

Figure 11.25

Rural Priority Areas in England

Rural Priority Areas

Areas designated by Regional Development Agencies as being in need of assistance. Grants are available to support integrated rural development and to assist individual enterprises. Projects may also qualify for EU Structural Funds.

EU Structural Funds

These funds are the EU's main instrument for supporting social and economic restructuring, and account for more than one-third of the EU's budget. Regions have access to Structural Funds according to their status: there are three categories. *Objective 1* status applies to areas where the GDP per head is less than 75% of the EU average, such as Cornwall in the UK. *Objective 2* supports the economic and social diversification of areas with structural difficulties, including many rural areas with low population density, high dependence on farming, population loss or high unemployment. *Objective 3* involves only the European Social Fund to which all regions have access. For more details on Objective 1 and Objective 2 status, see under 'Instruments of policy and assisted regions' in Chapter 1.

England Rural Development Programme (ERDP)

This programme is the arm of the CAP that aims to support agricultural diversification, e.g. Rural Enterprise Grants.

EU Community Initiatives

A proportion of the Structural Fund budget is used to support specific community initiatives, including the LEADER+ programme which is aimed at innovative rural development projects proposed by local action groups.

Countryside Agency

This is a statutory body which advises the government on rural issues and also administers a range of schemes and grants in support of rural services, including rural transport.

Other organisations

Other bodies with direct involvement in rural issues include the Forestry Commission, English Nature, the Environment Agency, and English Heritage.

Several LEADER+ projects (Links between Actions for the Development of the Rural Economy) across Europe have concentrated on applying ICT in order to enhance job opportunities in rural areas. One was set up in the Western Isles, to carry forward a long-term strategy of development.

In 1989, Highlands and Islands Enterprise joined British Telecom in a £20 million investment to bring a better telecommunications infrastructure to the region. The assumption was that modern information and communications technology had removed the need for many office-based activities to be undertaken in urban locations. BT itself established a call-centre at Thurso, employing 70 people. The company used remoteness to advantage, reducing its overheads by locating in a low-cost area and gaining EU grants in the process.

The Western Isles ICT Advisory Service coordinates the latest stage in the process – a LEADER+ project, funded in part by the EU through Objective 1 funds. It aims to develop teleworking employment in rural areas. A publishing firm called Lasair now operates from the islands. Although it only has two office-based core staff, it employs 35 home-based teleworkers engaged in proofreading, indexing and copy-editing. All of this work can be done on a computer at home. LEADER funds go towards IT training so that people can take advantage of the opportunities and new firms can be attracted.

Key settlements reborn: the market town initiative

Over the last 40 years, planners have tended to focus new development on the larger settlements in rural areas. This policy has been adopted in areas of service decline, regardless of population trends, as a means of safeguarding and ensuring the survival of at least some rural services. By concentrating on a few centres, planners hope to maintain populations above the threshold levels needed for the viability of service functions.

In the 1950s and 1960s, key villages were a major feature of county structure plans, the extreme example being County Durham, in which 114 settlements were considered to have no long-term future at all. This policy tended to continue into the era of counterurbanisation for two reasons in particular:

1 Economies of scale – council services and infrastructure can be more cheaply provided if population is concentrated in a smaller number of larger settlements.

2 Opposition to new development is often less vehement than in small close-knit communities.

In planning terms, today's key settlements are the market towns. These towns have tended to grow faster than other settlements, and yet they have suffered disproportionately from service decline and competition from out-of-town centres. Village development is now not favoured, as it tends to do nothing to bolster rural services but increases commuting and car dependency. Planning guidance from central government states that counties should try to divert growth to existing larger urban areas (market towns and larger centres). The Rural White Paper identified market towns (Figure 11.26) as a key to rural regeneration, and subsequent programmes have followed up this lead in the following ways:

- **Retail services:** In structure plans for English counties there is now a strong presumption against out-of-town shopping developments, unless they can be proved to have no adverse effect on existing town centres.

- **Transport:** Market towns are seen as a crucial node, linking rural transport schemes to the wider inter-urban trunk network. In addition, concentrating development would serve to reduce car dependence.

- **Housing:** Market towns are targeted for most of the new housing provision in rural areas. Population growth would be in synchrony with employment opportunities and infrastructure.

- **Employment:** Market towns provide greater opportunities for industrial development, in terms of space, premises and workforce. Greater broadband cable coverage should enhance ICT access in towns across the country.

The emphasis is now not just on where to put new housing, but also on planning to encourage skills and employment opportunities, and improving the competitiveness of rural areas, thus boosting their economies and giving local people alternatives to out-migration.

Figure 11.26
Market towns as a focus for rural development

Affordable housing in a market town

A new ICT centre under construction in a market town

A busy high street in a small market town

Case Study: Regenerating East Anglia's market towns

In Norfolk, where 61 000 new houses are needed before 2011, growth is to be directed away from villages. Most of the new housing development in Norfolk is scheduled to go to the larger urban areas of Norwich, King's Lynn and Great Yarmouth, plus the larger market towns of Thetford and East Dereham. These places offer the best employment opportunities and allow for balanced growth. In other market towns such as Diss, Fakenham, North Walsham and Downham Market, growth will be allowed where it supports their function as service centres for the surrounding rural areas, and where it enhances their self-sufficiency. Smaller towns will be allowed development where it is in keeping with the character of the town, but villages are to be kept free of development in all but exceptional cases (Figure 11.27).

Figure 11.27

Market town initiatives in Norfolk

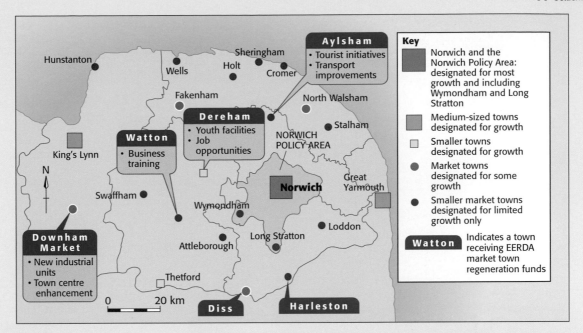

Following the White Paper, the Government offered £32 million for market town regeneration in or close to Rural Priority Areas. Bids were invited from settlements with populations of between 2000 and 20 000. The East of England Regional Development Agency (EERDA) chose six schemes, which shared grants totalling £1.4 million. The schemes have focused on creating new job opportunities, restoring commercial life in high streets, and improving transport facilities.

Integrated regeneration initiatives

The HEART of Suffolk scheme represents an integrated approach to the problems faced by young people in market towns (HEART = Housing, Employment and Rural Training). Out-migration from rural areas is often the result of a lack of affordable homes, and a lack of training and job opportunities. The scheme set up centres in each of seven small towns, including Framlingham, Bungay and Saxmundham. The centres provided bedsit accommodation, access to training, and careers advice. Transport services were coordinated to ensure access to job opportunities. The scheme should contribute to the local skills base and housing stock, and reduce out-migration of young people.

Case Study: Transport in Norfolk

Rural transport in Norfolk has undergone continuous decline, experiencing major crises such as the reduction in branch railway lines in the 1960s, and the consequences of privatisation in the 1980s (Figure 11.28). Surviving public transport is subsidised by the government through local councils, in order to protect unprofitable routes. In addition, new initiatives are encouraged through the Rural Transport Development Fund (individual grants for new services) and the Rural Transport Partnership Scheme which gives support to integrated schemes operated through local partnerships.

In East Anglia, 5 per cent of the population (more than 100 000 people) live in areas where car journeys to the nearest doctor's surgery take more than ten minutes, and where there is no daily return bus link (Figure 11.29). With reductions in scheduled commercial bus and rail services, increasing emphasis is being placed on community and voluntary transport projects that focus on the needs of the disabled and those with limited personal mobility.

In Norfolk this initiative takes various forms:

- **'Flexible feeder' projects** funded from 1998 under the Rural Bus Challenge scheme. Services

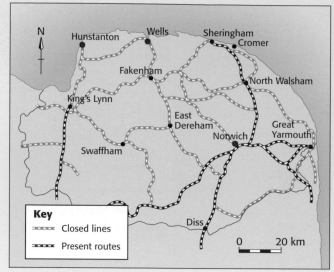

Figure 11.28

The destruction of the Norfolk railway branchline network

connecting villages to market towns like Wymondham and Downham Market are contracted out by the county council.

- **Community buses** – volunteer drivers provide timetabled local services, using vehicles owned by the council.
- **Rural transport partnerships** – these have been established in two areas of Norfolk since 1999, and involve community partnerships part-funded by the Countryside Agency.

Nevertheless, extensive rural areas remain without either regular bus services or community transport schemes. In these areas, 9 per cent of people do not own cars.

The East Norfolk rural transport partnership

This scheme was launched in 1999, with a grant of £250 000 over three years. The objective was to increase access to employment, education and local facilities in market towns. One minibus each serves the communities around the two market towns of North Walsham (see Figure 11.30) and Wymondham. These buses are semi-scheduled and pre-bookable, but have fixed times of arrival at transport interchanges in the two towns.

A similar scheme will serve isolated communities in West Norfolk and the Breckland, while in the Fens a partnership serving 32 villages operates a fleet of 14

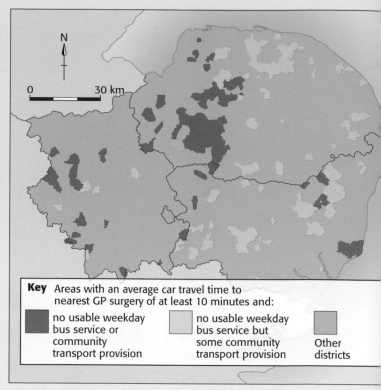

Figure 11.29

Access to GP services in East Anglia

vehicles, offering mobility for those without a car, and the disabled.

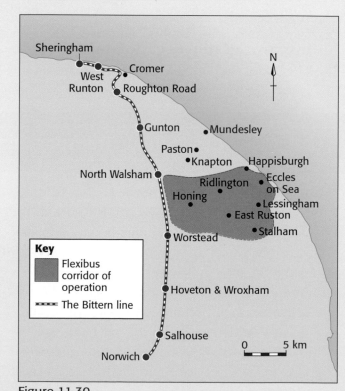

Figure 11.30

The North Walsham flexibus area

Case Study: Access and services in the Australian outback

In Australia, population growth has become concentrated on the fringes of the metropolitan zones in the coastal areas, most noticeably in New South Wales and southern Queensland and also in Western Australia (Figure 11.31). By contrast, the remote and lightly settled rural areas of the wheat and sheep-grazing belts and the outback have suffered chronic depopulation. This long-term rural exodus reflects the decline in agriculture and mining, partly through economic crisis and partly under pressure from the conservation lobby. The decline of services is part cause – and part consequence – of this net out-migration. In the period 1990–98, 1300 banks closed in rural areas. In 1999 the Australian Government adopted a series of measures to reverse the decline:

- banks and postal services would be provided in a network of 500 Rural Transaction Centres
- special payments would be made to keep GPs in country practices
- a rail link would be established between Darwin in the north and Melbourne in the south, through the country's rural heartland.

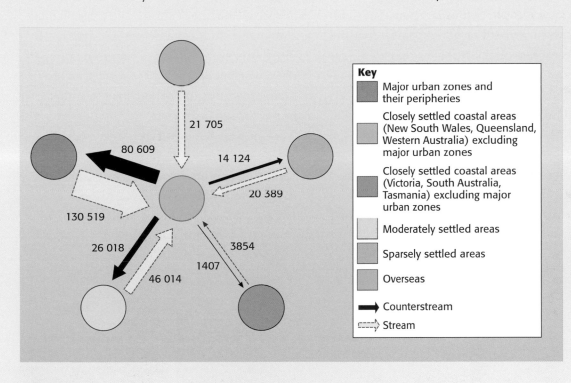

Figure 11.31

Migration streams in Australia, 1990–95

Key

- Major urban zones and their peripheries
- Closely settled coastal areas (New South Wales, Queensland, Western Australia) excluding major urban zones
- Closely settled coastal areas (Victoria, South Australia, Tasmania) excluding major urban zones
- Moderately settled areas
- Sparsely settled areas
- Overseas

→ Counterstream
⇢ Stream

21 705
80 609
14 124
20 389
130 519
26 018
3854
1407
46 014

Activity

1 Imagine you are preparing a small website aimed at rural communities and employers whose lines of business are IT-based. The aim of the site is to promote the use of ICT initiatives in combating rural employment problems. What opportunities would your site stress, and what would you say about the problems?

2 Write a critique of the key elements of initiatives aimed at regenerating English market towns.

3 Explain how, and in what sense, poor people in the countryside are 'doubly-deprived'.

- Intensive farming has reduced the extent of many habitats and reduced biodiversity.
- Environmental and agricultural policies converged in the 1980s and 1990s with the initiation of European agri-environmental programmes.
- Forestry programmes have increasingly sought to encourage multi-purpose uses.

Threatened habitats

Owing largely to the intensification of agriculture, and the growth of agri-business, natural habitats across Britain have retreated (see Figure 3.8 on page 39). Even though a slow-down in the rate of destruction of many threatened environments was witnessed in the 1990s, the UK has lost almost all its unimproved natural grasslands, 30 per cent of its upland heaths, 60 per cent of its lowland bogs and 43 per cent of its limestone pavements. The present pattern of land use in England, Wales and Scotland is shown in Figure 12.1.

Hedgerows

A hedgerow is a line of shrubs and trees planted and managed to form a permanent barrier. In 1950 there were about 1 million km of hedgerow, a half of which have since been lost.

Hedgerows are important for a number of reasons.

- They provide habitats that support a distinct ecological community (Figure 12.2). Insects support shrew populations; shrews and voles in turn support barn owls. The loss of hedgerows has been instrumental in a 70 per cent decline in barn owl numbers. Given the

Figure 12.1

Land use in Britain, 1998

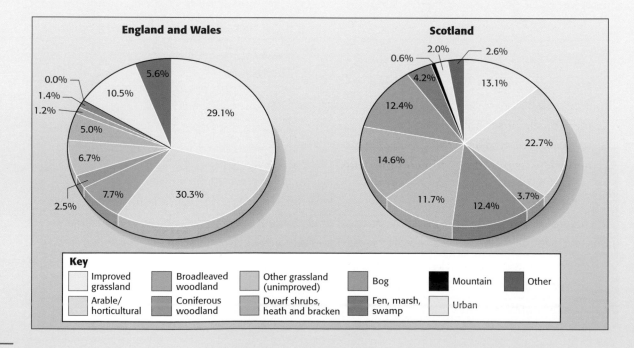

	Hedges on unmodernised farms	Wire fences on modernised farms
Mammals	20	5–6
Birds	37	6–9
Butterflies	17	0–8

Figure 12.2

Contrasts in species diversity in and around hedges and wire fences (number of species)

Figure 12.3

Weak control over spraying damages hedgerows

lack of woodland cover over England and Wales in particular, hedgerows assume even greater significance as a habitat. Hedges support on average 20 species of mammal, 37 species of bird, and 17 species of butterfly. By contrast, wire fences with sown grass are capable of supporting only 5 species of mammal and 6 species of bird. In 1962 hedgerows covered a greater area than all the country's nature reserves put together.

- Soil conservation – hedgerows reduce wind-speed and trap sediment, thus reducing erosion.
- In many areas, hedgerows contribute to landscape character. During the 1970s and 1980s in Britain, hedgerows were removed at a rate of 6000 km per year, changing the rural landscape into 'a vast featureless prairie' in the words of one writer. In Brittany, the **bocage** landscape (see Chapter 3) has undergone a similar transformation. Since the 1960s the 'débocage' associated with field amalgamation has opened up the landscape and radically changed its visual character.

Species diversity in surviving hedgerows has tended to fall, for several reasons:

- the impact of spraying with pesticides and herbicides, with spray drifting off the fields (Figure 12.3)
- mechanised hedge-cutting, which damages saplings
- the decline in traditional methods of hedge-laying, which opened up hedges and increased light and space, encouraging saplings
- the removal of trees to reduce shade effect, plus the impact of Dutch elm disease

- the tendency to plant new hedges with fewer species (e.g. mostly blackthorn, hawthorn, hazel).

Under the 1997 Hedgerow Regulations, farmers need permission to remove hedges, but losses still continue through neglect. In the 1990s there was no net loss in length of hedgerow, with new hedges cancelling out losses. Even so, new hedges cannot directly substitute for old, because older hedgerows tend to be more species-rich (Figure 12.4).

Species	Oldest			Youngest
Blackthorn	✔	✔	✔	✔
Hawthorn	✔	✔	✔	✔
Hazel	✔	✔	✔	✔
Oak	✔	✔		
Hornbeam	✔	✔	✔	
Field maple	✔	✔	✔	
Elder	✔	✔		
Birch	✔			
Willow	✔			
Sallow	✔			
Lime	✔			
Ash	✔	✔		
Alder	✔			
Holly	✔	✔		
Broom	✔	✔		
Beech	✔	✔		

Figure 12.4

Species diversity and the age of hedgerows

Chalk grasslands

The chalk downlands of England were deforested early, and for centuries the traditional land use was wheat-growing in the valleys and sheep-grazing on the slopes above.

Singular conditions (poor chalk soil and summer drought) produced a distinctive ecosystem of herbs, grasses, mosses, rare orchids, and butterfly and songbird populations. This natural community was preserved by sheep grazing which prevented any single species from dominating (Figure 12.5).

However, after the Second World War the higher returns for crops encouraged the extension of cultivation onto steeper slopes. The grasslands were systematically ploughed or re-seeded with quick-growing grasses, producing low species-diversity with few herbs. Eighty per cent of chalk grassland has been lost or damaged since 1940, and unimproved grasslands are now largely restricted to the steeper slopes, often on escarpments.

Where the land has not been improved it is often in too small and fragmented parcels for viable grazing, and has therefore reverted to scrub. This process contributed to a very rapid decline in chalk grasslands across England in the 1990s.

Wetlands

Wet grassland ecosystems have been in rapid decline across the country. Of the plants that have become extinct over the last 200 years, a third have been wetland species. The loss of wetland was fuelled by agricultural policies that made cereals more profitable than livestock, leading farmers to drain and convert wetlands, filling in the drainage ditches.

The Norfolk Broads contain a variety of wetland habitats, including fen, freshwater lakes, and grazing marshes. They provided a habitat for waders and wildfowl as well as rare water plants and animals such as the marsh harrier and the swallowtail butterfly. Drainage and improvement have led not only to the eutrophication of the Broads themselves, but also to losses of wildlife in ditches owing to the seepage of pesticide and to the creation of an 'arable desert'.

By 1987, 30 per cent of the drained marshes in the Broads had been converted to arable land. In 1984 plans were made to drain the Halvergate Marshes, which at 1200 hectares represented the largest single area of grazing marshland in Britain. The ensuing outcry led to the Broads Grazing Conservation Scheme, a £1.7 million scheme dedicated to paying farmers to operate in a traditional way. The scheme became the model for future action, and the area was among the first six designated Environmentally Sensitive Areas (ESAs). Under the scheme, farmers are paid to graze the area in a traditional way, and they qualify for an extra grant if they reduce fertiliser input and maintain the water levels in the dykes. The aim is to encourage more wildflowers and birds.

As a result of this scheme, and similar ones in the Somerset Levels, the decline in wetland areas has been reversed.

Figure 12.5

Grassland farming

a Traditional downland landscape: cereals on lower slopes and grassland on steeper slopes

b Unimproved grassland

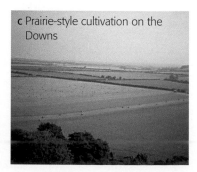

c Prairie-style cultivation on the Downs

Ancient woodland

Woodland represents the climatic climax vegetation cover for most of Britain (Figure 12.6) and once covered 80 per cent of the country. Today it covers about 10 per cent, although only about a third of that represents vestiges of the wildwood. The UK is one of Europe's least wooded countries. In comparison, France has 26 per cent of its area covered.

Ancient woods are defined as those with a continuous existence since 1600. They are characterised by great species diversity. Most were once managed, often by **coppicing** and pollarding (Figure 12.7), but are now largely neglected. Since the 1930s, 7 per cent of ancient woodland in England and Wales has been cleared and

Figure 12.7

An ancient managed woodland: pollarded trees in Epping Forest

38 per cent converted to plantation woodland.

Broadleaved woodland in England grew by 4 per cent during the 1990s, but problems remain.

- Eighty-five per cent is not protected with Site of Special Scientific Interest (**SSSI**) or National Nature Reserve (**NNR**) status.
- Only 14 woodland sites in England are over 300 hectares in size. More than 80 per cent of sites are smaller than 20 hectares.
- Most of the 1990s growth has been in urban areas.

In ecological terms, woodlands are vital for bird conservation, given that most of Britain's bird species are woodland-based (Figure 12.8).

Figure 12.8

Biodiversity in two contrasting woodlands

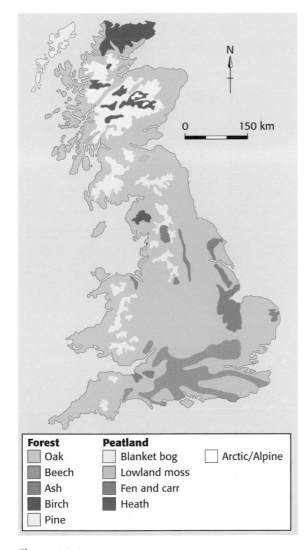

Figure 12.6

Climatic climax communities of Britain

Forest
- Oak
- Beech
- Ash
- Birch
- Pine

Peatland
- Blanket bog
- Lowland moss
- Fen and carr
- Heath

- Arctic/Alpine

Characteristics	Plegdon Wood, Essex	Lady Wood, Essex
Age of woodland	Ancient	Recent
Type of wood	Coppice with standards pre-1600	Coppice with standards established in 19th century
Size of wood	< 5 hectares	< 5 hectares
Tree species:		
Oak	✔	✔
Ash	✔	✔
Birch species	✔	✔
Hornbeam	✔	
Wych elm	✔	
Field maple	✔	
Goat willow	✔	
Field layer species:		
Lesser celandine	✔	✔
Wood anemone	✔	
Meadowsweet	✔	
Germander speedwell	✔	
Male-fern	✔	
Lords and ladies	✔	✔
Wood-sedge	✔	✔
False brome	✔	✔

The number of species depends on the diversity of tree species and the niches they create. The chiffchaff, for instance, prefers mature woodland, while the spotted flycatcher prefers woodland edges. By contrast, relatively few mammals are totally dependent on woodland habitats. Originally, woods were home to wild boar and beaver, but these were hunted to extinction. The red squirrel has been confined to coniferous woodlands in the north and the Isle of Wight. Woodlands are still home to deer and the grey squirrel (introduced from North America in around 1900 and considered by many to be a pest), but of the smaller mammals only the common dormouse is an exclusively woodland animal.

Lowland heaths

Heathlands support a significant proportion of the UK population of woodlark, nightjar and Dartford warbler. Heathlands have been prey to 'improvement' for centuries, with 84 per cent of the original lowland heath having been lost (Figure 12.9). By the 1970s, the remaining heathland habitats were small and fragmented, under threat from agricultural intensification and afforestation. Salvation came in the form of the declining profitability of arable farming, a reflection of the reductions in price support introduced in the 1980s. Most of the small loss of heathlands in the 1990s was the result of urban development.

Figure 12.9

Heathland vegetation on the Suffolk sandlings threatened by afforestation

The future of the uplands

The UK uplands (land over 240 metres) comprise the bulk of the remaining wild countryside and are home to the greatest amount of natural vegetation. Upland communities include woodland, grassland, bog and heath. Changes in land use on Bodmin Moor in Cornwall reflect the trends in the uplands at large (Figure 12.10).

Peat bogs represent waterlogged soils supporting bog mosses and sedge. They are threatened by afforestation, over-grazing (which causes trampling and nutrient enrichment), and burning. In some areas, they have also suffered from heavy recreational use, which breaks up the peat and causes erosion.

Since 1918 massive planting has changed the wooded character of some uplands, especially in Wales and Scotland where 'blanket forestry' has become visually intrusive (Figure 12.11).

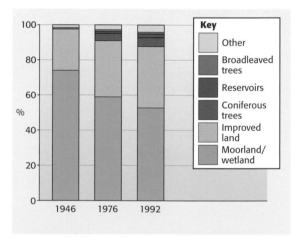

Figure 12.10

Land use change on Bodmin Moor, 1946–92

Figure 12.11

Afforestation on the Welsh borders

The word 'moor' is often used to denote all areas of uncultivated, unimproved grassland, heather, bracken or gorse. Upland areas lost 20 per cent of their moorlands between 1950 and 1980. The main pressures were agriculture and forestry. The Hill Livestock Compensation Allowance made it profitable to improve grassland and increase stocking levels, while grants and tax incentives for tree planting gave rise to 'blanket forestry' in some areas. In some areas, another threat was posed by the need for reservoirs for water storage.

In the uplands, the removal of the ancient forest cover, and subsequent use by livestock, resulted in dwarf shrub communities, dominated by the two heather species. This community may be maintained by shallow burning and grazing, but overgrazing leads to acid grasslands and a species-poor community dominated by grass and bracken. Undergrazing, on the other hand, can lead to a reversion to scrub and, ultimately, woodland. Thus, while heather moorlands are often perceived to be natural, they are, in fact, artificial and require careful management. In Wales, the Lake District and the western Pennines, acid grassland dominates, but further east, where rainfall is lower, managed heather moorland has survived.

Threats to the surviving moors include drainage, improvement, use of herbicides, wildfire, afforestation, inappropriate management, and recreational disturbance.

Moorland ecosystems are dominated by birds (Figure 12.12). The loss of moorland habitats led to a catastrophic decline in the population of black grouse, and affected the numbers of ptarmigan and golden eagles. Heather moors tend to be dominated by red grouse, golden plover and hen harrier. Today, the dominant mammals – sheep and, in Scotland, red deer – are domesticated animals. Otherwise, upland heaths support non-specific mammals like shrew, mouse, fox, weasel and stoat.

	Activity
1	Prepare an explanation of **a** the benefits of hedgerows to farmers and **b** the wider ecological benefits of hedgerows.
2	Most moorland environments have been created by human activity, so what are the arguments for protecting them? Answer this question with a series of concise bullet points.

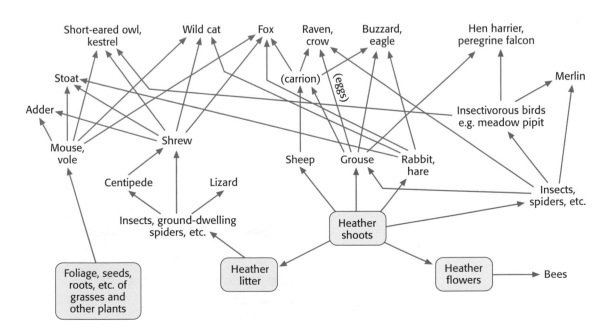

Figure 12.12

The food web in heathland environments

Declining biodiversity

Destruction or alteration of habitats has inevitably led to a decline in biodiversity. For example, the ploughing up of old grasslands in lowland areas has removed plants like bird's-foot trefoil, which in turn has eliminated the common blue butterfly from large areas.

Factors in declining biodiversity are:

- conversion to agriculture
- increased use of chemicals
- building development and road-building
- mineral workings
- drainage of wetlands
- afforestation
- poor land management.

The net effect of land use changes in the 40 years after the Second World War was a substantial reduction in biodiversity. Indicators of biodiversity include the area and character of woodland, the area and condition of SSSIs, and the population of wild birds. How these features have changed is outlined below:

- **Woodland:** There has been a long-term decline in the amount of ancient woodland. Surviving woodlands are often not managed, and new woodlands have, until recently, tended to be planted with a narrow range of species.

- **SSSIs:** while the total protected area has increased, 15 per cent of SSSIs have been found to be in an unfavourable or declining condition. Chalk grasslands are particularly vulnerable, yet two-thirds of the SSSIs in these localities were found to be in trouble.

- **The wild bird population:** birds are at or near the top of the food chain, so they are indicative of the state of many other wildlife species. Despite a slowdown in the 1990s, most species remain in decline (Figure 12.13). Agricultural intensification has resulted in a loss of winter food, largely through insecticides and herbicides. In addition, the switch from spring to autumn sowing has reduced the period when fields are occupied with stubble, a traditional source of winter food. Furthermore, the removal of hedgerows and small woodlands has resulted in a loss of nesting sites. The crops themselves used to provide nesting sites for farmland species like the skylark, but winter-sown cereals mature too quickly and become too dense for birds to establish nesting sites.

Until the 1980s, efforts to conserve habitats and species tended to occur independently from policies concerning agriculture. Early conservation measures, such as SSSIs, focused on creating special havens or reserves for wildlife. Elsewhere, farmers were being encouraged, albeit indirectly, to reduce biodiversity in the effort to grow more food. Protected areas thus tended to become isolated fragments enjoying special status. The two objectives came together during the 1980s, with conservationists arguing the need to look beyond the protected areas to the land around them. The decade saw the first systematic schemes offering payments to farmers to support conservation on farmland. These schemes grew

Figure 12.13

Declining population of wild birds in the UK, 1970–99

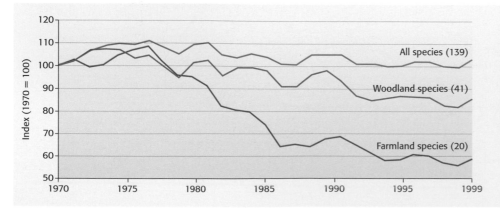

The skylark – a farmland bird once common but now under threat from intensive farming

in scope and coverage during the 1990s, with the establishment of agri-environmental programmes across Europe (Figure 12.14). Figure 12.15 shows two projects taking place under the Countryside Stewardship Scheme.

In 1992, the UK signed the Convention on Biological Diversity at the Rio Earth Summit, and subsequently launched a Biodiversity Action Plan, seeking to identify those habitats and species in greatest need of protection. Detailed national plans are being drawn up for each, and parallel work is going on locally.

Local Biodiversity Action Plans seek to conserve and enhance priority species and habitats within and beyond SSSIs. In the Peak District, separate plans have been drawn up for habitats and for species. For example, the plan for heather moorland identifies the need to improve the management of existing moors and is aimed at extending the total area covered. It also envisages the reintroduction of extinct species such as black grouse, the high brown fritillary butterfly and marsh club moss.

In the 1990s, agri-environment schemes proliferated and became available across the whole country, not just in specially-designated areas.

Countryside Stewardship Scheme

Payments are made for sensitive management activities, e.g. re-creating habitats, establishing wildlife corridors, and adopting measures to improve public access.

Arable Stewardship

Farmers are paid to undertake a range of measures, including limiting herbicide use, maintaining stubble through the winter, sowing spring rather than winter crops, and conserving field headlands. Capital grants are available for hedgerow laying and planting, and ditch restoration.

Hedgerow Initiative Scheme

Payments are made for the proper management of neglected hedges over a 10-year period.

Habitat Improvement Scheme

Encourages farmers to create new wildlife habitats by taking land out of cultivation for 20 years. This is intended to reinforce the set-aside scheme.

Woodland Grant Scheme/Farm Woodland Premium Scheme

Grants are available to farmers who create new woodlands or improve the management of existing ones.

Moorland Scheme

Farmers in upland areas are encouraged to improve moorland environments by reducing grazing densities and improving management regimes.

Figure 12.14

Habitat conservation in agriculture

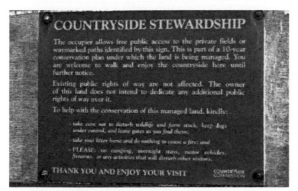

a Opening up more of the land for public access

b Woodland creation

Figure 12.15

Countryside Stewardship schemes

Activity

1   Explain why birds are a good indication of biodiversity.

2   With the aid of one researched example of each, explain how the following activities contribute to a decline in biodiversity:

   a   increased use of chemicals

   b   afforestation

   c   poor management of land.

Habitat conservation: protected habitats

Agri-environment schemes have contributed to a slowdown, and in some cases a reversal, of the loss of habitats in the 1990s (Figure 12.16). English Nature and the National Farmers Union have combined to produce a five-point plan for wildlife-friendly farming, pointing out that many schemes are low-cost or may even save money. Farmers are encouraged to:

- take stock of the natural assets on their farms and produce a farm map or conservation plan

- look after these natural assets by, for example, avoiding hedge-trimming in the bird-nesting season; matching grazing pressure to the environmental capacity of the land; clearing ditches only on one side at a time, or in rotation

- manage farm inputs and waste carefully, including the adoption of nutrient and waste management plans and the integration of codes of good agricultural practice for soil, water and air

- consider new opportunities for wildlife, such as creating new ponds and using set-aside opportunities intelligently

- join a scheme under the England Rural Development Programme.

SSSIs

Sites of Special Scientific Interest were introduced in 1949 in order to protect valued habitats, wildlife species or geological features (Figure 12.17). There are over 4000 SSSIs in England, covering over 1 million hectares, or about 8 per cent of the surface area (Figure 12.18). They represent the core conservation resource for the country.

When an SSSI is designated, owners and tenants are notified and they are then required to consult with the Countryside Agency before carrying out any changes in land use practice that might damage the scientific integrity of the site. At first, landowners were only obliged to consult and could still go ahead with damaging 'improvements'. SSSI designations could also be overridden by planners if jobs were at stake in proposed developments. In extreme cases, stronger protection was available under Nature Conservation Orders, but very few such designations were made. The arrangements were also very expensive, with farmers demanding compensation for 'income forgone'.

SSSIs now have greater protection. Under an Act passed in 2000, conservation agencies can refuse consent for damaging activities, and

Figure 12.16

Changes in area covered by particular habitats in England, 1990–98

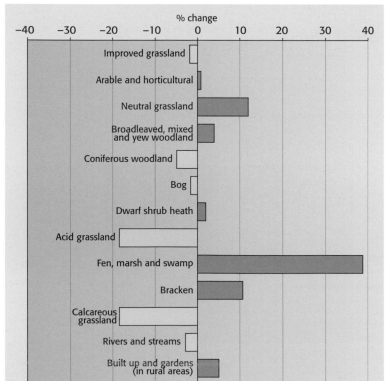

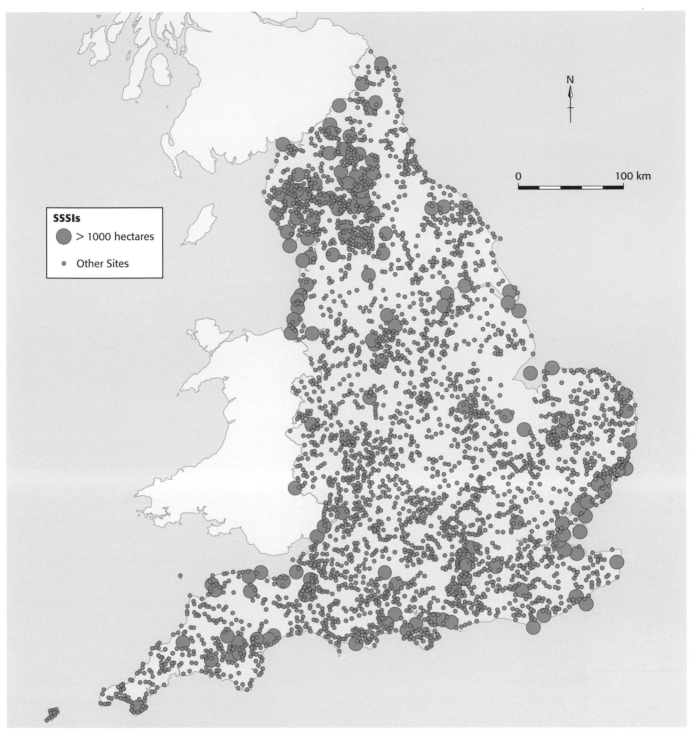

Figure 12.17

Sites of Special Scientific Interest in England

Figure 12.18

Coverage of conservation areas in England

	% land area
Sites of Special Scientific Interest	8.0
Special Areas of Conservation	5.0
Special Protection Areas	3.9
National Nature Reserves	0.6
National Parks	7.6
Areas of Outstanding Natural Beauty	15.6

heavier penalties may be incurred for damage to sites.

Thirteen per cent of SSSIs are damaged every year (Figure 12.19). In one well-publicised case, at Offham Down near Lewes in Sussex, a farmer ploughed up a major part of an SSSI in 1997 in order to gain from large EU subsidies to grow flax. He did the ploughing at night, using high-powered lamps to guide him. At Grove Farm,

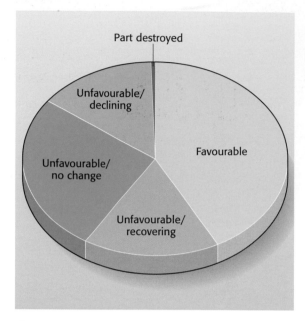

Figure 12.19

The condition of SSSIs in England

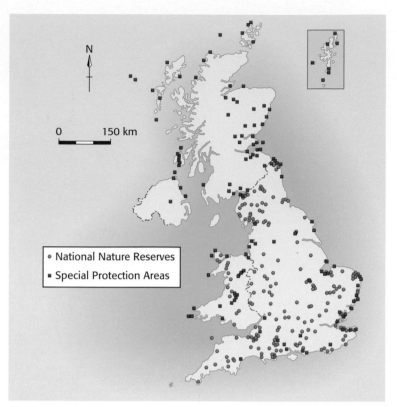

Figure 12.20

Areas designated for habitat conservation

near Yeovil, the owner's response to SSSI designation in 1987 was to plough up one of the meadows. Although the meadow was restored under a Nature Conservation Order, the owner continued to refuse to discuss any long-term management agreement, and demanded hefty payments in return for conservation. Despite the cost to the taxpayer, public access remains denied to most of this SSSI.

Nature Reserves

There are 200 National Nature Reserves (see Figure 12.20) covering over 80 000 hectares in England alone. These sites are also SSSIs, but are owned and administered either by English Nature or by charitable trusts. In addition, there are 635 local nature reserves owned by local authorities and covering almost 30 000 hectares. Nature reserves are managed primarily for the purpose of nature conservation, and they protect some of the most important areas of wildlife habitat.

The European context

In the 1990s the EU launched the 'Natura 2000 network', an ecological network of sites of international significance aimed at conserving rare and vulnerable habitats in representative biogeographical environments across the continent. Under various EU directives, the UK has designated some of its sites as **SPAs** (Special Protection Areas) with a focus on bird habitats. It is also in the process of nominating **SACs** (Special Areas of Conservation) for the protection of habitats of non-bird species. In these areas, measures are aimed at preventing any further decline in vulnerable species. However, even this level of protection is not proof against assault from development schemes. Spain's National Hydrological Plan aims to stave off a shortage of water in the south by diverting water from the Ebro system in the north-east. This project, involving a large-scale dam and reservoir, and river channel modification schemes, will adversely affect 82 Natura 2000 sites.

The Arctic National Wildlife Refuge in Alaska, and the two adjoining Canadian National Parks, together constitute North America's largest protected area (Figure 12.21). The tundra environment supports polar bear, musk ox, caribou and gray wolf communities. But there is a dilemma, in that the area is also rich in fossil fuel reserves. Drilling would disrupt caribou calving grounds and migration routes, and might compromise wilderness integrity, as well as posing the risk of a repeat of the 1989 *Exxon Valdez* disaster. In Canada all industrial activity is completely banned in National Parks, but in Alaska most citizens are in favour of development. This comes as no surprise – owing to Alaska's oil and gas wealth they receive a dividend from the state government instead of paying state income tax. Attempts to initiate exploratory drilling met with opposition in the 1990s, but the Republican administration in Washington has shown support for the oil industry.

Figure 12.21

Oil exploration and the Arctic National Wildlife Refuge

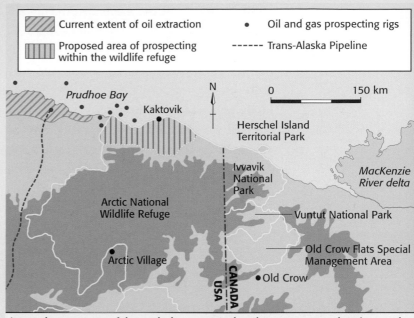

'More than two out of three Alaskans report that they support exploration on the coastal plain of the Arctic National Wildlife Refuge. A vast majority of Alaskans continue to support opening the ANWR to oil and gas exploration.'
www.anwr.org/features/support.htm

'Drilling will not serve as a long-term solution for our supposed energy crisis. Ruining the wilderness character of the Arctic Refuge forever would equate to less than a 180-day supply of oil.' www.protectthearctic.com

Size matters

Attempts to preserve endangered species by designating specially protected areas have not always succeeded, and there are many examples around the world of failed nature reserves. In 1923, a hilltop in Panama was made into an island by the creation of an artificial lake. Subsequent monitoring of Barro Colorado established that the island lost an average of 10 species per decade. The critical factor appears to have been size.

On islands the number of species is directly proportional to the area of the island (Figure 12.22). Many conservationists have concluded that nature reserves should be as large as possible. The fragmentation of natural communities does seem to increase the risk of extinction, as is evident from studies of chalk grasslands. Large areas are an advantage because:

- they increase the chance of preserving entire ecological communities

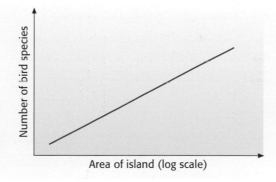

- they provide a more effective buffer against human interference
- species at higher trophic levels have larger area requirements, and if higher-level predators disappear, the *whole* ecosystem is likely to change.

Some conservationists argue that a large number of smaller reserves would maximise protection against disease and fire, but they agree that higher predators would be endangered. An additional problem with fragmentation is that the lack of communication between the

Figure 12.22

The species–area relationship: the example is for bird species on an island

individual reserves reduces the chance of migration of species in the event of external shocks and disturbances, such as climate change.

In Canada, the size of National Parks reflects competition from logging, mining and agriculture in surrounding areas. An area of around 1000 km² is required to support a viable population of wolves; much more is needed for bears. In actual fact, only 6 of the 39 parks are as large as the minimum critical area required for large mammals. Wolves and bears survive in the smaller parks only because there is sufficient wilderness in the areas beyond the park boundaries. A recent study has highlighted the dangers of relying on small fragmented 'islands' of conservation in a sea of habitat-destroying development.

Concerns about the fragmentation of conservation initiatives helped to move the EU agricultural policy further towards environmental practices in farming as a whole, not just in selected areas.

Case Study: Panworth Hall Farm

Panworth Hall Farm occupies 263 hectares in south Norfolk, near Swaffham. Over the last 25 years it has become more specialised in terms of arable crops (Figure 12.23), but diversification measures have been wholeheartedly adopted, as shown in Figure 12.24. Included in these measures are:

- **Set-aside** Land has been set aside on a non-rotational basis around the farm in order to maximise the conservation impact. It has been left uncultivated in strips of up to 20 metres around the **field headlands** with the intention of increasing the effective width of hedgerow habitats and encouraging populations of insects, butterflies, hares and songbirds. In addition, the strips have been drilled with kale, sunflower and turnip to provide for pheasants and partridges. The idea is to create areas where birds can nest and feed safely (Figure 12.25).

- **Countryside Stewardship Scheme** The farm management plan has involved the planting of new hedges, as well as grass margins to protect ditches from spray-drift. Beetle banks have been built up – these are small ridges sown with hummocky grasses, an ideal habitat for nesting birds and insects as well as fieldmice and voles. Water courses are protected from pollution by a 6 metre grass margin on either side.

- **Woodlands** A series of small (2 hectares) woods was established, with mixed species, to act as a refuge for game birds, as well as owls, songbirds, deer, voles and insects.

The result has been a significant increase in songbird populations. Grants from the government for conservation have compensated for the lost farming income, and shooting has become established as a recreational activity. The landowner reports: 'I can honestly say now that I get more pleasure out of the work we do in conservation than I do from day-to-day farming.'

	1975	2000
Winter wheat	84	128
Winter barley	44	–
Spring barley	36	–
Sugar beet	30	49
Oilseed rape	14	–
White turnip	6.5	–
Peas	22.5	32
Grass	18	18
Other	8	8
Set-aside	–	18
Countryside Stewardship	–	4
Woodland	–	6
Total	263	263

Figure 12.23

Changing land use on Panworth Hall Farm, 1975–2000 (hectares)

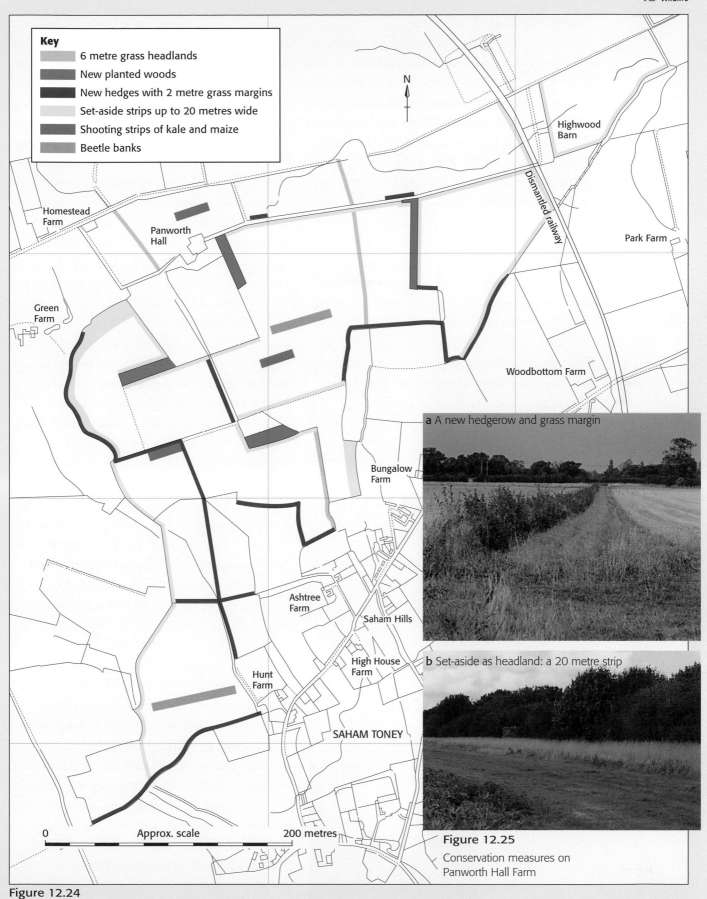

Key
- 6 metre grass headlands
- New planted woods
- New hedges with 2 metre grass margins
- Set-aside strips up to 20 metres wide
- Shooting strips of kale and maize
- Beetle banks

N

Highwood Barn

Homestead Farm

Panworth Hall

Dismantled railway

Park Farm

Green Farm

Woodbottom Farm

Bungalow Farm

a A new hedgerow and grass margin

Ashtree Farm

Saham Hills

High House Farm

Hunt Farm

SAHAM TONEY

0   Approx. scale   200 metres

b Set-aside as headland: a 20 metre strip

Figure 12.25

Conservation measures on Panworth Hall Farm

Figure 12.24

Agri-environmental schemes on Panworth Hall Farm

Sustainable forestry

After centuries of deforestation, the trend was reversed after 1918 with the creation of the Forestry Commission, which was responsible for increasing the country's self-sufficiency in timber products (Figure 12.26). The impact was felt largely on the uplands where afforestation took the form of huge expanses of conifer plantations, often dominated by a single species. In north Wales in the 1970s, Sitka spruce accounted for 71 per cent of new planting. Conifer monoculture has had several negative environmental impacts, including the acidification of soils and water, a reduction in ground flora (owing to the presence of a closed canopy for the whole year), and altered wildlife habitats. The more positive outcomes have included a reduced dependence on imports, and increased employment in rural areas.

Figure 12.26

Tree cover in the UK, 1995

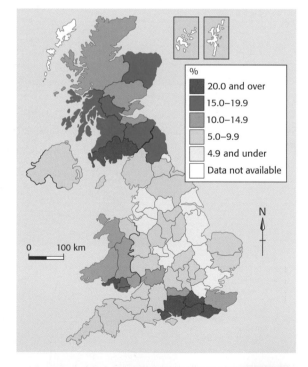

%

20.0 and over

15.0–19.9

10.0–14.9

5.0–9.9

4.9 and under

Data not available

0   100 km

N

Figure 12.27

Woodland management at Garston Wood

Since 1980 there have been significant changes in forestry practice, including less regimented planting, a greater mixing of species, and the increased use of broadleaved and native species. However, the most significant impact has been in terms of the objectives of forestry, as directed by the Forestry Commission through its management arm, Forest Enterprise. Timber production remains a central objective, but to this has been added the objectives of recreation and conservation. This more diverse approach has given rise to so-called 'consensus forestry' or 'multipurpose forestry'. The largest-scale example of this strategy is the plan for a 518 hectare National Forest in the East Midlands.

Multipurpose forestry still has to deal with conflicts if it is to be sustainable. The different objectives sometimes clash when it comes to detailed management issues. For example:

- **Open areas** These areas are good for conservation, providing a wide variety of niches, especially for deer, as well as recreation (picnic) facilities, but they reduce the potential for timber production and encourage weed growth.

- **Dead trees** Dead trunks are good for nature conservation because they provide habitats for birds and insects, but in amenity terms they represent safety hazards.

An interesting small-scale example is Garston Wood, an SSSI owned by the Royal Society for the Protection of Birds, which occupies 35 hectares on Cranborne Chase in Dorset. It is an ancient coppiced woodland in which management maintains a plagioclimax, preventing reversion to oak woodland (Figure 12.27). It functions as a sustainable resource in three senses:

- **Conservation** – the wood is rich in bluebells, wood anemones and primroses, a habitat for nightingales, turtle doves, badgers and fallow deer.

- **Recreation** – the wood is easily accessible, with a car park and signed paths.

- **Commercial wood production** – the hazel is still coppiced to meet local demand for hurdles and thatching spars.

a A multipurpose forest

b Visitor pressure

c Recreation facilities

Figure 12.28

Moors Valley Country Park
and Forest, Dorset

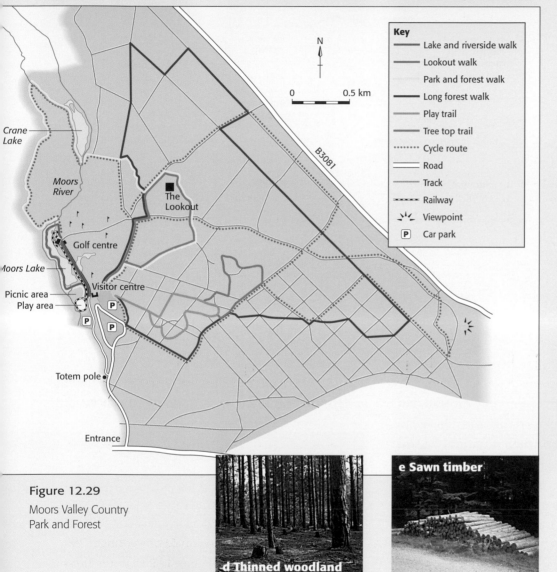

Key

— Lake and riverside walk
— Lookout walk
— Park and forest walk
— Long forest walk
— Play trail
— Tree top trail
····· Cycle route
— Road
— Track
---- Railway
☀ Viewpoint
Ⓟ Car park

N

0   0.5 km

Crane Lake
Moors River
Moors Lake
Moors River
The Lookout
Golf centre
Visitor centre
Picnic area
Play area
Totem pole
Entrance
B3081

Figure 12.29

Moors Valley Country
Park and Forest

d Thinned woodland

e Sawn timber

This lowland river valley was once largely grazed heathland, with some Scots pine woodlands around boggy tracts. It was planted with Corsican pine, covering 1500 hectares, but it is now run as a country park with recreational uses combined with commercial forestry. The layout of the Park is shown in Figure 12.29.

Sections of the forest with an area of 2–3 hectares are thinned annually for five years, and then clear-felled and replanted. The products of thinning are used for fencing, pallet wood and chipboard, while the felled timber (2500 trees per year) is used for construction.

This managed woodland is the setting for intensive recreational use, with a visitor centre, play areas, a narrow-gauge railway, golf course, and a dense network of woodland trails and cycle routes.

Activity

1   Explain why one large protected conservation area is generally seen as preferable to lots of smaller ones. Draw up a list of the possible exceptions, at different scales, to this principle.

2   Describe the environmental problems that have arisen as a result of large-scale afforestation in upland areas. Outline ways in which current management practices have sought to overcome these problems.

Part Four

Hazardous Environments

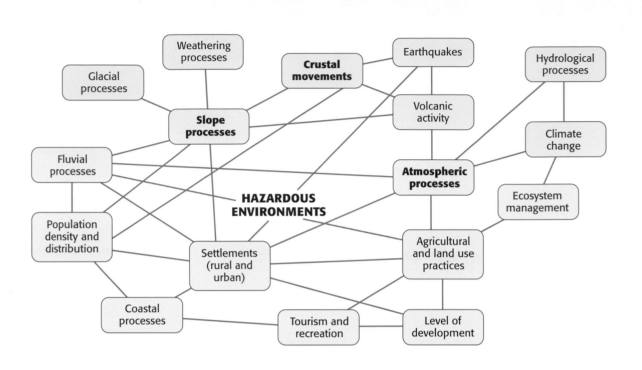

Thinking synoptically: hazardous environments

Introduction

Natural hazards are physical events or processes that have the potential to cause loss of life and damage to property. A **disaster** occurs when a natural hazard materialises and causes the extensive destruction of property and, quite often, a large numbers of fatalities. The severity or magnitude of a disaster depends not just on the scale of the hazard itself, but also on human factors, such as population distribution and density and economic development. Disparities in social and economic development between richer and poorer countries readily expose the differences between them in coping with disasters arising from natural hazards. Comparisons of **mitigation** and **resilience** measures produce marked – but not always expected – contrasts between nations of differing levels of economic development.

Part Four is divided into three chapters. Chapter 13 addresses the distribution, nature and impacts of crustal movements and the efforts made to reduce the variety of primary and secondary natural hazards

Figure 4.A
Mount Ruapehu erupting in New Zealand, 1995

associated with them. The distribution of major volcanic eruptions (Figure 4.A) and earthquakes is related to the structure of the Earth and, in particular, requires an understanding of plate tectonics.

Chapter 14 examines the hazards relating to movements of rock, soil and snow on slopes (Figure 4.B). Case studies provide an explanation of the rising number of landslides in developing countries, and methods taken to reduce slope hazards are also discussed. In order to understand this category of hazards, it is necessary to know how they are linked to rock types and geological structure, to the processes of weathering and erosion, soil type, hydrology, crustal movements and climate. Again, population density, population distribution and land use are important factors to take into account when examining the potential impact of these hazards.

Chapter 15 focuses on the nature and impact of tropical cyclones, hurricanes and tornadoes. Our knowledge of the formation, spatial and temporal distribution of tropical cyclones and hurricanes is closely bound to an understanding of energy budgets and the global distribution of winds and pressure systems. The impacts of **tropical storms** have considerable consequences for agriculture and food production, **tourism**, education and health, especially in less developed countries (see Figure 4.C). Differences between nations in terms of access to information about the development and movement of tropical cyclones, and the availability of measures to reduce their impact, is an important theme of this chapter.

The wider picture

Disasters stemming from natural hazards are usually reported as one-off events with a strong emphasis on the impacts of the moment, such as damage to buildings, loss of life and the speed – or lack of it – with which aid arrives. The longer-term consequences are,

Figure 4.B

Landslide, Santa Tecla, El Salvador, January 2001

Event	Date	Location	Population density (persons/km²)	Wind speeds	No. of deaths	Estimated cost	Cost as % of state GDP
Hurricane Hugo	September 1989	South Carolina, USA	43	211–250 km/h	20	US $ 7000 million	3.2%
Cyclone 07B	November 1996	Andhra Pradesh, India	261	175–220 km/h	1059	US $ 1303 million	3.7% *

* Percentage of the state's annual economic plan for 1997–98

Figure 4.C

Comparison of the impacts of two tropical cyclones

however, likely to be greater than the event itself. While these consequences will be much the same regardless of the cause and nature of the disaster, their impact will inevitably vary according to a country's economic, cultural, social and political circumstances. In practice, the greatest difference between countries, and between different communities, lies not in how they cope with the immediate problems of a disaster, but in their capacity to marshal resources to reduce its long-term effects. Even greater variation is apparent in the precautions they take to prevent natural hazards from ever causing disasters in the first place. Coping with natural hazards, whatever their nature or scale, must go beyond, and well beyond, a simple understanding of the geophysical processes involved.

Few, if any, countries can be regarded as completely successful in avoiding the adverse consequences of natural hazards, but only a handful of cross-national disaster studies have ever been carried out, making it difficult to establish the full long-term impact of disasters on different nations. Certainly, it is not at all safe to assume, for example, that less economically developed countries (LEDCs) will necessarily suffer greater long-term harm than more economically developed countries (MEDCs). Where people are used to a lifestyle based on the ready availability of consumer goods, and where reliance on a complex infrastructure of communications and services is high, the post-disaster recovery phase may take longer and cost more. On the other hand, for countries striving to develop their economies, the total cost of disasters in delaying, and even preventing, economic investment may be enormous.

Political, cultural and social attitudes are significant influences on how well nations and communities cope with the long-term impacts of disasters. Studies have shown that the quality of recovery planning has much more to do with local than national government, and that local officials commonly prefer to be perceived as doing something to help after the event rather than drawing up contingency plans in advance. Furthermore, local officials may not always be trained in hazard perception or identification, thus allowing more and more people to live in hazardous areas. This shortcoming is likely to be found in both more and less economically developed countries.

Ideally, the mitigation of long-term impacts should be guided by a country's, or a community's, vision of itself as a sustainable and resilient entity in the face of future disasters. In order to achieve this state of affairs, however, coordination of effort is necessary. Tightly-knit and organised communities, with all groups working together, are better placed than those where different interests are allowed to come into conflict. Strong links with political, social and economic institutions are likely to assist recovery, reduce the degree of isolation often caused by disasters, and lessen the need for long-term external aid. Ironically, it may take a disaster to trigger the development of policies and plans for coping competently with future events. Political and social priorities may be revised in the light of the loss of human life, and the inclusion of groups of people formerly disregarded by the planning process may emerge as a positive benefit. International agreements may also be needed, but may be difficult to secure when one nation's safety depends on another modifying its plans for economic advancement. For example, in south-east Africa in early 2000, the release of excess water from dams in neighbouring Zimbabwe aggravated the already severe flooding in Mozambique, adding to the scale of the disaster and its long-term consequences. Planned international cooperation will clearly be required to avoid a similar occurrence in the future.

When examining the case studies presented in the following chapters you should keep in mind the general economic, cultural, social and political backgrounds of the regions concerned. You will already be broadly familiar with these conditions from studying other aspects of the geography of contrasting countries from across the globe.

Essay questions

1 Discuss the view that the impact of natural hazards owes more to the level of development of a country, or region, than to the magnitude of the event.
2 Discuss the effectiveness of planning responses to earthquake hazards.
3 How important are human factors in explaining the causes of hazards resulting from mass movements?

Suggestions for further reading

D. Alexander (1995) *Natural Disasters*, UCL Press.

E. A. Bryant (1991) *Natural Hazards*, Cambridge University Press.

D. Chester (1993) *Volcanoes and Society*, Arnold.

K. Donert (2001) 'What are hurricanes?' *GeoActive* 12 (244), Nelson Thornes.

S. Frampton *et al.* (2000) *Natural Hazards*, Hodder & Stoughton.

G. O'Hare (2001) 'Hurricane 07B in the Godavari delta, Andhra Pradesh, India: vulnerability, mitigation and spatial impact' *Geographical Journal* 167(10): 23–38.

S. Oliver (2001) 'Natural hazards, some new thinking' *Geography Review* 14 (3): 2–4.

L. Newstead (2001) 'Montserrat volcanic eruptions 1995–1998' *Geofile* No.401, Nelson Thornes.

S. Ross (1998) *Natural Hazards*, Stanley Thornes.

J. Salmond (1994) 'Hurricanes: a predictable phenomenon' *Geography Review* 8(1): 117–22.

K. Smith (2001) *Environmental Hazards*, Routledge.

J. Whittow (1980) *Disasters*, Pelican.

Websites

Volcano World:
http://volcano.und.nodak.edu

Geo Resources (useful on volcanoes, earthquakes, landslides, hurricanes and tornadoes):
www.georesources.co.uk

US Geological Survey:
http://landslides.usgs.gov

North American Avalanche Centers:
www.avalanche.org

Cooperative Institute for Metrological Satellite Studies (CIMSS):
http://cimss.ssec.wisc.edu

University of Colorado:
www.colorado.edu/hazards

Kingston University:
www.king.ac.uk/~ce_s011

13 Hazards resulting from crustal movements

KEY THEMES

● A major hazard is present where plate boundaries coincide with large centres of population.

● Volcanoes and earthquakes can trigger a variety of primary and secondary hazards, especially on slopes.

● Earthquakes cause higher fatalities than volcanic eruptions.

● Monitoring of crustal movements has the potential to reduce loss of life from volcanic eruptions and earthquakes.

● Sharp contrasts exist between rich and poor countries in levels of preparedness and resilience to hazards arising from crustal movements.

The global distribution of crustal movement hazards

A majority of earthquakes and volcanic eruptions occur near plate boundaries (Figure 13.1). At destructive margins or boundaries that are created by collisions of either oceanic plates or oceanic and continental plates, complex changes in the subduction zone cause partial melting of the upper mantle and the oceanic and continental crusts (Figure 13.2). Melting occurs at about

100–200 km below the ground and the resulting magma eventually finds its way to the surface to produce explosive volcanoes. Friction in the subsiding zone brings about earthquakes in what is called the Benioff zone, which extends to a depth of about 700 km. Below this level, earthquakes cease because the plates are assimilated into the mantle. Arcs of volcanic islands characterise the subduction process taking place between two oceanic plates. Earthquake-prone

Figure 13.1

Location of the major plate margins, earthquakes and volcanic eruptions referred to in the text

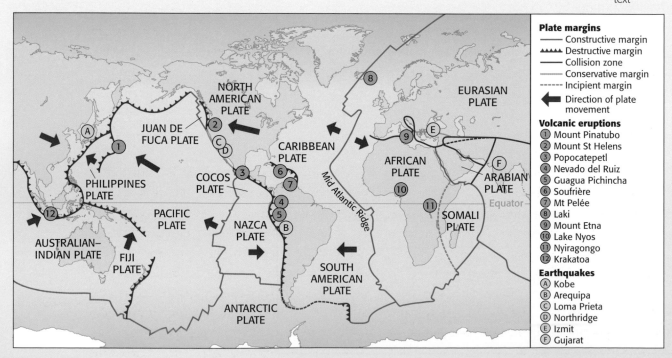

Plate margins
—— Constructive margin
▲▲▲▲ Destructive margin
—— Collision zone
—— Conservative margin
----- Incipient margin
◀ Direction of plate movement

Volcanic eruptions
① Mount Pinatubo
② Mount St Helens
③ Popocatepetl
④ Nevado del Ruiz
⑤ Guagua Pichincha
⑥ Soufrière
⑦ Mt Pelée
⑧ Laki
⑨ Mount Etna
⑩ Lake Nyos
⑪ Nyiragongo
⑫ Krakatoa

Earthquakes
Ⓐ Kobe
Ⓑ Arequipa
Ⓒ Loma Prieta
Ⓓ Northridge
Ⓔ Izmit
Ⓕ Gujarat

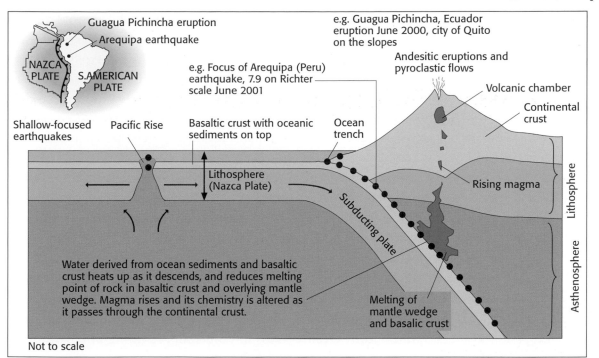

Figure 13.2

Formation of earthquakes and volcanic eruptions at the boundary of the South American continental and Nazca oceanic plates

ranges of fold mountains, such as the Andes in South America, reveal the collision of oceanic and continental plates. Where two continental plates collide, shallow earthquakes are likely but volcanic activity will be minimal. On the other hand, where continental plates slide past one another and a good deal of frictional resistance is encountered, for example along the San Andreas fault in California, earthquakes – often strong ones – are common. Volcanic eruptions are also possible along this type of plate boundary.

At constructive margins, such as the Mid-Atlantic Ridge, diverging plates allow mantle rocks to rise and, as pressure is released, melting occurs. The resulting magma moves towards the surface to produce lava flows and low-angle shield volcanoes. Shallow earthquakes may also occur but these margins are most clearly marked by volcanic islands.

A few volcanic eruptions occur within, rather than at the edges of, crustal plates. Such volcanoes form where plates move over hot spots created by convection currents rising from the mantle. The Hawaiian volcanoes have been produced in this way. The most active volcanic eruptions occur above the hot spot, but as the plate underlying the islands has moved slowly away to the north-west, the volcanoes that developed actively over the hot spot have become dormant.

Earthquakes may also occur within plates rather than at the margins. Pressure at plate boundaries is believed to cause stresses within the plate, leading to earthquakes. Earthquakes may also occur in response to changes in the distribution of magma well below the surface of the ground. Human activities can also encourage earthquakes to occur. Some are caused by subsidence following deep mining, while others are triggered by controlled nuclear explosions. Yet others are produced when reservoirs are filled and the weight of the water causes stress in the underlying rocks. Water may also help to lubricate and activate faults.

The natural characteristics of the Earth's crust create potential hazards where earthquakes and volcanic eruptions coincide with large centres of population. Thus earthquakes that occur in localities that are remote from people or their property are not, by definition, hazards. A majority of volcanic eruptions and earthquakes are located around the Pacific plate margin, an area also favoured for settlement. Japan is a good example. It is a country where a large percentage of the population is clustered in three major cities, all of which have experienced large earthquakes, notably Kobe in 1995. Indonesia, located at the junction of three plates, is also at risk. Many of that country's 150 million people live on highly fertile volcanic slopes, and two-thirds of all deaths caused by volcanic activity have occurred on such slopes where heavy tropical rainfall also brings about secondary hazards such as mudflows. The area between Indonesia and Japan is also highly susceptible to **tsunami**, which are large sea waves generated by volcanic and earthquake events. Other highly hazardous areas include the northern Andes and the Caribbean, which are also on plate margins. Colombia and Ecuador have several active and highly explosive snow-capped volcanoes, which can create dangerous mudflows. Over 90 per cent of earthquake-related deaths occur in LEDCs, and this is a reflection of the fact that **human vulnerability** is often more important than the magnitude of the event itself. In contrast, the highest property damage occurs in the MEDCs such as the USA and Japan.

The impact of volcanoes and earthquakes on life and property
Volcanic hazards

Constructive margins such as mid-ocean ridges produce gently-sloping volcanoes and lava plateaus because **basic lavas** tend to be relatively free-flowing. Eruptions are more effusive and less explosive and occur more frequently than those at destructive margins because the lava is less viscous and less rich in gases. In contrast, at destructive margins **intermediate** and **acidic lavas** form steep-sided volcanoes because the lava is highly viscous and rich in gases. Between eruptions magma collects underground, and over time pressure is exerted on the solidified lava above until eventually it gives way and a fresh layer of lava and **ash** is deposited. Successive eruptions, each depositing a layer of lava and ash, produce a composite or **strato-volcano**. Very

viscous lava, trapped by a solid plug of lava, may eventually break through a weakness in the side of a volcano causing a highly explosive lateral blast or **basal surge**. Hot spots such as the Hawaiian islands produce low-sided, spreading cones made of basalt. Eruptions are frequent and fountains of lava are often thrown high into the air.

Lava flows, poisonous gases and **pyroclastics** are all primary hazards associated with volcanic events. Carbon monoxide, carbon dioxide and hydrogen sulphide released from eruptions, or from lava flows, can asphyxiate humans and animals. Such events are rare – one example was the explosive release of carbon dioxide which occurred in 1986 at the volcanic Lake Nyos in Cameroon, resulting in the deaths of nearly 2000 people.

Lava flows generally extend for between 1 and 4 km and are between 10 and 100 metres thick. Basic lavas extend further and are thinner than acidic flows. Flows do not normally cause loss of life, although there have been exceptions, such as when lava spilled from a crater during an eruption of Nyiragongo in Zaire in 1977 and flowed rapidly downhill, killing 72 people. The main threats posed by lava flows are the destruction of crops and homes, and the rendering of soils temporarily infertile. In 1783 extensive flows from the 25 km long Laki fissure in Iceland overran farmland, while fluorine gas contaminated grass, killing livestock and causing a famine that claimed 10 000 lives. In November 2000, sulphur dioxide gas and ash emitted from Mount Popocatepetl, an active volcano in Mexico, threatened 30 000 people living in nearby villages, many of whom were prevented from reaching fields to harvest their maize. Vineyards and orange groves on the slopes of Mount Etna in Sicily have been periodically destroyed by flows. The July 2001 eruption damaged a ski station and threatened to overrun the village of Nicolosi, a village of 5000 people.

Pyroclastic falls are produced when volcanic material is thrown into the air during explosive eruptions. They are generally associated with more explosive, acidic volcanoes. The size of the material deposited during a pyroclastic fall varies from less than 4 mm to greater than 32 mm in diameter.

A widespread component of pyroclastic falls is ash. The distribution of this deposit is influenced by wind direction, and its thickness declines away from the volcanic vent. Ash can cover wide areas, burying soil, blocking rivers and roads, contaminating grazing land and water supply, ruining crops, starting fires, damaging machinery and aircraft engines, as well as asphyxiating or causing breathing difficulties in animals and humans. Heavy falls of ash can also cause roofs to collapse, as in the case of the Mount Pinatubo eruption. More indirectly, ash particles can affect temperatures and rainfall. Particles can absorb and scatter solar radiation leading to a reduction of surface temperatures. They can also act as condensation nuclei encouraging rainfall.

Case Study: Mount Pinatubo, Philippines

In June 1991, Mount Pinatubo on the island of Luzon in the Philippines (Figure 13.3) erupted and sent an ash cloud 35 km into the sky. The previous eruption had occurred 500 years before and the mountain had since become covered in dense forest, so many of the 100 000 people resident on its slopes were unaware that they were living on a volcano.

Precursors to the eruption were several earthquakes and emissions of ash and steam. Between 12 and 15 June 1991, large volumes of ash and pyroclastic material flowed down the mountain, destroying homes and agricultural land on the rich volcanic slopes. Heavy rain from Typhoon Yunga mixed with the ash to create mudflows or **lahars**. Ash silted-up rivers, causing them to overflow and flood villages and crops. About 300 people were killed from the effects of lahars and from the collapse of roofs under the heavy weight of the wet ash. A total of 60 000 people were evacuated from the slopes immediately before the eruption – otherwise the death toll would have been much higher. A further 500 people died as the result of the poor conditions in relocation camps, and from lahars that occurred from time to time in the years following the eruption.

The eruption also released large quantities of sulphur dioxide, which combined with water to create a haze that reduced global temperatures by 0.4°C in 1992–93. Two US military bases on the island were seriously damaged and have since closed, bringing economic hardship for those local people who depended on the bases, directly or indirectly, for their employment.

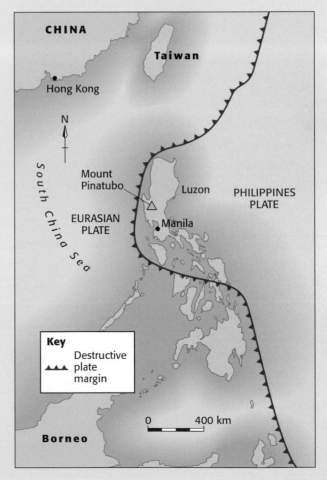

Figure 13.3

The location of Mount Pinatubo

One of the most devastating hazards associated with volcanic eruptions is a **pyroclastic flow** or **nuée ardente**. A hot, glowing cloud of gas and rock fragments, often riding on a cushion of air trapped underneath it, moves rapidly down the mountainside at speeds of up to 100 km/h, destroying all before it. In the 20th century, this form of eruption was responsible for 70 per cent of all volcano-related deaths. The hazard is associated with acidic volcanoes and is thought to occur when pressure builds up behind a plug of viscous solidified lava in a volcanic vent. Eventually the plug is broken and there is a highly explosive eruption. One of the most devastating nuée ardentes in history occurred when Mont Pelée, a strato-volcano on the Caribbean island of Martinique, erupted in 1902. The flow moved rapidly downslope, asphyxiating 29 000 people and destroying the town of St Pierre. Pyroclastic flows are sometimes preceded by a basal surge – a lateral explosion from the side of a volcano such as occurred when Mount St Helens erupted in 1980.

Case Study: Mount St Helens, Washington, USA

On 18 May 1980, Mount St Helens, a snow-covered strato-volcano in the Cascade Range in Washington State, USA, erupted after a dormant period of 123 years (Figure 13.4). Indications of an impending eruption were a swarm of earthquakes measuring 3.0 on the **Richter scale**, a small ash and gas eruption in late March, and a developing bulge which had been detected by tiltmeters on the north flank of the volcano.

On 18 May an earthquake measuring 5.1 on the Richter scale, caused by an injection of magma under the north flank, triggered a **debris avalanche**. A mixture of rock, glacier ice and soil flowed into Spirit Lake and then down North Fork of the Toutle River, filling the valley with 100 metres of debris. As the avalanche moved away, the magma plug and groundwater suddenly de-pressurised, creating a lateral blast of hot gases which exploded from the north side of the volcano and travelled rapidly northwards, flattening trees for up to 25 km and lowering the summit of the mountain by 400 metres. This blast, which overtook the avalanche, caused many of the 57 fatalities that occurred as the combined result of blast and pyroclastic injuries, burns, and the inhalation of poisonous ash and gases. The blast was followed by pyroclastic flows. The avalanche and the blast exposed the magma conduit and an ash cloud rose 20 km into the sky and spread north-eastwards, covering the town of Yakima, some 150 km away, with 1.5 cm of ash.

The ash made roads slippery and reduced visibility. Fish, some in hatcheries, perished as ash fell into lakes and streams, clogging their gills and raising the temperature of the water. Crops were destroyed, or subsequently produced low yields, because ash settled on leaves, impeding photosynthesis. Electricity supplies were interrupted and sewers were blocked, and the ash damaged car engines. Melted snow and ice, together with water displaced from Spirit Lake, mixed with the ash to create lahars which were responsible for most of the property damage that occurred, as roads, houses and bridges in the Toutle Valleys were destroyed. Sediment eventually found its way into the Columbia River, reducing the size of the shipping canal, which subsequently had to be dredged. Although the volcano had been carefully monitored prior to the eruption, the scale and timing of the eruption were not predicted.

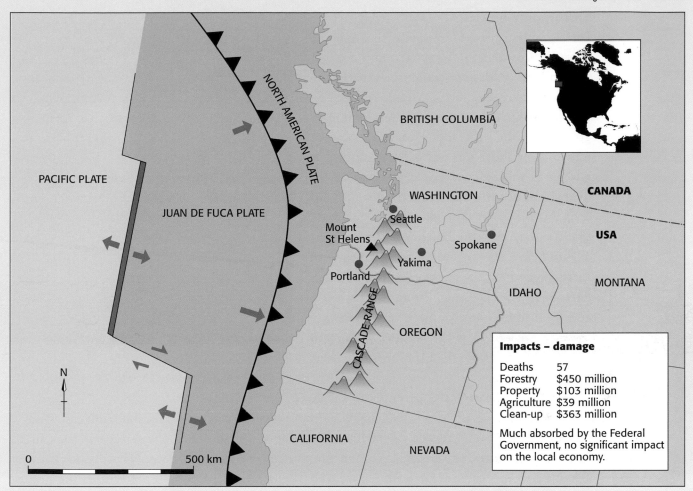

Figure 13.4

The location of Mount St Helens and impacts of the eruption

Within the figure:

PACIFIC PLATE

JUAN DE FUCA PLATE

NORTH AMERICAN PLATE

BRITISH COLUMBIA

WASHINGTON

Seattle

Mount St Helens

Spokane

Yakima

Portland

CASCADE RANGE

OREGON

IDAHO

MONTANA

CANADA

USA

CALIFORNIA

NEVADA

N

0   500 km

Impacts – damage

Deaths   57
Forestry $450 million
Property $103 million
Agriculture $39 million
Clean-up $363 million

Much absorbed by the Federal Government, no significant impact on the local economy.

Activity

1 With reference to the Mount St Helens case study:

  a Explain which plate movements were responsible for the eruption.

  b The eruption is well known for the variety of its products. Draw a diagram summarising the hazards it created.

  c Suggest reasons why 57 people died, given that an eruption in May was expected.

2 Suggest why the Pinatubo eruption was ten times larger than that of Mount St Helens.

3 Research the reasons for the higher number of fatalities in the Pinatubo eruption.

4 Long-term effects of natural hazards are often more damaging than the short-term impacts. To what extent is this true for the Mount St Helens and Pinatubo eruptions?

Earthquake hazards

Earthquakes are caused by stresses that build up along lines of structural weakness until friction is overcome and the strain is released in a sudden movement along a fault plane. The point at which the stress is released underground is called the **focus**, and the location immediately above this on the Earth's surface is known as the **epicentre**. Deep-seated earthquakes can occur up to 700 km below ground level, but the most damaging earthquakes are shallow-focused – that is, they occur less than 40 km below the surface. The magnitude of earthquakes is measured on the Richter scale. Earthquakes with a magnitude of between 5 and 8 cause the most damage. Another more subjective measure is the **Modified Mercalli scale**, which describes the likely physical effects of an earthquake.

Earthquakes cause the ground to shake, which encourages buildings and bridges to collapse, roads and railways to buckle, and pipes carrying water, sewage and gas to fracture. Leaking gas pipes often create a fire hazard, and in the 1906 San Francisco earthquake it was fire that killed more people than the collapsing buildings. Loss of historic buildings can damage tourism, especially for LEDCs which may depend heavily on foreign earnings. For example, Arequipa in Peru, a World Heritage Site containing many historic buildings and an important 19th-century cathedral, was hit by an earthquake in June 2001 (Figure 13.5).

A large earthquake tends to cause more damage than a smaller event, but much will depend on the duration of the shaking, rate of acceleration of the movement, and distance from the epicentre. The time of day when the hazard strikes also influences the number of fatalities; the highest number occur during the night, or in the cool of the day when people are asleep or at work. Large numbers of fatalities often occur in LEDCs because many buildings in urban areas may have been poorly and hurriedly constructed and regulations are

Figure 13.5

Clearing debris in Arequipa, Peru, after the earthquake in June 2001

ignored (see the Gujarat and Izmit case study). Homes made of adobe, a type of clay brick common in LEDCs, are also prone to collapse. It is estimated that 90 per cent of the homes damaged by the earthquake that hit Peru in June 2001, and which resulted in 47 deaths and 550 injuries, were made of adobe and roofed with sheets of corrugated iron.

The nature of the underlying geology and soils also influences the degree of damage that is caused. Buildings constructed on soft sediments such as alluvium, sands and clays are at greater risk of collapse than those built on solid rock. For example, the central area of Mexico City was extensively damaged by an earthquake in 1985 partly because it is constructed on an old lake-bed. Often a number of factors coincide. The earthquake that struck Kobe in 1995 caused widespread damage and 5300 deaths because the area was densely populated, many buildings had been constructed on soft sediments and landfill, and it happened at lunchtime when food was being prepared on open fires. The fires, encouraged by high winds, quickly spread, causing significant loss of life.

Gujarat

In January 2001, the state of Gujarat in India experienced an earthquake measuring 7.9 on the Richter scale (Figure 13.6). The epicentre was 20 km north of the town of Bhuj. It was the most powerful earthquake to hit India since 1950. An estimated 30 000 people were killed and 150 000 injured, and 1 million were made homeless as a result of the disaster. The fatalities were so high because the earthquake was strong and it struck a newly industrialised area of India. Large numbers of unskilled, landless labourers had recently moved here from all over India to find work and were accommodated in poorly designed buildings. Many people were inside the buildings when the earthquake struck, watching the anniversary celebrations of the Indian Republic on television. Several large towns were badly damaged, including Bhachau, Anjar and Bhuj. More than half of the homes and four hospitals in Bhuj, a town of 150 000, were destroyed. Ahmadabad, the state capital and a booming diamond-cutting and textile centre, was also affected. Temples dating from the 9th century in the neighbouring region of Saurashtra were destroyed. The museum in Bhuj, which contained valuable artefacts dating from the medieval period when the city was on an important trade route, was destroyed.

Gujarat is located in a highly tectonic area where earthquakes have occurred in the recent past. It is an economically important Indian state and has received a lot of foreign and domestic investment. It is rich in natural resources and includes Kandla, India's largest port. As a consequence of its prosperity many companies offered help after the disaster.

Izmit

In August 1999, an earthquake measuring 7.4 hit western Turkey (Figure 13.7). The epicentre was near the industrial city of Izmit, 88 km from Istanbul. Twenty thousand people were killed. Multi-storey apartment blocks collapsed, minarets fell, roads and bridges were destroyed, power-lines were brought down, and a fire started at a large refinery near the city. The earthquake also caused a tsunami in Izmit Bay, which smashed many boats. After the earthquake

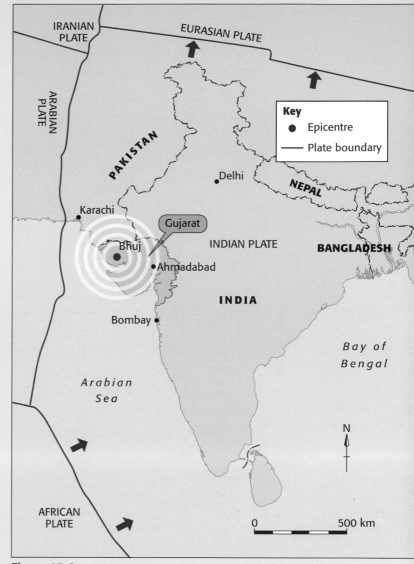

Figure 13.6

Location of the Gujarat earthquake

many people, fearing aftershocks, attempted to leave the city, causing severe road congestion.

Several factors contributed to the high number of fatalities. There was no obvious warning, which prevented evacuation, and the earthquake occurred at 3.00 am when many people were asleep inside buildings. Many who died were living in poorly-constructed buildings recently erected to accommodate migrant workers who had moved into the area to take advantage of the booming economy.

The earthquake was caused by movement along an active transform fault which is located across northern Turkey. The Anatolian fault is near the surface and can be seen from ground level. Movement along the fault has produced an earthquake stronger than 6.7 on the Richter scale every 6 years for the past 50 years.

In November 1999, a further earthquake hit Duzce, a town halfway between Istanbul and Ankara. The earthquake measured 7.1 on the Richter scale and killed 374 people. Istanbul, also on the fault-line and home to 9 million people, could also be struck in the near future. Like Izmit, Istanbul has recently experienced considerable economic growth and an influx of migrants who live in poor-quality housing.

Figure 13.7

Location of the Izmit earthquake

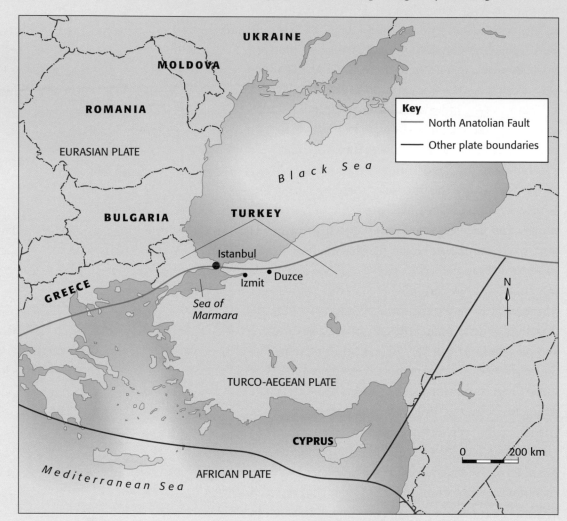

Secondary hazards

Both volcanic eruptions and earthquakes are responsible for a range of secondary hazards, including lahars, mudflows, tsunami, rock falls, snow and rock avalanches, and **landslides** and **glacial bursts**. Landslides, snow and rock avalanches and rock falls are more commonly associated with earthquakes (see Chapter 14), but may also be triggered by volcanic activity. Slope failure and building collapse may be encouraged by **soil liquefaction**.

Lahars are estimated to cause 10 per cent of all volcanic-related fatalities. They can travel up to 100 km/h and cover 300 km² of land. They may be formed in a number of ways; some authorities distinguish between primary lahars, created as the result of the eruption itself, and secondary lahars produced by other causes. A lahar may form when rainfall, sometimes encouraged by volcanic dust acting as condensation nuclei, mixes with ash. Alternatively, ash may mix with water from another source, such as a crater lake which has burst during an eruption. Yet others are produced when ash combines with water from snow-caps melting during an eruption, or from rivers impounded by nuée ardentes which eventually breach. Mudflows can bury houses, block roads, destroy bridges, cover soil and crops, and impound or silt-up rivers, eventually causing flooding. In areas of high rainfall they can continue to threaten settlements well after the eruption, as in the case of the Pinatubo eruption. One of the worst recent disasters occurred when Nevado del Rúiz, a high strato-volcano in Colombia, South America, erupted in 1985. Part of an ice-cap melted and the water combined with ash to create a lahar which travelled at 45 km/h down the Lagunillas valley. The mudflow removed soils, buildings and trees, and at the canyon mouth spilled out over the town of Armero, crushing or suffocating 20 000 people who were buried under an 8 metre thick flow.

Tsunami are large sea-waves which drown people living in coastal settlements and damage property. They are relatively rare events associated with crustal movements which cause a sudden vertical or horizontal displacement of sea water. Such displacements may stem directly from earthquakes that register 6.5 or more on the Richter scale, or they may be caused by coastal volcanic eruptions creating massive rock movements in the form of landslides. Commonly, tsunami average 6 metres in height, but are known to reach 30 metres. Narrow bays and inlets can concentrate their power. Japan and Indonesia are highly prone to these waves, many of which are locally generated. Others, which develop in the Pacific basin, affect the Hawaiian Islands and the area between Japan and Alaska and down the west coast of South America. A majority of tsunami form in the Pacific basin because this area is tectonically unstable and it contains a large expanse of ocean. Some 22 countries around the basin are at risk.

The worst known disaster occurred when Krakatoa in Indonesia erupted in 1883. The disturbance of the crust created by the eruption displaced a great volume of sea water and produced a tsunami 35 metres in height, which drowned 36 000 people in the Pacific basin. Other parts of the world, however, are not free of risk. In Europe in 1775, the death of 30 000 people occurred as a direct result of a tsunami created by an earthquake centred on Lisbon in Portugal. On an even greater scale is the mega-tsunami which is predicted to occur should part of the unstable Cumbre Vieja volcano on the Canary Island of La Palma collapse into the sea (Figure 13.8). Within five minutes of the collapse, scientists predict that a dome of water about 1.5 km in height would be created which, in turn, would generate waves up to 100 metres high travelling outwards in every direction at initial speeds of up to 800 km/h. Waves close to this height would reach the Saharan coast of Africa in less than an hour, while Britain would experience waves in the order of 12 metres after six hours. The impact on the other side of the Atlantic Ocean would be even greater. Here, it is predicted that tsunami close to 40 metres in height would reach the eastern seaboard of North America just nine hours after the landslide. Such waves would inflict serious devastation up to 9 km inland, effectively destroying the major eastern cities. While many natural hazards are perceived as local events, the predicted magnitude of the La Palma collapse, despite its origin in a relatively remote and lightly-peopled location, is likely to be so extensive that countries positioned well away from it will be seriously affected. At the same time, it is hard to see how effective precautions might be taken by any nation to mitigate the ensuing disaster.

Landslides may be triggered by injections of highly viscous magma under the volcano at a shallow depth prior to an eruption. Slopes become oversteepened, creating debris avalanches as in the case of the Mount St Helens eruption.

A **glacial burst** occurs when a volcano erupts beneath a thick ice-cap, melting a large volume of ice. Water then flows down the valley, threatening life and property. This process occurred in Iceland in 1996 when a volcanic eruption under the Vatnajökull ice-cap melted basal ice, which collected in a sub-glacial lake. Water eventually

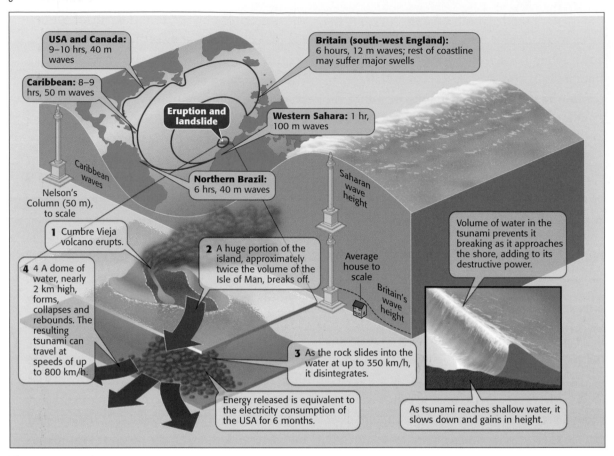

USA and Canada: 9–10 hrs, 40 m waves

Britain (south-west England): 6 hours, 12 m waves; rest of coastline may suffer major swells

Caribbean: 8–9 hrs, 50 m waves

Eruption and landslide

Western Sahara: 1 hr, 100 m waves

Caribbean waves

Nelson's Column (50 m), to scale

Northern Brazil: 6 hrs, 40 m waves

Saharan wave height

1 Cumbre Vieja volcano erupts.

2 A huge portion of the island, approximately twice the volume of the Isle of Man, breaks off.

Average house to scale

Britain's wave height

Volume of water in the tsunami prevents it breaking as it approaches the shore, adding to its destructive power.

4 4 A dome of water, nearly 2 km high, forms, collapses and rebounds. The resulting tsunami can travel at speeds of up to 800 km/h.

3 As the rock slides into the water at up to 350 km/h, it disintegrates.

Energy released is equivalent to the electricity consumption of the USA for 6 months.

As tsunami reaches shallow water, it slows down and gains in height.

Figure 13.8

The impact of the predicted Canary Island tsunami

escaped and flowed down a valley, destroying bridges and roads. Fortunately the event was predicted and no lives were lost because roads had been closed beforehand.

Responding to perceived levels of danger

People living in hazardous environments can take a number of measures to reduce the impact of a disaster. For **risk management** to be effective, all the necessary measures need to be planned and implemented together; in reality such an integrated approach is rarely achieved. The ability to manage hazards effectively is strongly related to a country's level of development – which is why the scale of a disaster is often a function of human vulnerability rather than the magnitude of the physical event. A precursor to effective hazard management is **risk assessment** (Figure 13.9). This procedure

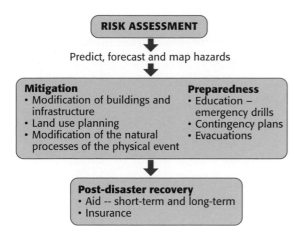

Figure 13.9

Steps to reduce exposure to hazards

identifies hazards that might occur, as well as their likely probability, magnitude, and social and economic impacts. It also involves assessing the ability of a society to cope with a disaster.

One method of predicting when a volcanic eruption or earthquake is likely to occur is to examine the pattern of past events. There is some evidence to suggest that earthquakes re-occur at regular intervals, an observation explained by the tendency for pressure at a fault to build up at a constant rate and then be released. For example, the Parkfield fault in California appears to have a **recurrence interval** of 22 years. Another approach is to identify localities along active fault-lines where earthquakes have *not* occurred – zones known as **seismic gaps** – and then to assume that pressure is building up and that a failure is likely to occur in the near future.

Despite improvements in technology only one earthquake has ever been successfully predicted, that which occurred in Haicheng in China in 1976. One difficulty with earthquake prediction is that faults can move in different ways. Another problem is that knowledge of fault locations is incomplete, which is why the 1995 Kobe earthquake in Japan and the Northridge earthquake in California in 1994 were not predicted.

Volcanic events are easier to predict than earthquakes because there is usually more warning of the impending eruption, and the location where the event will occur is known. As previously noted, acidic volcanoes produce less frequent but more explosive eruptions than basic volcanoes. Nevertheless, there are difficulties. The existence of long dormant periods between eruptions from acidic volcanoes means that patterns are difficult to detect simply because records have not been kept for long enough. Some volcanoes, such as Mauna Loa in Hawaii, exhibit a random pattern of eruptive behaviour, whereas in other cases – Hekla on Iceland for example – the likelihood of eruption increases steadily with the passage of time from the previous eruption. Another difficulty, well illustrated by the eruption of Mount Etna in July 2001, is that vulcanologists cannot be certain from where, and in which directions, the lava will travel.

So-called 'vital signs' immediately preceding an earthquake or volcanic eruption are very useful in forecasting the occurrence of a hazardous event. Foreshocks are often a precursor to a major earthquake, and earthquake activity often increases prior to a volcanic eruption as magma moves towards the surface. This movement may also cause the sides of a volcano to change shape, or the ground surface to deform or bulge. These changes can be detected by tiltmeters which measure alterations in ground-slope angles. Serial satellite images taken near volcanoes over a known period of time can also detect changes in the shape of the ground. Other indications of an impending eruption are changes in the temperature and chemistry of the steam in warm springs and the lava within volcanic vents. Other vital signs include localised uplift or subsidence of the land and changes in the **electric resistivity** of the country rock. Some people have also reported changes in animal behaviour prior to an earthquake.

While the occurrence of tsunami is closely linked to crustal disturbances, their ability to cause destruction at locations well away from their point of origin makes local-scale predictions more difficult. Where they occur frequently, they may be preceded by a draw-back of water along the coast, which local people recognise as a warning of the need to retreat to higher ground. Elsewhere, warnings may be given only if tsunami are observed in sufficient time while they are still moving across the open ocean.

The findings from a risk assessment exercise can inform decisions about which mitigation measures to take. Hazard maps can identify locations at highest risk and places where mitigation efforts should be focused. Risk can be reduced by:

- attempting to physically modify the event
- constructing hazard-resistant buildings and infrastructure
- educating people about the dangers posed by hazards
- issuing warnings
- devising evacuation and emergency plans
- land use planning.

Mitigation measures fall into two basic categories: those aimed at intervening in the natural processes of the hazard, and those designed to reduce its impact. Included in the former category are attempts to reduce the build-up of stress along fault lines by injecting liquids to lubricate rock movement. Most measures, however, fall into the latter category. Rock barriers and channels may be constructed to divert lava flows, as for example in the July 2001 eruption of Mount Etna. Water can be sprayed onto the surface of a lava flow to cool and slow it down. The speed of a flow can also be reduced by direct bombing of the lava, which encourages cooling by exposing more of it to the air. Infrastructure and buildings can be strengthened to resist earthquake shaking. Buildings enclosed in a steel frame with deep foundations and cross-beams to support walls and floors are more likely to survive an earthquake than those without these modifications. The installation of automatic systems to shut off electricity and gas supplies is beneficial in preventing fire, which is a common secondary hazard associated with earthquakes. Bridges made of reinforced steel and concrete resist shaking, while flexible gas and water piping is less likely to fracture than rigid pipes. Steeply-pitched roofs on homes in volcanic areas help to shed the heavy, wet ashfall which otherwise would cause them to collapse. Shortcomings in building design and lax adherence to building codes are often the reasons for the high level of fatalities caused, especially by earthquakes in the economically poorer countries of the world. Officials may ignore building regulations if they appear to be discouraging investment and the development of the country.

In highly developed localities such as California, the construction of earthquake-resistant housing has resulted in fewer deaths during earthquake events (Figure 13.10). However, some buildings inevitably pre-date the introduction of improved strengthening techniques and, moreover, there is now concern that a heavy reliance on structural solutions may encourage people to continue to live in hazardous zones when other locations would be preferable.

Education, emergency planning, warnings and evacuations can all reduce the impact of a disaster but they depend for their success on improving the **risk perception** of those living in hazardous environments. Education measures include informing the public of the risks and explaining what they should do in the event of a volcanic eruption, for example. Video footage about volcanic hazards shown to local people prior to the eruption of Pinatubo helped to persuade them to evacuate. In California, guidance is widely available about what to do should an earthquake occur; earthquake drills are common in schools, and contingency plans for the deployment of emergency services are in place should a disaster occur. Past experience suggests that it is vital to reach earthquake victims quickly before they die from shock, hypothermia or injury and, therefore, effective planning is essential. In LEDCs the fact that this help is not usually available immediately accounts for the high level of fatalities.

Improvements in the monitoring of earthquakes and volcanic eruptions has significantly reduced the loss of life in recent times when warnings and evacuations are heeded. The

Earthquake	Loma Prieta	Northridge
Location	Epicentre 16 km east of Santa Cruz and 95 km south of San Francisco	Epicentre at Northridge, an urbanised suburb of Los Angeles, 32 km north-east of central Los Angeles
Date	5.04 pm, 17 October 1989	4.31 am, 17 January 1994
Magnitude (Richter scale)	6.9	6.8
Cause	Movement along the San Andreas fault; Pacific Plate moving north on a locked section	Movement along the newly identified San Fernando thrust fault
Fatalities	67	66
Estimated losses	US $600 000 million	US $30 000 million
Impacts	• Section of San Francisco–Oakland Bay Bridge collapsed, killing motorists • Airports closed • Fire consumed city block in Marina district of the Bay area • National Guard called out to control looting in Oakland • Modern high-rise buildings throughout the area sustained little damage • Candlestick Park sports stadium filled with spectators but withstood severe damage • Some buildings collapsed in Santa Cruz • Marina district in San Francisco suffered from being built on silty sands which experienced liquefaction	• Block of apartments in Northridge collapsed • Fire destroyed homes in Sylmar and Granada Hills • Cars exploded from intense heat • Roads buckled and bridges collapsed • Expensive yachts sank in marinas • Exclusive shopping centre – Rodeo Drive – damaged • University campus severely damaged and replaced with 450 temporary 'huts' • Power failures in central Los Angeles • Buildings made of wood and reinforced concrete withstood the tremor

Figure 13.10

Two notable late 20th-century earthquakes in California

development of tsunami warning systems has also considerably reduced the loss of life in the coastal areas around the Pacific Ocean. The Pacific Tsunami Warning System (PTWS) was set up in 1948 and involves 23 nations. Some 69 seismic stations and 65 tidal stations, located within and on the edges of the Pacific basin, monitor earthquakes and unusual wave movements and send the information to a centre in Hawaii. In turn, this centre issues warnings Pacific-wide by teletype or telephone. More local systems, such as that established to monitor tsunami behaviour around Japan, provide further information.

Tsunami can take up to 20–25 hours to traverse the Pacific Ocean, which provides plenty of time to issue warnings and carry out evacuations, although false alarms do sometimes occur. The majority of tsunami are, however, generated by earthquakes close to land and travel very fast, allowing coastal inhabitants perhaps only 10 minutes to evacuate. In these circumstances, the PTWS is ineffective. One solution to this problem has been to set up a reliable and inexpensive system called THRUST

(Tsunami Hazard Reduction Utilising Systems Technology). When an earthquake equal to, or greater than, 7 on the Richter scale occurs within 100 km of the coastline, an accelerometer sends a signal to a geostationary satellite above the Pacific Ocean. The signal is decoded and wave-level movements are then monitored. If these movements suggest the likelihood of a tsunami, then a message is sent directly to the nations at risk. The system, which is still in its infancy, has undergone successful trials in Chile.

Unfortunately warnings are sometimes ignored because people with no past experience think they can cope, or insufficient information is provided about the scale and timing of an impending disaster. Warnings are also not heeded because people fear their homes will be looted. Too many false warnings, or alternatively no warnings at all, can also quickly erode public confidence. For example, 72 000 people were evacuated from Soufrière on Guadeloupe in 1976 but no eruption subsequently occurred. In the case of the Nevado del Rúiz tragedy the government was aware of the risks but failed to issue warnings in sufficient time because it was unwilling to pay for the costs of a premature, or an unnecessary, evacuation.

Careful land use planning can also reduce the impact of a disaster. Hazard maps may be prepared to indicate areas where future housing or industrial development might be at risk. Buildings constructed across active faults, or on soft sediments, are at particular risk should an earthquake occur. In other respects, however, these locations may appear to be ideal sites because they are near markets and have a good infrastructure. In addition, competition for land may limit the choice of available sites and lead developers to build despite the risks. In Japan, land-use zoning measures have been employed to reduce the impact of tsunami on coastal settlements. Where attempts have failed to persuade fishermen to abandon their livelihood and to move inland, defensive structural measures have been employed. Sea walls, break-waters and the planting of trees along the coast have all helped to dissipate wave impact. Housing is also set back from the shoreline as a matter of good practice.

Persuading people not to live in hazardous environments is often difficult. People continue to live on the sides of active volcanoes because the weathered soils are very fertile. Others live on unstable slopes on the edges of urban areas because land is in short supply. Despite the risk of tsunami, people still live in coastal settlements, especially around the Pacific basin, because such localities are relatively flat and provide ready opportunities for trading and fishing.

Emergency aid and insurance can help spread the cost and reduce the level of suffering after a disaster. Insurance is available in MEDCs, but much less so in LEDCs. Aid is provided by governments and a wide range of non-governmental organisations (NGOs) such as the Red Cross and Oxfam. Spontaneous international appeals are frequently launched in cases of severe suffering. Immediate relief measures include supplying food, blankets, tents, water containers and medical supplies. The rate of recovery or resilience following a disaster exposes the differences between rich and poor countries. A lack of fresh water, poor sanitation and overcrowding in temporary camps invariably encourages the spread of disease, especially in LEDCs where it is often difficult to distinguish between disaster aid and long-term aid once the emergency is over. While disaster aid may bring many immediate benefits it can also create longer-term problems. For example, funds may have to be diverted from development programmes to rebuild homes and infrastructures, or the use of expensive equipment may not be supported for long enough with technical expertise or spare parts. Food aid may lower market prices and distort the local economy. Aid may also encourage dependency beyond reconstruction, and money may fall into the hands of a ruling elite rather than be distributed to those most in need. The psychological problems brought about by the loss of homes and relatives, and as a result of injuries, are often not addressed.

Activity	
1	Explain the difference between risk assessment and risk perception.
2	Mount Etna is Europe's most active volcano. What are the arguments for and against compulsory resettlement of people away from areas at risk?
3	Although monitoring has improved, why are earthquakes, and to a lesser extent volcanic eruptions, still difficult to predict?
4	The Nevado del Ruiz disaster stemmed from a moderate eruption but killed 23 000 people; the Pinatubo eruption was the second largest in the 20th century but only 300 people died. What lessons should we learn from this discrepancy?
5	Produce a diagram showing those aspects of the natural and built environments that need to be kept under constant review in areas where earthquakes are likely.

14 Slope hazards

KEY THEMES

- Slope failure is often induced by a combination of factors or events.
- Human activities can encourage or cause slope movements.
- Fatalities from landslides are rising in LEDCs.
- Some slope hazards are linked to crustal and atmospheric hazards.

Slopes and mass movements

The sudden movement downslope of large volumes of rock, soil or snow under the pull of gravity can be regarded as a hazard where it threatens life or property (Figure 14.1). Movement of surface rocks and soil can be encouraged by several factors, often acting together, as in the case of the Vaiont Dam disaster (see page 207).

Causes of movement

Heavy or prolonged rainfall, snowmelt or a change in land use can increase the amount of water held in the pores between soil and rock particles. Gradually **positive pore pressure** builds up and breaks the bonding between the particles which then lose their internal cohesiveness. Slope failure commonly follows.

Progressive physical, chemical and biological weathering can also encourage slope instability. Porous rocks and those with dense bedding planes and joints are particularly susceptible to processes such as frost-shattering, wetting and drying, and heating and cooling, all of which loosen rock and soil. Faults, bedding planes and joints also act as slip-planes along which mass movement can occur.

Marine or river erosion, spring sapping, or human activities, such as road and railway construction, undercut and steepen slopes, leading to their failure. Removal of material from the base of a slope by marine or fluvial processes, lateral unloading, or through human activities such as mining and building, also destabilises slopes.

Accumulation of snow or scree, or an increase in rock bulk density as the result of heavy rainfall, adds extra weight to a slope and this form of overloading can also cause failure. Housing developments, or the dumping of spoil on slopes, may have a similar effect. Earthquakes or vibrations produced by blasting, drilling or the movement of heavy vehicles can also trigger movement on slopes. Deforestation, overgrazing and urbanisation all have the effect of altering

Figure 14.1

Homes in Honduras buried by mud that flowed down a steep hillside following a period of heavy rainfall in 1998

positive pore pressure and soil water movement which, in turn, encourage slope failure.

Areas of the world that are highly susceptible to slope hazards include earthquake zones, areas of very steep relief, localities that have been deforested or overgrazed, places covered by **tephra**, and areas of high precipitation, including those affected by tropical cyclones. For example, Japan is a high-risk area because earthquakes and tropical storms are common. Hong Kong is vulnerable because it has a dense population largely clustered at the base of steep, unstable slopes composed of deeply-weathered granite. Settlements in northern Italy are also prone to slope movements because they are located in a tectonically active area of easily weathered sedimentary rocks and, in addition, the area has been subject to deforestation. Landslides are common in Rio de Janeiro because increasing numbers of poor people live on steep, unstable slopes on the edge of the city.

Categories of mass movement

Mass movements are broadly classified into three types: falls, slides and flows (Figure 14.2). A **rockfall** is the simplest form of mass movement. The hazard commonly occurs on steep slopes greater than 40° formed in well-jointed rock. Progressive weathering, an increase in bulk density and positive pore pressure all readily encourage falls to occur. A common trigger mechanism is an earthquake, as in the case of the 1970 Nevado Huascarán landslide in Peru – see the case study on page 208.

A rock slide occurs when large slabs of rock break away and move down a slip-plane, the material breaking only at the base of the slope. Two types are recognised: **rotational** and **translational slides**. Rotational sliding is encouraged by positive pore pressure together with the undercutting and removal of material at the base by fluvial or coastal erosion. Rotational sliding in alternating bands of relatively soft rock such as

Figure 14.2

Types of slope movement

Primary mechanism	Type of mass movement	Materials in motion	Nature of movement	Rate of movement
FALL	Rockfall	• Detached blocks of rock	Individual blocks fall from steep faces	Extremely rapid
	Debris/earth fall	• Detached masses of soil	Soil masses topple when support is lost	Very rapid
SLIDE	Translational slide	• Unfractured rock mass	Shallow slide more or less parallel to ground surface	Very slow to extremely rapid
		• Fractured rock	Shallow slide more or less parallel to ground surface	Moderate
		• Rock debris or soil	Shallow slide of deformed or undeformed masses of soil	Rapid or very slow
	Rotational slide	• Rock	Rotational movement along concave failure plane	Moderate to extremely slow
		• Rock debris or soil	Rotational movement along concave failure plane	Slow
FLOW	Mudflow	• Predominantly clay-sized particles	Confined elongated flow	Slow
	Slow earthflow	• Predominantly sand-sized particles	Confined elongated flow	Slow
	Rapid earthflow	• Clay soils	Slide followed by extensive lateral spreading	Very rapid
	Debris flow	• Mixture of fine and coarse debris	Flow usually confined to existing drainage lines	Very rapid
	Rock avalanche	• Rock debris, plus ice and snow in some cases	Catastrophic large-scale movement over several kilometres; landscape features obliterated	Extremely rapid
	Snow avalanche	• Snow and ice, plus rock debris in some cases	Catastrophic fall or slide	Extremely rapid

sandstones and clays is often referred to as 'slumping'. Here water builds up in pore spaces in the permeable sandstone causing pressure on the impermeable clay below. The clay layer may act as a lubricating surface encouraging failure. A rotational slide that occurred at Ancona in central Italy in 1982 was caused by sudden heavy rainfall which increased positive pore pressure and resulted in the loss of 280 homes.

The translational slide occurs when a block glides on a bedding plane parallel to a slope. The Vaiont Dam disaster in Italy began as a translational slide but became transformed into a **debris slide**.

Case Study: The Vaiont Dam disaster, Italy

One of the worst disasters in the 20th century occurred in the Piave valley in north-eastern Italy in October 1963. A debris slide with a volume of 240 million cubic metres fell into the reservoir behind the Vaiont Dam (Figure 14.3). This dam was completed in 1960 after four years' work, during which time concern was expressed by engineers that relatively small debris slides on the south side of the reservoir were a possibility as the accumulating water created instability in the adjacent bedrock. A slide of 700 000 cubic metres occurred in November 1960. Concrete injections were made in an attempt to strengthen the bedrock, and between October 1961 and September 1963 the water level in the reservoir was raised and lowered according to the perceived level of risk. However, on 9 October 1963, at a time when the reservoir was two-thirds full, the major slide occurred. A 100 metre wave of water overtopped the dam and spilled down the valley, killing 3000 people in the towns of Pirago, Villanova and Longarone. The slide itself lasted 45 seconds, and it took just 7 minutes for the wave to overwhelm the downstream settlements; the dam remained more or less intact.

Several factors contributed to the Vaiont disaster. The rocks making up the walls of the reservoir dipped down into the Vaiont valley, which facilitated movement under gravity as a translational slide. Alternating bands of limestone and clay allowed water to build up between impermeable and permeable layers, thus lubricating the sliding process. A number of fractures across the strata also increased the risk of movement. As the reservoir was filled, rocks near the edge were saturated and positive pore pressure increased. Heavy rains during August and September 1963 increased the bulk density of the rock. Relatively small slides had been observed in the months leading up to the disaster and, had the slopes been drained and the foot of the slope stabilised, the disaster might have been prevented. The fact that the area had a history of slides did not appear to have been taken into account when the dam and reservoir (the latter designed to be the third largest in the world) were initially planned.

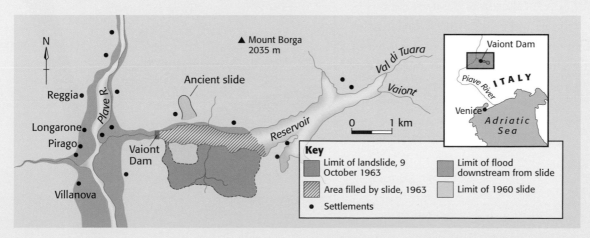

Figure 14.3

The Vaiont Dam disaster, Italy

Mudflows are common on steep, unvegetated slopes composed of fine-grained materials such as tephra or clays. Clays have tiny pore spaces and when moist they are cohesive and will resist movement, but eventually positive pore pressure will cause failure. In May 1998, 54 people were killed by mudslides which affected the town of Sarno in southern Italy.

Earthflows contain less water and therefore move slowly and travel shorter distances than mudflows. Once movement starts it appears to extend upslope. One of the worst disasters arising from this sort of hazard occurred at Aberfan in South Wales in 1966 when a mine spoil-tip 250 metres in height became saturated by rain and collapsed to bury part of the town, killing a total of 144 people including 116 children.

Debris avalanches are catastrophic events involving the rapid movement of rocks, soils and sometimes ice fragments. They may flow for considerable distances, sometimes riding on a cloud of compressed air, as in the case of the Mount St Helens (see page 194) and Huascarán disasters. Additional water can transform the movement into a **debris flow**.

Case Study: The Nevado Huascarán landslides

In January 1962, part of the west side of Nevado Huascarán, a high peak in the Peruvian Andes, fractured (Figure 14.4). A debris flow estimated to consist of 13 million cubic metres of material travelled at 170 km/h down the mountain, killing 4000 people in the town of Ranrahirca and eight other towns. Part of the granite-jointed vertical face gave way with no obvious trigger.

In May 1970 an offshore earthquake in the Pacific Ocean measuring 7.7 on the Richter scale triggered rock and snow avalanches on the same mountain. Initially the movement started as a rockfall, but it soon transformed into a debris avalanche and then a debris flow comprising a total of about 100 million cubic metres of material moving at speeds up to 300 km/h. The overall vertical drop of the material was in excess of 4000 metres and it travelled 16 km laterally. A lobe of debris 30 metres thick buried the town of Yungay, killing 18 000 people. Similar mass movements continue to be a threat in this area today.

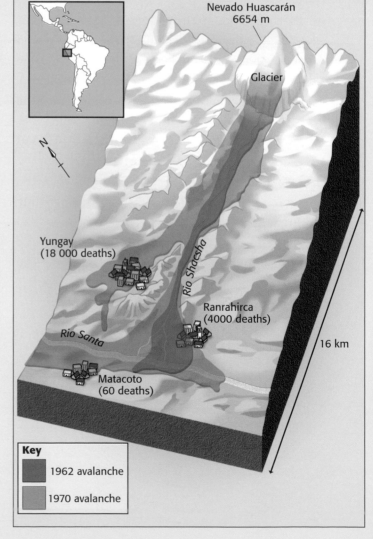

Figure 14.4

The Nevado Huascarán landslides

The sudden movement of snow down a slope under gravity is known as a snow avalanche. **Slab avalanches** are more hazardous than **loose snow avalanches** because large areas can give way without warning. Avalanches tend to occur on intermediate slopes of between 25 and 45°. On gentler slopes there is less likelihood of movement, whereas very steep slopes cannot support the thickness of snow, and so pack failure can occur. North- and east-facing slopes in the northern hemisphere are particularly prone to avalanches because snow stabilises more slowly where temperatures are lower. Wind can also encourage falls by redistributing snow from windward to leeward slopes, causing overloading. Common causes of pack failure include heavy snowfall, rain, a sudden thaw, skiers, climbers or snowmobiles traversing a slope, earthquakes, and vibration from machinery or trains. Fracture points often occur at a point of stress such as at a break of slope. The tendency for repeated avalanches in the same locations suggests that certain conditions favour their development more than others.

The impacts of slope instability

Landslides can bury communities, cover soils and destroy trees and crops. They can also block rivers which may eventually burst, causing flooding. Fatalities from slope movements are rising glob-ally because more people, especially in the poorer regions of the world, are settling on unstable slopes in tectonically active areas and in areas of high rainfall. Mismanagement of land in these areas may also contribute to slope failure. Two examples of slope failure in Central America, each with a different cause, are given in Figure 14.5.

Reducing the risk of disaster

Careful studies of risk-prone areas are an important first step in reducing the risk. Studies of slope angles, rock types and structures, active fault-lines, land uses, weather events and evidence of past failures can be used to compile a slope hazard map. The resulting information is useful to planners and local authorities, who may choose to restrict development at vulnerable sites such as the base of steep slopes or the entrance to canyons. Furthermore, vital signs of an impending disaster are often observable. Changes in slope, as detected by tiltmeters, cracking and soil creep, are all indications of potential movement. Warnings of heavy rainfall or tropical storms can highlight the risk of landslide hazards, but persuading people to move is often difficult.

Where potentially hazardous areas cannot be avoided, a number of mitigation measures can reduce the risk of slope failure. One approach is to regrade slopes by unloading the top and

Figure 14.5
Landslides in Central America

November 1998

Hurricane Mitch causes landslides. 1500 people are killed when a crater lake in Casitas volcano, swollen by rainfall, overflows and creates a mudslide that buries homes in 6 metres of mud. Slides around Tegucigalpa, the capital of Honduras, are encouraged by deforestation for fuelwood and the spread of population on marginal unstable slopes.

January 2001

Landslides in San Salvador kill 600 people, triggered by an earthquake in the Pacific Ocean.
In Santa Tecla, a suburb of San Salvador, poorer homes are destroyed while better constructions remain standing.
In Las Colinas, another suburb, 500 middle-class homes are destroyed by a mudslide. Landslides also close the Pan-American Highway.

MEXICO

Gulf of Mexico

BELIZE

GUATEMALA

HONDURAS
Tegucigalpa

San Salvador

Casitas volcano

NICARAGUA

Caribbean Sea

Epicentre

COSTA RICA

PANAMA

EL SALVADOR

PACIFIC OCEAN

N

0   600 km

loading the toe or base. Drainage can alter soil and rock positive pore pressures and bulk density. Vegetation cover reduces the impact of rainfall, plant roots bind soil particles together, and transpiration helps to dry out the slope. Movement can also be restrained by artificial means through the construction of walls, buttresses, ground anchors, drainage channels, cables, nets and bolts. Figure 14.6 shows a range of engineering measures taken to reduce the risk of movement on a hillside in Japan. In some instances, however, authorities are reluctant or unwilling to pay for expensive defences because private companies profit from land speculation and development.

Avalanche hazards have increased in recent years because of the growth of winter recreational activities in mountainous areas. Risk has increased particularly in Europe because of the relatively high winter population densities in the Alpine areas. Seemingly innocent activity can trigger snow avalanches (Figure 14.7) which bury victims who then die from suffocation, hypothermia, shock or snow impact. For example, one climber was killed and another buried in 4 metres of snow while traversing a wind-loaded, 30° slope with a north-east aspect in the Mission Mountains in Montana, USA, in January 1998. The slab released was 100 metres wide and fell downslope for 266 metres before coming to a halt. In another incident, a snowmobile triggered a slab avalanche 30 metres wide on Sawtell Peak in Idaho. The east-facing, 36°, wind-loaded slope had recently received half a metre of new snow.

Avalanches also damage trees and buildings and disrupt lines of communication. The build-up of snow on steep slopes can be prevented by controlled releases using explosives. Fences can be erected to intercept snow in collecting zones, whereas further downslope walls, wedges, tree planting and the construction of snow-sheds over railways and roads can all reduce the impact of an avalanche. Avalanche maps are available which grade slopes according to the level of

avalanche risk, and weather reports are used to update the information. The availability of effective search and rescue in these areas following an event is vital, as the chances of survival reduce severely after 1–2 hours.

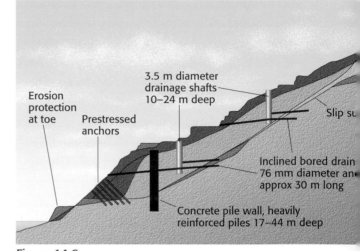

Figure 14.6

Engineering measures taken to reduce the risks of landslides

Figure 14.7

A snow avalanche near Trois Vallées in the French Alps

	Activity
1	What lessons can be learned from the Vaiont Dam disaster?
2	Write an assessment of the extent to which the Central American landslides were natural.
3	Despite the risks, people still continue to live on, or at the base of, steep slopes. Suggest why this should be so in **a** developed countries and **b** developing countries.

15 Atmospheric hazards

KEY THEMES

● Tropical cyclones comprise the main form of atmospheric hazard in many parts of the world. They occur at a range of scales with widely different primary and secondary impacts.

● The long-term impacts of disasters caused by atmospheric hazards vary substantially between the more and less economically developed countries of the world. In LEDCs, the long-term impacts are often equally or more damaging than the events themselves.

● While improvements in monitoring have reduced the number of fatalities in many countries, the level of property damage remains high.

● Although tornadoes are much smaller disturbances they pose a severe threat across wide areas and can cause intense localised damage.

Tropical cyclones, hurricanes and tornadoes

A **tropical cyclone** is a general term for an area of intense low pressure, high winds, torrential rain, thunder and lightning and swirling cloud which occurs in the tropics. Its main features are shown in Figure 15.1. They are initiated when converging trade winds create local disturbances in easterly airflows near the Equator. Pressure begins to fall at the surface, which encourages warm moist air to rise, creating local convection cells. Tropical cyclones vary in scale from tropical disturbances to **hurricanes** and are most readily classified according to windspeed. Tropical disturbances are characterised by variable winds of low strength and pose few problems. **Tropical depressions** are noticeably more developed features and are

Figure 15.1

The main features of a tropical cyclone

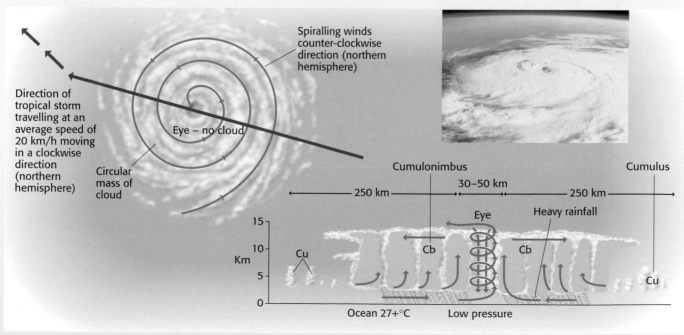

Spiralling winds counter-clockwise direction (northern hemisphere)

Direction of tropical storm travelling at an average speed of 20 km/h moving in a clockwise direction (northern hemisphere)

Circular mass of cloud

Eye – no cloud

Cumulonimbus

Cumulus

250 km — 30–50 km — 250 km

15

10

Km

5

0

Eye

Heavy rainfall

Cu

Cb

Cb

Cu

Ocean 27+°C   Low pressure

defined by windspeeds up to 63 km/h. **Tropical storms** are defined by windspeeds of between 64 and 118 km/h and hurricanes by winds above 119 km/h.

Only a few tropical disturbances and depressions evolve into larger tropical storms and hurricanes because, for these to develop, a number of conditions must be met. Humidity should be constantly high and the sea surface temperature must be at least 26–27°C. The warmth encourages evaporation from the ocean surface, and as the water vapour rises and cools to form clouds and rainfall, the latent heat released by the condensation process helps to perpetuate atmospheric instability. The disturbance must occur more than 5° North or South of the Equator in order to ensure that the Coriolis force is strong enough to encourage rising air to rotate (the force is zero at the Equator). It is also necessary for pressure, lapse rates, windspeed and wind direction to be almost constant vertically through the atmosphere so that pockets of rising air become organised into a cohesive cell. A strongly divergent flow of air aloft is required in order to provide the suction needed to draw more moisture-laden air upwards.

Once formed, tropical storms track westwards at average speeds of 15–25 km/h under the influence of prevailing winds. They move rather like a spinning-top, constantly in touch with the warm ocean which provides them with the necessary energy, rotating counter-clockwise in the northern hemisphere and clockwise in the southern hemisphere. As pressure continues to fall, windspeeds may increase to hurricane force – 119 km/h or more. Tropical cyclones dissipate on moving over land or a cooler sea because the energy supply obtainable from a warm, wet surface is cut off.

As Figure 15.2 shows, most tropical cyclones form on the western side of large oceans where high pressure cells are less strongly developed, allowing air to rise from the surface. The

Figure 15.2

The global distribution of tropical cyclones

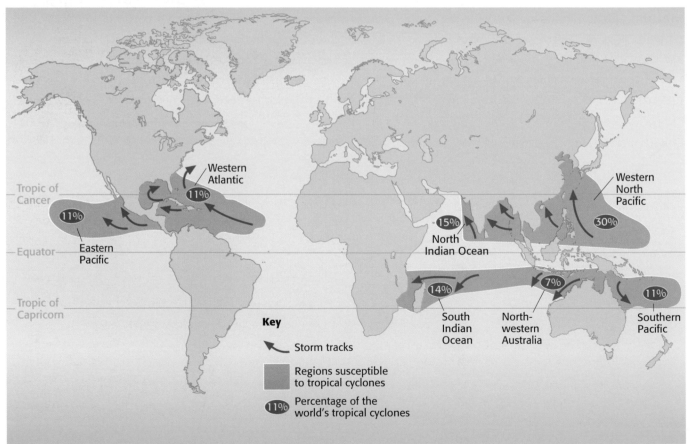

western North Pacific produces the largest number annually. No storms develop in the tropical South Atlantic or the eastern South Pacific because surface water temperatures are usually too low. Tropical cyclones are known as **hurricanes** in the Caribbean and Atlantic Ocean, **typhoons** in the western Pacific and **cyclones** in the Indian Ocean. Many hurricanes tend to move west towards the Caribbean and Central America and then track north-west, then north and eventually east out over the Atlantic again. Tropical cyclones develop during the summer months between June and October in the northern hemisphere and between December and May in the southern hemisphere.

Tornadoes (Figure 15.3) are much more localised events but their strong winds can cause considerable damage. When developed over water they generate waterspouts. Exactly how tornadoes develop is uncertain. They seem to form where a cold dry layer of air overlies a warm moist layer and when local heating of the ground surface, or a vigorous cold front, triggers a vortex of rotating air. Tornadoes can occur singly or in families. Rotating windspeeds are typically 150–200 km/h but they can gust up to 500 km/h. Tornado tracks are on average only 50–100 metres wide and 2–5 km in length. Tornadoes travel across the surface at about 30–60 km/h and are normally in contact with

the ground for a maximum of 20 minutes, but not all of them touch down.

A lack of information means that the global distribution of tornadoes is difficult to map but they are common in the USA and north-west Europe. In the UK they are a winter phenomenon associated with cold fronts and deep low-pressure systems. In the USA they occur in spring and early summer when warm moist air moves up from the Gulf of Mexico and meets cold dry air descending the eastern side of the Rockies. They are particularly common in Texas, Oklahoma and Wisconsin.

Figure 15.3

A strongly developed tornado sweeping across the countryside

Case Study: The Oklahoma tornado, 1999

In May 1999 tornadoes crossed the US states of Oklahoma and Kansas killing 43 and injuring 700 people (Figure 15.4). Houses were damaged and power-lines brought down. There were at least three dozen tornadoes covering territory from Oklahoma City in the south to Wichita, 320 km to the north in Kansas. This area (Figure 15.5), known as Tornado Alley, is renowned for tornadoes; there can be up to 40 or 50 a year. In 1999, hundreds of people were evacu-ated after warnings were issued, although continuing thunderstorms in the area hampered rescue efforts. The tornadoes were on average 0.8 km wide in Oklahoma, increasing to 4.8 km nearer Wichita. Most were in touch with the ground for less than half an hour. In the national context, tornadoes kill about 80 people per year in the USA. Mobile homes and cars are frequently wrecked and trees and houses in the paths of tornadoes are invariably extensively damaged.

Figure 15.4

Damage inflicted on homes by the 1999 Oklahoma tornado

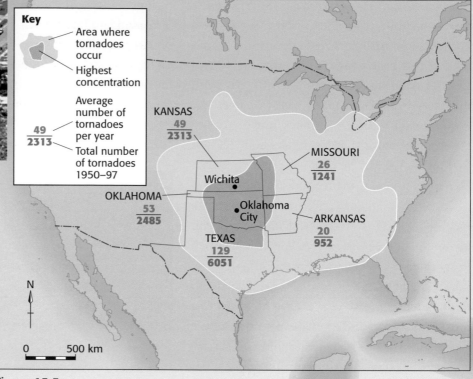

Key

Area where tornadoes occur

Highest concentration

Average number of tornadoes per year $\frac{49}{2313}$

Total number of tornadoes 1950–97

KANSAS $\frac{49}{2313}$

MISSOURI $\frac{26}{1241}$

Wichita

OKLAHOMA $\frac{53}{2485}$

Oklahoma City

ARKANSAS $\frac{20}{952}$

TEXAS $\frac{129}{6051}$

N

0   500 km

Figure 15.5

The location of tornado-prone areas in the USA

The consequences of atmospheric hazards

Atmospheric hazards are responsible for more deaths and damage to property than any other type of hazard. One country particularly prone to tropical cyclones is Bangladesh, a low-lying, densely populated area that is exposed to cyclones which develop in the Bay of Bengal. Other hazard-prone areas include Japan, the Philippines, the Caribbean and the Atlantic coast of the USA, especially Texas, North and South Carolina and Florida.

The impacts of a tropical cyclone depend upon its intensity, speed of movement and the distribution and vulnerability of the population affected. Slow-moving storms cause more damage than those that travel faster because they influence areas for longer. High relief can intensify rainfall – a factor that contributed to the damage inflicted by Hurricane Mitch which hit Central America in 1998.

The most serious hazard associated with a tropical cyclone is the **storm surge**, which can raise the sea-level by several metres, especially if it coincides with a high tide. Surges arrive about five hours before the storm itself. They are produced by a combination of wind-driven waves which pile up water along the coast and low pressure which encourages the sea-level to rise. Surges can result in high death tolls and cause extensive damage to property and crops. More indirectly, the intrusion of salt-water can adversely affect crops and soils. A lack of fresh water and contamination of sewerage systems may also lead to outbreaks of disease. Valuable export crops such as bananas and coffee, which provide countries in the Caribbean, for example, with foreign earnings, are also lost.

Another hazard is high winds, which can gust to 250 km/h. These damage shipping, coastal defences, housing, trees and power-lines. Severe rainfall can result in river flooding which may wash away homes, roads, railways, crops and livestock (see the Mozambique case study on page 218–219). Rainfall can cause secondary hazards such as the landslides in Central America described in Chapter 14.

Coping with atmospheric hazards

The power of tropical cyclones can be modified by seeding the clouds with dry ice or silver iodide. This type of event modification is not always successful, however, and the iodide is also a pollutant. In Florida, experiments are now underway using a non-polluting highly absorbent gel in an attempt to reduce the power of hurricanes. Flakes of Dyn-O-Gel, which can absorb a quantity of moisture up to 2000 times their own weight, work on the principle that if sufficient moisture can be drawn out of the rising air, then the release of latent heat that occurs during the process of condensation will be reduced, and the storm's energy supply cut down.

The construction of sea-walls, maintenance of sand dunes and the planting of mangroves can all reduce the impact of a storm surge. Water- and wind-resistant buildings, raised floors and the placing of power-lines underground, as practised in Florida, can also help to limit damage. River embankments may also be strengthened against flooding.

Storm shelters provide protection for coastal communities in India and Bangladesh, although they are not always used. For example, when Cyclone 07B hit Andhra Pradesh in India in November 1996 (see Figure 15.7), shelters remained unused because they were not provisioned with food and water and some people were afraid that the poorly maintained structures might collapse. Those who suffered most in this cyclone were the poor, rural, coastal communities where homes were made of mud with thatched roofs. In contrast, more wealthy people where brick and concrete houses suffered less. The better-off were also the first to receive aid after the disaster because their homes were in the most accessible areas.

Monitoring the movement and development of tropical storms, coupled with the issuing of warnings, is regarded as the key line of defence against atmospheric hazards. The path taken by a tropical cyclone can be tracked using geostationary satellites and coastal radar. The information provided is then used to issue warnings and initiate evacuations. However, one feature of tropical cyclones that makes it difficult to forecast the exact position where they will strike the land is that they wobble. Forecasters also tend to be cautious in making predictions because false alarms may incur substantial unnecessary costs and undermine public confidence.

At present, the most widely monitored tropical cyclones occur in the Atlantic and Caribbean. Improvements in tracking have reduced the number of fatalities in the USA, as the case study of Hurricane Hugo (page 216) shows. Here people were given advice about what to do before the hurricane struck, and updates were provided on the expected location, arrival and intensity of the storm. Potential storm damage was assessed using the **Saffir-Simpson scale**, which grades tropical cyclones on a scale of 1 to 5.

Material losses from hurricanes striking the USA remain high because an increasing number of people, many of whom are wealthy, are moving to the south-east coastal states. This trend is causing concern to the authorities who are worried that the existing infrastructure may no longer be capable of evacuating enough people before a hurricane arrives. Moreover, it estimated that 80 per cent of the people living in these vulnerable areas have no previous experience of hurricanes, and therefore their perception of the risks involved is low. Furthermore, the availability of insurance is considered to be encouraging a sense of complacency.

Case Study: Hurricane Hugo and the Carolinas

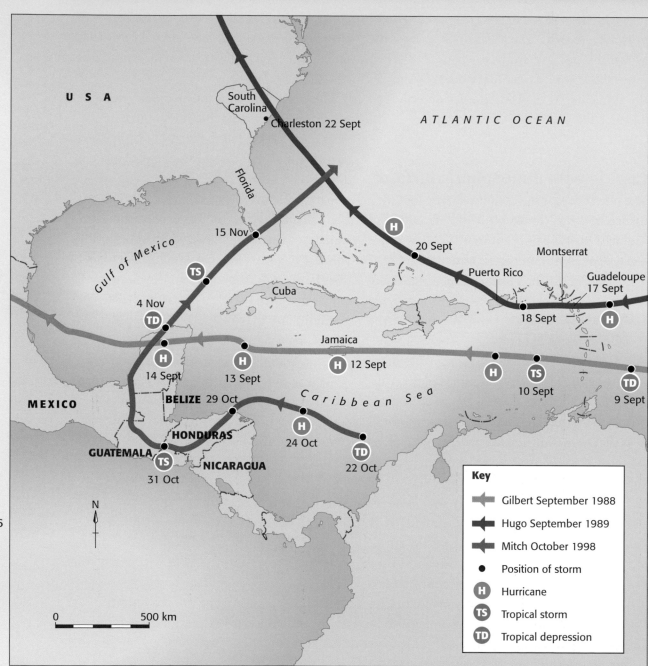

Figure 15.6

The tracks of three major Caribbean hurricanes: 1988, 1989 and 1998

After causing considerable damage in the Caribbean (Figure 15.6), Hurricane Hugo made landfall just east of Charleston in South Carolina at midnight on 22 September 1989. It then tracked north-west over North and South Carolina, sustaining hurricane-force winds for a distance of 240 km before dying out.

A 5.8 metre storm surge, coincident with a high tide, combined with the high winds to cause considerable property damage along the coast. Houses fronting the beach (especially single-storey homes), barrier-island developments and millions of tonnes of sand were swept away. Inland, forestry was severely damaged. The total estimated cost of the damage in the Carolinas was US$ 7000 million. This high figure arose because not only did the hurricane initially strike a highly developed coastal area, but high winds were also maintained for a considerable distance inland.

The passage of the hurricane across the Caribbean had been carefully observed, but forecasters were uncertain where landfall would occur and therefore issued warnings for the coastal area between the Florida/South Carolina border in the south and Cape Lookout, North Carolina in the north – a distance in excess of 600 km. People had been advised to stock-up with food, water and medical supplies and to secure their property. Hospitals were made ready and the National Guard and emergency services were put on alert. Evacuations from vulnerable coastal locations were complete before the hurricane arrived, a factor that explains the relatively low death toll of 20. Water and electricity supplies were fully restored within two weeks of the disaster.

Poor countries such as Bangladesh have also taken steps to improve warning systems but evacuation is difficult because there is little high land to act as a refuge, and roads and inter-island transport are poor. Sometimes warnings are inadequate. In the case of the 1996 Andhra Pradesh cyclone, the densely populated, poor fishing communities were given little indication of the impending disaster. Many people lost their lives as a storm surge hit the coast causing extensive flooding. Some had ventured out to sea in boats without radios which otherwise might have been used to give warnings. Similar problems were encountered when a cyclone struck neighbouring Orissa in 1999.

Activity
Study Figure 15.6 and an atlas map of the region.
1 Calculate the number of days it took for Hurricanes Gilbert and Mitch to develop from a tropical depression into a hurricane.
2 Briefly describe the track of both hurricanes, noting the main population centres and relief barriers over which they passed.
3 Rainfall intensified as Mitch passed over Honduras. Can you suggest why?
4 What mechanism would account for both Gilbert and Mitch gaining in strength again as they passed over the Gulf of Mexico?
5 Both hurricanes produced high winds which defoliated trees and heavy rain that caused landslides. How would defoliation have contributed to the landslides?
6 Gilbert and Mitch destroyed the banana crop in Jamaica and Honduras respectively. Suggest other industries which would have also lost valuable foreign earnings.
7 High winds and heavy rain produced by both hurricanes destroyed agricultural storage facilities. Outline the consequences of this damage for the economies of the countries involved.

In November 1999 a cyclone hit the Indian state of Orissa (Figure 15.7). It is estimated that 10 000 people lost their lives, although figures are imprecise because some victims were migrant workers and others lived in shanty towns. About 1.5 million people were made homeless, and hundreds of villages and 323 000 hectares of land were destroyed. The cyclone caused extensive damage to the rice crop which was almost ready for harvesting and which, in normal years, would have supplied India with 10 per cent of its needs. The cyclone also felled coconut trees, and destroyed coffee plantations, sugar cane and jute. Incidences of cholera and typhoid increased after the cyclone.

Orissa is one of the poorest regions of the world, with a GNP of $200 per capita. It has a literacy rate of only 49 per cent. Two-thirds of Orissa's population is dependent on agriculture, which contributes up to 60 per cent of the GDP. Had early warning systems been available, many lives could have been saved. Many people were unaware that a cyclone was approaching, and of the 50 cyclone shelters available, more than half were unused. Cyclones are common in this area and this was the second storm to hit the region in a month. A cyclone in 1990 produced a 6 metre storm surge which affected 20 million people and destroyed 2 million homes.

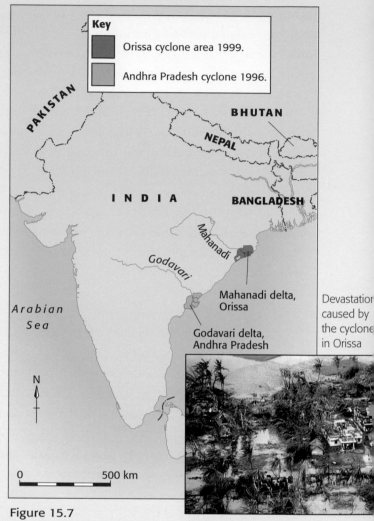

Key
Orissa cyclone area 1999.
Andhra Pradesh cyclone 1996.

PAKISTAN

BHUTAN

NEPAL

I N D I A

BANGLADESH

Mahanadi

Godavari

Arabian Sea

Mahanadi delta, Orissa

Godavari delta, Andhra Pradesh

Devastation caused by the cyclone in Orissa

N

0   500 km

Figure 15.7
The location of the 1999 Orissa and 1996 Andhra Pradesh cyclones

In March 2000, severe river flooding affected the lower reaches of the Limpopo, Save and Zambesi rivers in Mozambique (Figure 15.8). About 1 million people were displaced and at least 200 died. Many head of livestock were drowned and the valuable rice crop was destroyed. The main north–south road linking the main settlements, and many bridges, were washed away. So much water accumulated behind the Kariba Dam in Zambia that, to avoid structural damage, spillways were opened which

increased the flood risk in the lower Zambesi region.

People climbed trees and telegraph poles and waited on roofs to be rescued by helicopter or boat. Mozambique appealed to the international community for helicopters, tents, sheeting, blankets, cooking utensils and water tanks. As the floods receded, concern grew that cholera, dysentery and malaria would increase.

Flooding is not uncommon in the Mozambique lowlands, but the annual seasonal rains were particularly heavy. The arrival of Cyclone Aline in late February deposited heavy rain on an already saturated land, tipping the balance. Poor land management was also partly to blame because overgrazing, urbanisation and wetland drainage had altered water movements in the river catchments.

Mozambique is a poor country, but since the civil war ended in 1992 it has received a lot of foreign investment and its GNP had grown rapidly. The flooding represented a major setback to the country's rate of economic development. Although international appeals often provide post-disaster assistance to LEDCs, they are often faced with overwhelming problems which make it very difficult to prioritise needs at difficult times. Mozambique is no exception.

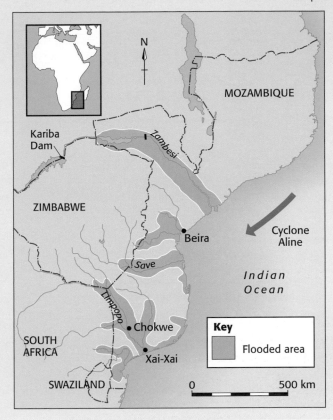

Figure 15.8

The main areas affected by flooding in Mozambique

Land-use planning strategies and controls can also help to reduce the risks posed by tropical storms. Measures include restricting or setting back development from the coast, and using such areas for low-value activities. Adopting these measures is, however, difficult in MEDCs because coastal sites are often considered to be prime locations for development. In LEDCs people living on coastal deltas and floodplains are unwilling to move because the soils are highly fertile and the sea provides an income from fishing. Moreover, they may lack the means to move and have little choice but to stay.

Tornadoes, like hurricanes, can be tracked. The US authorities issue warnings when atmospheric conditions are conducive to tornado formation. The likely damage which a given tornado might produce is measured on the five-point **Fujita scale**. Further warnings are given when tornadoes are suspected or sighted.

	Activity
1	With reference to the Mozambique case study: **a** Suggest why the rebuilding of roads, bridges and railways was perceived by the international community as vital in the immediate aftermath of the disaster. **b** Saturated soils were a clear indication that a hazard might occur. What lessons can be learned from the disaster that followed?
2	Produce a table summarising the impacts of Hurricane Hugo on the Carolinas and the cyclone that hit Orissa.
3	Top-down, structural and monitoring measures appear to be inadequate in Orissa. What lessons can be learned from this situation?
4	Why might cyclones that hit Bangladesh and India be perceived as creating or perpetuating a cycle of poverty?

Glossary

Absolute poverty A condition in which a person lacks sufficient earnings to provide for the basic requirements of existence.

Acidic lava Lava with more than 66 per cent silica content; it is viscous, slow-flowing and associated with explosive volcanic activity.

Agribusiness Large-scale, capital-intensive farming, using modern technology such as machinery and agro-chemicals to produce cash crops for food and industry at minimum cost for maximum profit.

Agri-environmental programme Farming activity combined with conservation measures designed to sustain agriculture without harming the natural environment.

Ash Fine-grained pyroclastic material produced by a volcanic eruption.

Automobile dependence When the layout of the built environment and the location of amenities is such that car ownership becomes more or less essential.

Backwash effects The movement of people, capital and resources from the periphery to the core of a country or region.

Basal surge Sudden lateral eruption from the side of a volcano.

Basic lava Lava with a silica content between 45 and 52 per cent; it is fluid, free-flowing and spreads far before solidifying.

Biodiversity The variety of different species of plants and animals in an ecosystem.

Bocage Rural landscape of north-west France characterised by small fields separated by substantial hedges and lines of trees.

Brownfield site A site for housing, industry or commerce that has previously been developed but has since fallen into dereliction.

Cairns Group A coalition of 18 agricultural exporting countries, formed in 1986, that has sought to put pressure on the EU to reduce the level of support to its own farming sector, and open up European markets to international competition.

Carrying capacity The level of tourist activity beyond which the impact on the host economy and environment becomes unacceptable.

Comparative advantage The economic benefit to a country or region specialising in the production of goods (or services) for which it has a particular advantage (e.g. natural resources, low labour costs).

Congestion The delay imposed by one vehicle on another.

Coppicing Trees cut close to ground level every few years; the trees then grow again from the stool.

Cumulative causation The theory that initial advantages for industrial and economic growth lead to a series of virtuous growth cycles.

Debris avalanche Catastrophic movement of rocks, soil and sometimes ice fragments downslope.

Debris flow As *Debris avalanche* but contains much more fluid.

Debris slide As a *Translational slide* but material is more broken up.

De-industrialisation A sudden and steep decline of a country's or region's industrial base.

Depopulation An absolute decrease in the population of a country or region.

Disaster The realisation of a hazard resulting in extensive loss of property and/or life.

Disinvestment The closure of factories and plant in a region. The term is often used to describe the decisions of *Transnational corporations* to restructure their operations and/or transfer production elsewhere.

Earthflow Rapid movement of soil and loose material down a slope aided by water and characterised by an upper convex scar, a tongue, and an alluvial fan at the base.

Ecological footprint The amount or area of land required by a settlement to provide it with food, water and wood at prevailing levels of consumption.

Electric resistivity The degree to which rock can conduct an electric current.

ESA Environmentally Sensitive Area.

Eutrophication The nutrient enrichment of water and the consequent depletion of oxygen by the accumulation of chemicals from fertilisers, farm wastes and sewage. Nitrogenous fertiliser and manure cause algae to multiply, using up oxygen and blocking out light. Decomposition of the algae by bacteria uses up still more oxygen. Fish and other organisms are starved of oxygen and die.

Extended metropolitan region In Southeast Asia, an area where urban and rural differences are blurred because of rapid urban sprawl and increases in personal mobility.

Extensification A reduction in the intensity of farming in order to protect the environment and/or eliminate food surpluses.

External economies Cost advantages or potential savings obtained from sources outside the individual firm.

Field headland The area around the edge of a field where tractors turn and which may become compacted, giving lower yields and more weeds. Under conservation schemes, headlands are often turned into wildflower margins or countryside access strips; under organic farming, they may be left as beetle banks.

Foreign direct investment (FDI) Inward investment by a foreign company (usually a *Transnational corporation*) in a country or region.

Formal economy Work that is regulated, legal, generally well-paid and requiring skills or training.

Fujita scale A five-point scale measuring the rotational speed of a tornado: F1 = 118–180 km/h; F5 = over 420 km/h.

GDP per capita Gross domestic product is the total value of goods and services (excluding overseas investments) in a country or region divided by its population. It is a convenient measure of wealth or development.

Glacial burst A sudden release of water melted by a volcanic eruption under a glacier; also called a *jökulhlaups*.

Green belt An area surrounding a city in which urban development is usually prevented.

Greenfield site Land not previously used for urban development.

Growth boundary An area surrounding a city in which urban development is usually prevented (USA).

Growth pole An area or region where planners concentrate investment. The aim is to create a critical mass which produces self-sustaining, cumulative growth.

Honeypots The most popular, and often the most accessible, leisure sites visited by people.

Human vulnerability The characteristics of an individual or group in terms of their capacity to anticipate, cope, resist and recover from a natural hazard.

Hurricane A tropical cyclone with sustained surface wind speeds of greater than 119 km/h.

Informal economy Work that is easy to obtain, often illegal or unregulated, and generally small-scale with few opportunities for upward mobility.

Initial advantage The reason or reasons why an economic activity first located in a place.

Intermediate lava Lava with a silica content between 52 and 66 per cent; its properties are midway between those of *Acidic lava* and *Basic lava*.

Lahar A Javanese word for a mudflow of volcanic ash.

Landslide General term for a downslope movement of rock or soil along a slip plane.

Loose snow avalanche Loose snow which falls from a point and spreads downslope as an inverted V-shaped scar.

Mitigation Measures taken to reduce the impact of a hazard.

Modified Mercalli scale A 12-point scale describing the physical effects of an earthquake: I = earthquake recorded but felt by a very few; XII = total damage.

Monoculture Farming systems which concentrate almost exclusively on one crop.

Mudflow As *Earthflow* but composed of finer-grained material and a higher water content.

Multifunctionality The idea that food production is only one of agriculture's functions. Other functions include supporting rural communities, conserving habitats and wildlife, maintaining the appearance of the rural landscape, etc.

Multiple deprivation When the various dimensions of deprivation experienced by an individual reinforce one another.

Natural decrease An excess of deaths over births in a country or region.

Natural hazard A natural event or process that has the potential to cause loss of life and/or damage to property.

New town A planned settlement designed to manage urban growth.

Nitrate vulnerable zones Areas defined by the EU where water resources are at risk from nitrate contamination. Farmers who limit the use of nitrate fertilisers in these areas receive compensatory payments for loss of yield.

NNR National Nature Reserve.

Nuée ardente A type of *Pyroclastic flow* containing a high percentage of hot gases.

Pluriactivity Agricultural diversification, whereby farmers gain income from activities other than farming.

Polarisation When the income gap between the richest and poorest in society increases.

Pollarding Trees cut at about 2.5–4 metres above the ground, and allowed to grow again to produce successive crops of wood.

Population potential A measure of the accessibility of a specific place to surrounding populations.

Positive pore pressure Pressure exerted on rock or soil particles as water builds up in pore spaces.

Pyroclastic fall Rock fragments and lava that solidify in the air, fall back to earth and accumulate as layers on the sides of the volcano and surrounding area.

Pyroclastic flow A very hot cloud of volcanic gases, dust, steam and rock fragments which flows down the side of a mountain.

Pyroclastics Material ejected from a volcano as molten lava which cools to a solid in the air, or solid material ejected by fragmentation of surrounding rock or solidified lava.

Recreation Activities undertaken voluntarily for personal enjoyment in leisure time.

Recurrence interval The time (on average) that elapses between two events which are of equal, or greater than equal, magnitude.

Relative poverty A condition in which a person does not have sufficient earnings to acquire what their society regards as sufficient for well-being and esteem.

Renewable resource A natural resource that is either inexhaustible (e.g. solar energy) or follows a biological or physical cycle of continuous renewal (e.g. water).

Resilience A measure of the rate of recovery from a stressful experience.

Re-urbanisation The demographic and economic revival of the central districts of cities.

Richter scale A logarithmic scale ranging from < 1 to > 8, which measures the magnitude of an earthquake as recorded on a seismograph; developed by Charles Richter.

Risk assessment An objective measure assessed by experts about the probability that a hazard will occur, together with expected damage, less the mitigation measures taken to reduce the loss.

Risk management Strategies for reducing the threat to life and property imposed by a hazard while at the same time accepting unmanageable risk.

Risk perception A subjective assessment of the risk of a hazard occurring, based on individual intuition/awareness and experience of past events.

Road or congestion pricing Charging motorists for access to particular roads or zones, in which fees are often adjusted between peak and off-peak periods.

Rockfall Blocks that break off along lines of weakness on steep slopes and then fall freely.

Rotational slide Movement of material down a curved slip-plane; characterised by a stepped profile and backward rotational movement.

SAC Special Area of Conservation.

Saffir-Simpson scale A five-point scale of damage potential created by hurricanes, based on windspeed, air pressure, depth of coastal flooding and other likely impacts: Category 1 = 119–152 km/h winds, pressure 980 mb, little damage; Category 5 = + 250 km/h winds, pressure 920 mb, extensive damage.

Seismic gap Part of an active fault where an earthquake has not occurred for at least 30 years.

Slab avalanche A cohesive layer of snow which breaks away from an underlying layer leaving a fracture line.

Glossary

Smart growth Policies designed to prevent urban sprawl.

Social exclusion A combination of poverty and powerlessness that prevents an individual, group or neighbourhood from fully participating in society.

Soil liquefaction A process by which water-saturated sands and silts temporarily lose their strength because of shaking and behave as a liquid.

SPA Special Protection Area.

Spread effects The dispersal of economic activity, capital and wealth from a core region to the periphery.

Squatter settlement A settlement of usually self-built housing on land not legally owned by the residents.

SSSI Site of Special Scientific Interest.

Stocking density The number of head of livestock on a specific area of land.

Storm surge Rise in sea-level caused by a cyclone – may be up to 8 metres.

Strato-volcano A volcano consisting of ash and lava.

Sustainability The ability to continue a particular practice indefinitely. In particular, it involves the capacity of an agricultural system to carry on into the future without unacceptable pollution, depletion or destruction of its natural resources.

Teleworking Forms of employment that involve working away from traditional office workplaces – from computer terminals and telephones – in call centres or at home.

Tephra See *Pyroclastics*.

Tornado A violently rotating column of air which descends from a cumulonimbus cloud and is visible as an inverted cone.

Tourism Recreational or leisure activities that involve an overnight stay away from home.

Translational slide Downslope movement of a rock block often along a bedding plane, parallel to the dip of underlying strata.

Transnational corporation (TNC) A very large company with factories and/or offices in more than one country and which markets products and/or services worldwide.

Travel poverty Low standards of living exacerbated by a lack of personal mobility, with no car and high dependence on public transport in a remote rural area.

Tropical cyclone A general term for an area of intense low pressure, high winds, torrential rain, thunder and lightning and swirling cloud which occurs in the tropics.

Tropical depression A *Tropical cyclone* with windspeeds up to 63 km/h.

Tropical storm A *Tropical cyclone* with windspeeds of 64–118 km/h.

Tsunami Japanese word for a harbour wave; large sea-waves generated by earthquakes, landslides or volcanic eruptions.

Urban agglomeration A large urban area containing several formerly discrete nuclei which have merged together (i.e. a conurbation).

Urban growth The increase in numbers of people living in cities.

Urban sprawl Low-density settlement extending beyond the boundaries of built-up areas, usually dependent on the use of automobiles.

Urbanisation The process by which a greater proportion of a country's population lives in towns and cities.

Index

Index

Index

Acknowledgements

We are grateful to the following for permission to reproduce photographs:

Art Directors/Trip Photography 1Dv (Smith), 1.20 (Rogers) 2.2 (Grant), 2.12 (Fairman), 4.3 (Sanders), 4.5 (Turner), 4.15 (Davis), 7.14 (Wiseman), 7.17 (Clegg), 8.9 (Rogers), 12.13 (Witts), 14.7 (Vikander), 15.3 (Picturesque); Associated Press Ltd 4B (LA PRENSA), 15.7 (PTI); A Braithwaite 12.27; R Cae – Brittany (Hodder & Stoughton) 11.7; Cephas 3.13 (Champollion); James Davis 2.3, 2.5, 5.23; J Engelheart 10.17; Mary Evans Picture Library 1.21; Eye Ubiquitous 4.8 (Cumming), 2B (Miessler), 2C (George); E Greenhalgh 11.10; Clive Hart 1.5, 2D, 5.30, 7.18, 3D, 9.3, 9.11, 9.18, 9.20, 9.21, 9.26, 10.4, 12.3; Tim Hart 6.19, 7.21; Holt Studios 1Dii, 1Diii; Impact Photos 2.16; London Aerial Photo Library 1.26, 9.17; Lulea University 2.13; Magnum Photos 6.10, 6.11, 14.1; Network Photographers 1.8 (Goldwater), 2.8 (Silvester); Panos Pictures 6.22; Peterhead Port Authority 3.20; Popperfoto 8.7, 10.7, 4A, 13.5, 15.4; P Ralli 12.25; Rayosol 2.4; Michael Raw 1Di, 1Div, 1.25, 2.18, 3.9, 3.14, 4.11; Roves Farms, Wiltshire 9.29; Kevin Stannard 10.1, 10.9, 10.12, 10.14, 10.17, 10.19, 10.22, 11.5, 11.6, 11.9, 11.18, 11.26, 12.5, 12.7, 12.9, 12.11, 12.15, 12.28; Still Pictures 4.14, 6.15 (Lehrfreund), 8.11 (Glendell), 9.28 (Arbib); Craig Taylor Photography 3.18; Prof. Tim Unwin 9.12.

We would like to thank the following for permission to use their material in either the original or adapted form:

1E Eurostat 1995–98; 1.8 *The Independent on Sunday* 30 April 2000; 1.14, 1.15, 1.16 Eurostat; 1.22 From Keeble, in R.J. Chorley & P. Haggett (eds) *Socio-economic Models in Geography* Methuen 1967; 2.17 'Good cause to be brassed off' by Peter Hetherington, *The Guardian* 16 March 1998; 3.8 M. Raw (2001) *Geography in Place*, 2nd edition; 3.10 & 3.12 R. Dalton & C. Canévet 'Brittany: a case study in rural transformation' *Geography* 84 No.1 January 1999; 3.17 'Atlantic fish stocks in peril, survey reveals' by Paul Brown in *The Guardian* 1 July 2000; 4.2 M. Raw (1989) *Resources and Environment* Unwin Hyman; 4.10, 4.12, 4.13 Swedish Environment Protection Agency 1999 *Facts about Swedish Policy: Acid Rain*; 4.16 Bananalink; 2A UN Population Division *World Urbanization Prospects* (1996 Revision); 5.1, 5.3, 5.4 UN Population Division 2001; 5.5 & 5.10 Adapted from A. Gilbert & J. Gugler (1992) *Cities, Poverty and Development* OUP; 5.6 & 5.9 D. Drakakis-Smith (2000) *Third World Cities* 2nd edn Routledge; 5.7 & 5.8 UNCHS, 1996; 5.12 UN 1988; 5.13 & 5.14 G. O'Hare (2001) 'Urban renaissance: new horizons for Rio's favelas' *Geography* 86/1; 5.15 Social Trends 2000; 5.16 Statistics Canada 2001; 5.17 P. Ogden & R. Hall (2000) 'Households, reurbanisation and the rise of living alone…', *Urban Studies* 37/2; 5.21 J. Rigg (1997) *South East Asia* Routledge; 5.24 D. J. Stewart (1996) 'Cities in the desert' *Annals of the Association of American Geographers* 86/3; 5.26 Maryland Office of Planning 2001; 5.32 New East Manchester 2001; 6.1 National Statistics; 6.4 & 6.13 Social Exclusion Unit 1998; 6.5 'The ghost of Christmas Past…' by D. Dorling et al, *British Medical Journal* 2000 321, 23 December; 6.6 World Bank 2000; 6.7 'The Road to Trauma' by Ian Roberts in *The Guardian* 9 May 2001; 6.8 M. Pacione (1977) *Britain's Cities* Routledge; 6.9 A. Power (2000) 'Poor areas and social exclusion' Centre for Analysis of Social Exclusion, London School of Economics; 6.12 Neighbourhood Renewal Unit 2001; 6.14 DETR 2000; 6.17 R. P. Otter and S. Lloyd-Evans (1998) *The City in the Developing World* Longman; 6.18 UN 1995; 6.20 UNCHS 1996; 6.21 ILO; 6.23 P. Kelly (2000) 'Rethinking the local labour market' *Singapore Journal of Tropical Geography* 20/1; 7.1 & 7.4 World Bank Development Indicators 2001; 7.2 T. Hart (2001) 'Transport and the City' in R. Paddison (ed.) *Handbook of Urban Studies*, Sage; 7.3 Indian Government statistics; 7.5 National Travel Surveys; 7.6 Social Trends 1996; 7.8 Texas Transportation Institute, 2001; 7.9 DETR 1998; 7.10 Brookings Institute 2000; 7.11 Newman &

Kenworthy (1989) *Cities and Automobile Dependence* Gower; 7.13 Adapted from R. Tolley and B. Turton (1995) *Transport Systems, Policy and Planning* Longman; 7.20 *Towards an Urban Renaissance*, Final Report, Urban Task Force, DETR 1999; 7.22 R. Simmonds & G. Hack (eds) (2000) *Global City Regions* Spon Press; 8.2 & 8.16 World Bank World Development Report 1992, *Development and the Environment* 1992; 8.3 B. Sengupta, 1999; 8.4 Panayotou 2001; 8.5 World Bank 2001; 8.6 World Bank *Pollution Abatement Handbook* 1998; 8.7 BBC News online: 3 April 2001 following new anti-pollution laws; 8.8 Barcelona City Council 2001 (website); 8.10 UNCHS 1996; 8.12 OECD 1997; 8.14 A. Read 'Where there's muck there's brass', *Area* 33/1 and UNCHS (Habitat) An Urbanizing World 1996 OUP; 8.15 H. Girardet (1999) *Creating Sustainable Cities* Green Books; 8.17 A. Wright & H. Girardet (1999) *Towards an Urban Renaissance: Report of the Urban Task Force* DETR; 8.19 British Social Attitudes Survey, 1999; 8.20 McGranahan & Satterthwaite 2000; 8.21 Greater London Authority *The Mayor's Transport Strategy*, June 2001; 3A Steve Bell in *The Guardian*; 3B 'Farmers angry over move to protect last "wild" lands' by Severin Carrell in *The Independent on Sunday* 26 August 2001; 3C, 9.4, 9.16, 9.25 DEFRA, ERDP 2000-6; 9.2 I. Bowler *The Geography of Agriculture in Developed Market Economies*; 9.5, 9.8, 9.23, 11.19, 12.13, 12.16, 12.19 Countryside Agency *The State of the Countryside* 2001; 9.6 & 9.7 R. Haines-Young et al (2000) *Accounting for Nature* DETR; 9.10 DEFRA; 9.12 Prof. Tim Unwin; 9.14 K. Spencer & G. Nagle 'Environmental Issues in Europe' *Geofile* 284, April 1996 (Nelson Thornes); 9.17 Reading Agricultural Consultants; 9.19 Countryside Agency (1997) *Agricultural Landscapes: a third look*; 9.22 & 11.14 DEFRA England Rural Development Programme Section 5; 9.24 B. Ilbery (ed.) *The Geography of Rural Change* Longman; 9.29 NFU 164 Shaftesbury Av, London OR Roves Farm Visitor Centre, Sevenhampton, Wiltshire; 10.5 K. Atkinson (2001) 'New National Parks in the Canadia North' *Geography* 86/2; 10.10 *National Geographic* August 2001; 10.16 J. Engleheart; 10.20 R. Prosser et al *Landmark AS Geography* Collins; 10.21 OS map extract: 1:25 000 Outdoor Leisure Map 24; 10.23, 11.15, 11.25 Countryside Agency; Peak District National Park Management Plan; Peak National Park Authority; 11.1 *Regional Trends 34*, Crown Copyright 1999; 11.2 US Census Bureau; 11.3 US Dept of Agriculture Economic Research Service; 11.7 R. Case *Brittany* Hodder & Stoughton; 11.8 G. Lewis (2000) 'Changing places in a rural world' *Geography* 85/2; 11.12 *The Times* 5 September 2001; 11.16 Countryside Agency Teleworking & Rural Development (RDC); 11.17 *One North East* Regional Economic Strategy for the North East; 11.20 Countryside Agency Survey of Rural Services 1997; 11.21 J. Chaffey *Managing Environments in Britain and Ireland* Hodder & Stoughton; 11.22 Countryside Agency *The State of the Countryside 2000: the South West*; 11.23 CPRE; 11.28 J. Cator & T. Jones *Social Geography* Arnold; 11.29 A. Lovett et al (2000) 'Accessibility of primary health care services in East Anglia' School of Health Policy and Practice, Research Report No.9; 11.30 www.ruraltransport.com/page5. html; 11.31 G. Lewis (2000) 'Changing places in a rural world' *Geography* 85/2; 12.1 R. Haines-Young et al (2000) *Accounting for Nature*; 12.2 A. Goudie *The Human Impact on the Natural Environment* Blackwell; 12.4 M. Harding; 12.6 & 12.12 A. Kidd *Managing Fragile Ecosystems* Hodder & Stoughton; 12.8 H. Read et al *Woodland Habitats* Routledge; 12.10 D. Jones & S. Essex (1999) 'Land use change in the British uplands' *Geography* 84/1; 12.17 English Nature 2001; 12.23 P. Ralli; 12.24 D. C. Ralli; 12.26 Regional Trends 34 Crown © 1999; 12.29 Moors Valley Country Park, Horton Road, Ashley Heath, Ringwood; 14.2 Adapted from D. J. Varnes (1978) in R. L. Schuster and Krizek (eds) *Landslide Analysis and Control*, National Academy of Sciences Report 176, Washington DC; 15.2 After Pielke 1990; 15.5 Adapted from Miller 1971.

Every effort has been made to reach the copyrightholders. The publishers would be pleased to hear from anyone whose rights they have unwittingly infringed.